The Military History of Late Rome AD 425–457

For my wife Sini, and children Ari and Nanna

The Military History of Late Rome AD 425–457

The Age of the Warlords
Aetius vs. Attila

Dr. Ilkka Syvänne

Pen & Sword
MILITARY

First published in Great Britain in 2020 by
Pen & Sword Military
An imprint of
Pen & Sword Books Ltd
Yorkshire – Philadelphia

ISBN 978 1 84884 853 5

Printed and bound in the UK by TJ International Ltd,
Padstow, Cornwall.

MIX
Paper from
responsible sources
FSC® C013056

Pen & Sword Books Limited incorporates the imprints of Atlas, Archaeology,
Aviation, Discovery, Family History, Fiction, History, Maritime, Military,
Military Classics, Politics, Select, Transport,
True Crime, Air World, Frontline Publishing, Leo Cooper, Remember
When, Seaforth Publishing, The Praetorian Press, Wharncliffe
Local History, Wharncliffe Transport, Wharncliffe True Crime
and White Owl.

For a complete list of Pen & Sword titles please contact

PEN & SWORD BOOKS LIMITED
47 Church Street, Barnsley, South Yorkshire, S70 2AS, England
E-mail: enquiries@pen-and-sword.co.uk
Website: www.pen-and-sword.co.uk

Or

PEN AND SWORD BOOKS
1950 Lawrence Rd, Havertown, PA 19083, USA
E-mail: Uspen-and-sword@casematepublishers.com
Website: www.penandswordbooks.com

Contents

Acknowledgements

Acknowledgments are due to the very same persons that I mentioned in the first book. I thank both Professor Geoffrey Greatrex for his recommendation and the commissioning editor Philip Sidnell for accepting my book proposal. Special thanks are also due to Matt Jones, Barnaby Blacker, Tara Moran and other staff at Pen & Sword for their stellar work and for the outstanding support they give for the author. The end result has also benefited from discussions with friends dealing with Attila and Aetius some of which actually took place well over a decade ago.

I also thank my family Sini, Ari and Nanna for their patience.

Thanks are due to my father and to my late mother who unknowingly also contributed to this volume by bringing back books and photos from Sicily in May 2005. I gave that trip as a gift to my parents but little did I know that I would be able to incorporate material brought back by them nine years later after their visit of the city of Agrigento on 26 May 2005 so that the book was basically finished by July of the same year. However, the book has been partially updated especially with photos during the editing process.

I also want to thank in particular Vicus Ultimus, the famous Polish re-enactor group, for their outstanding contribution and support in the form of photos. Without their efforts the book would be a lot less colourful.

None of the above bears any responsibility for any possible mistakes or strange views that remain in the book. Those are the sole responsibility of the author.

List of Plates

List of Maps

Introduction

The intention of this book, the fourth in a series of seven, is to present an overview of all the principal aspects of Roman military history during the years 425–457. The structure of the book follows the reigns of the emperors in chronological order, and the events and wars are also usually presented in chronological order. However, for the sake of ease of reading some events that took place in one particular sector of the empire are grouped together. The uneven survival of evidence means that there are huge gaps in our knowledge and that some of my conclusions are only my best educated guesses.

The text follows the same principles as the previous books and includes direct references to the sources only when my conclusions can be considered controversial or new or otherwise in need of such. I have also not included descriptions or analyses of the sources used and their problems, because there exists expert literature devoted to this subject. Some general comments, however, are in order. All of the period sources had their limitations. The narrative histories were restricted to dealing with only certain types of information (mainly politics and wars) and followed the literary models set before them. The chronicles usually give only the very barest of details. The ecclesiastical histories concentrated mainly on the religious events. The panegyrics and orations were also naturally restricted by the genre. All of the authors writing within the Roman Empire had to take into account the fact that they wrote under dictators who had the power over life and death. We should also not forget the personal goals of the authors which naturally varied. The quality of the Armenian, Georgian, Arabic and Persian histories etc vary greatly, and in contrast to the Roman material also present legendary material that has to be sifted through carefully. Nevertheless, in places these sources allow one to shed light on otherwise murky events.

When I refer to some chronicle for example by Cassiodorus, *Chronica Gallica* (452, 511), Hydatius, Isidore of Seville, Jordanes (*Romana*), Paulus Diaconus, Prosper, etc, the exact point of reference can be found in the annalistic dating even when I do not always state this in the narrative. These sources are conveniently collected in the MGH series, which is available online, for example from Internet Archive.

In this study when I refer to Spain I mean the whole of the Iberian Peninsula including Lusitania (modern Portugal). However, when I refer to Britain, I mean only the portion under Roman control. This solution has been adopted solely for the sake of making referrals easier.

As far as the language, transliteration, and titles are concerned I have usually adopted the easiest solutions. I have used the transliterations most commonly used except in the case of Greek military terms which I have generally transliterated so that I have maintained the original F of the Greek instead of using the PH. I have also adopted the practice of the Oxford University Press and used capital letters for all offices which could be held by only one person at a time. I have also used capital letters for all specific types of troops and military units. However, when I have referred to several office holders simultaneously (e.g. *comites*/counts, *duces*/dukes) I have used small letters.

All illustrations, drawings, maps and diagrams etc. have been drawn and prepared by the author unless stated otherwise. I have used the Barrington Atlas as the principal source for the maps.

Abbreviations

a.455	year 455/AD 455
Cav.	Cavalry
CGall. 452	Chronica Gallica 452 (Chron. Min., Mommsen, Berlin 1892)
CGall. 511	Chronica Gallica 511 (Chron. Min., Mommsen, Berlin 1892)
Com. Dom.	Comes Domesticorum (Count of Domestics)
CRP	Comes Rei Privatae (Count of the Privy Purse)
CSL	Comes Sacrarum Largitionum (Count of the Sacred Largess)
GC	Gallic Chronicle
HI	Heavy infantry
Hydat.	Hydatius
Inf.	Infantry
Isid. HRGVS	Isidorus of Seville, *Historia de regibus Gothorum, Vandalorum et Suevorum*
LHF	Anon. *Liber Historiae Francorum*
LI	Light infantry
Mag. Eq.	Magister Equitum (Master of Horse)
Mag. Ped.	Magister Peditum (Master of Foot)
Mag. Eq. et Ped.	Magister Equitum et Peditum (Master of Horse and Foot)
MGH	Monumenta Historia Germaniae
MGH AA	Monumenta Historia Germaniae Auctores Antiquitissimonum
MVM	Magister Utriusque Militiae (Master of All Arms of Service)
MVM Praes.	Magister Utriusque Militae Praesentales (Praesental MVM)
Mag. Mil.	Magister Militum (Master of Soldiers)
Mag.Off.	Magister Officiorum (Master of Office)
Marc. Com. or Marc.	Marcellinus Comes
Or.	Orations
PLRE1	See Bibliography
PLRE2	See Bibliography
PP	Praefectus Praetorio (Praetorian Prefect)
PPI	Praefectus Praetorio Italiae et Africae (PP of Italy and Africa)
PPIL	Praefectus Praetorio Illyrici
PPG	Praefectus Praetorio Galliarum
PPO	Praefectus Praetorio Orientis
PSC	Praepositus Sacri Cubiculi (Leader of Sacred Bedroom)
PVC	Praefectus Urbis Constantiopolitanae (Urban Prefect of Constantinople)
PVR	Praefectus Urbis Romae
QSP	Quaestor Sacri Palatii (Questor of the Sacred Palace)
REF1	See Bibliography
REF2	See Bibliography

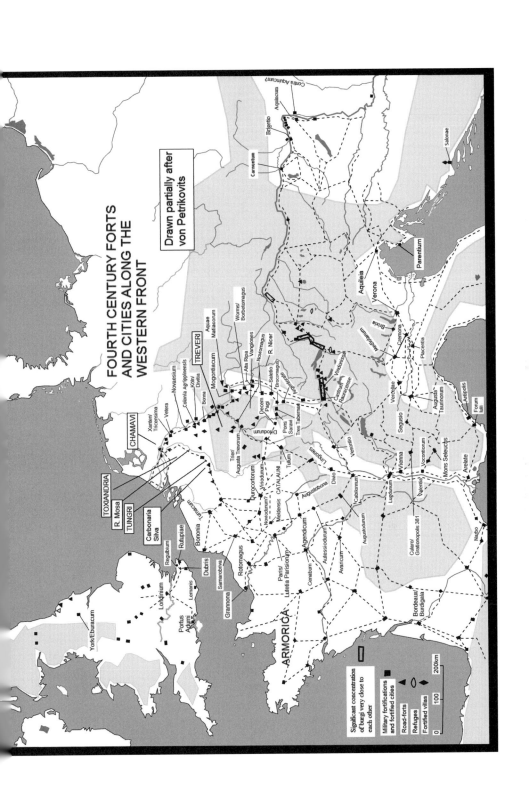

FOURTH CENTURY FORTS
AND CITIES ALONG THE
WESTERN FRONT

Drawn partially after
von Petrikovits

CHAMAVI

TREVERI

TOXIANDRIA
R. Mosa
TUNGRI
Carbonaria
Silva

ARMORICA

CATALAUNI

York/Eburacum
Londinium
Portus Adurni
Lemanis
Regulbium
Rutupiae
Dubris
Samarobriva
Bononia
Grannona
Rotomagus
Paris/ Lutetia Parisiorum
Cenabum
Agendicum
Autessiodurum
Avaricum
Augustobona
Bordeaux/ Burdigala
Cularo/ Gratianopolis 381
Augustodunum
Lugdunum
Vienna
Valentia
Vocontiorum
Narbo
Arelate
Mons Seleucis
Segusio
Augusta Taurinorum
Antipolis
Forum Iulii
Vesontio
Vercellae
Divio
Cabillonum
Lingones
Andematunnum
Tullum
Mediolanum
Nevirodunum
Durocortorum
Augusta Treverorum
Trier/
Divodurum
Pons Saravi
Tres Tabernae
Decem Pagi
Salerio
R. Nicer
Saletio
Brocomagus
Vangiones
Worms/ Borbetomagus
Aquae Mattiacorum
Mogontiacum
Alta Ripa
Bonna
Köln/ Divitia
Colonia Agrippinensis
Novaesium
Vetera
Xanten/ Tricensima
Castra Vindonissae
Rauracense
Augusta
Brugg
Mediolanum
Brixia
Verona
Aquileia
Cremona
Placentia
Parentium
Aquincum
Brigetio
Carnuntum
Contra Aquincum?
Salonae
R. Mosa
Tungror
Turcoriorum

Significant concentration
of burgi very close to
each other

Military fortifications
and fortified cities

Road-forts

Refuges

Fortified villas

0   100   200km

The Balkans.

Drawn after J.J. Wilkes
(2005, 126-127) and
Barrington Atlas with
some changes.

--- Roads
— Rivers

100km
100 miles

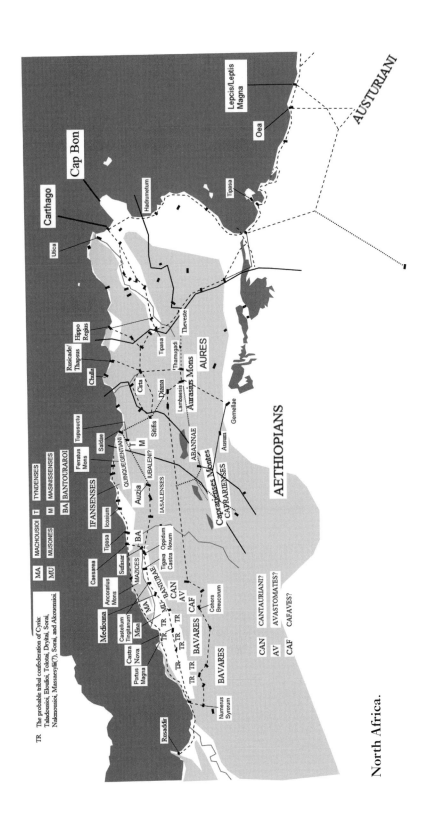

TR   The probable tribal confederation of Cynic:
Taladousioi, Eboulioi, Tolotai, Drysitai, Sorai,
Nakmousioi, Massaesyloi(?), Sorai, and Akouensioi.

MA	MACHOUSIOI	T	TYNDENSES
MU	MUSONES	M	MASINISSENSES
		BA	BANTOURAROI

Cap Bon

Carthago

AUSTURIANI

Lepcis/Leptis Magna

Oea

Utica

Hadrumetum

Tipasa

Rusicade/Thapsus

Hippo Regius

Chullu

Tipasa

Theveste

Cirta

Thamugadi

AURES

Diana

Aurasips Mons

Tupusuctu

Lambaesis

Sitifis

Ausum

Gemellae

Saldae

Ferratus Mons

QUINQUEGENTIANI

ABANNAE

Icosium

Auzia

IUBALENI?

Capraienses Montes

CAPRARIENSES

IFANSENSES

Tipasa

IASALENSES

AETHIOPIANS

BA

Caesarea

Sufasar

MAZICES

Oppidum Castra Novum

Ancorarius Mons

MA

MU

BANURAE

Tigava

CAN

Mediouna

Castellum Tingitanum

AV

CAF

Cohors Breucorum

Castra Nova

Mina

TR

TR

Portus Magna

TR

TR

BAVARES

TR

TR

CAN   CANTAURIANI?

BAVARES

AV   AVASTOMATES?

Numerus Syrorum

CAF   CAFAVES?

Rusaddir

North Africa.

Arabia.

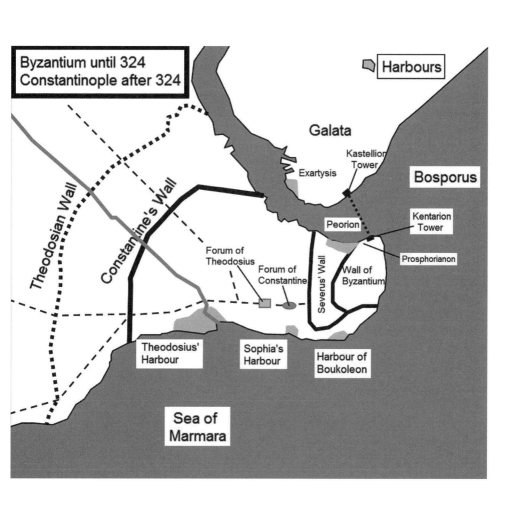

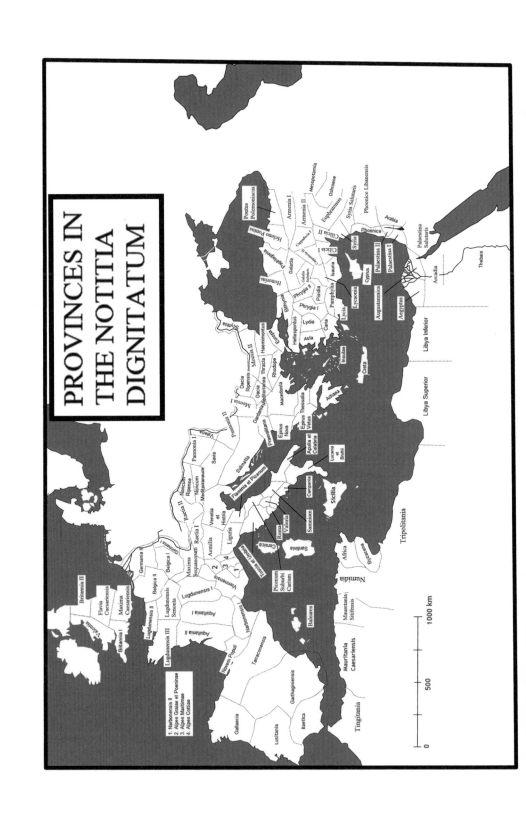

PROVINCES IN
THE NOTITIA
DIGNITATUM

1. Narbonensis II
2. Alpes Graiae et Poeninae
3. Alpes Maritimae
4. Alpes Cottiae

0   500   1000 km

Spain.

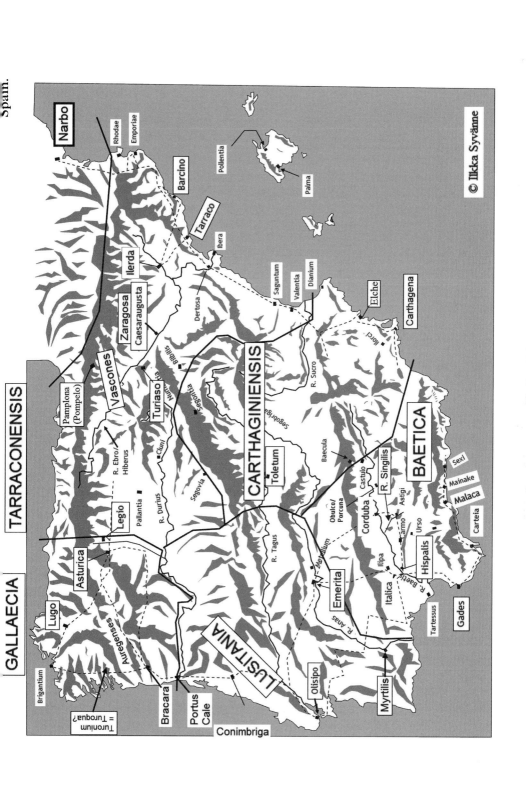

© Ilkka Syvänne

Neighbourhood of Rome.

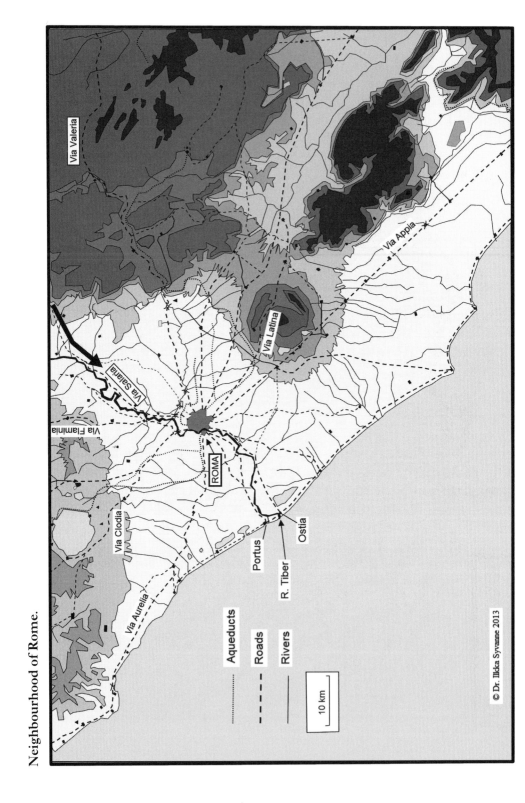

Via Valeria

Via Flaminia

Via Salaria

Via Latina

Via Appia

Via Clodia

Via Aurelia

ROMA

Portus

R. Tiber

Ostia

Aqueducts

Roads

Rivers

10 km

© Dr. Ilkka Syvänne 2013

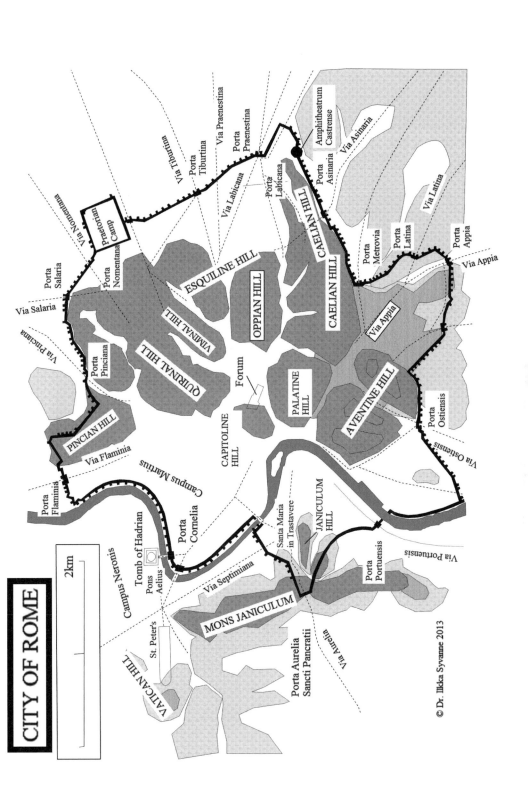

CITY OF ROME

2km

Porta Flaminia
Via Flaminia
PINCIAN HILL
Porta Pinciana
Via Pinciana
Porta Salaria
Via Salaria
Porta Nomentana
Via Nomentana
Praetorian Camp
Via Tiburtina
Porta Tiburtina
Via Praenestina
Porta Praenestina
Amphitheatrum Castrense
Porta Asinaria
Via Asinaria

QUIRINAL HILL
VIMINAL HILL
ESQUILINE HILL
OPPIAN HILL
Via Labicana
Porta Labicana
CAELIAN HILL
CAELIAN HILL

CAPITOLINE HILL
Forum
PALATINE HILL
AVENTINE HILL
Porta Metrovia
Porta Latina
Via Latina
Porta Appia
Via Appia
Via Appia

Campus Martius
Porta Ostiensis
Via Ostiensis

Campus Neronis
Tomb of Hadrian
Pons Aelius
Porta Cornelia
Santa Maria in Trastavere
JANICULUM HILL

St. Peter's
VATICAN HILL
Via Septimiana
MONS JANICULUM
Porta Portuensis
Via Portuensis

Porta Aurelia Sancti Pancratii
Via Aurelia

© Dr. Ilkka Syvänne 2013

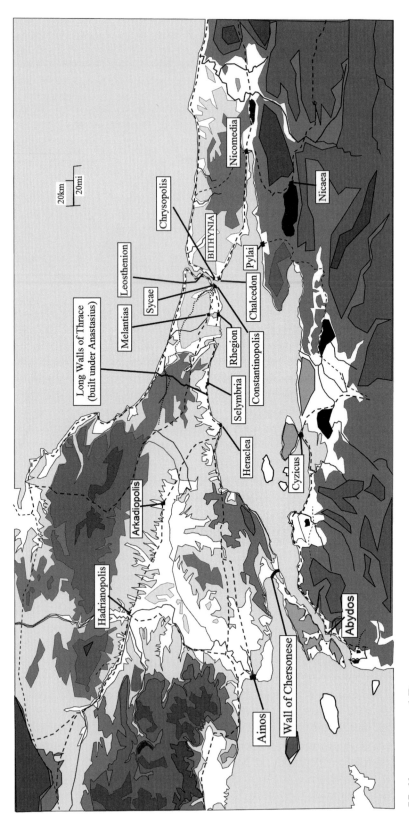

Hellespont and Bosporus.

Chapter One

Introduction: The Roman Empire in 425

The General Situation

Thanks to successful East Roman intervention in West Roman affairs the two halves of the Roman Empire stood united once again in 425. The empire had somehow managed to weather out the disasters caused by Honorius's ruinous racist policies. The West Romans still had to deal with the revolts of the Federate Visigoths and possibly also the revolt of the Franks even if their revolt is mentioned for the first time in 428. The Roman Army of Gaul was also in revolt, but it was in revolt only against the usurper John that the East Romans had just overthrown, so it proved easy for the new government to obtain its support.

Despite the fact that the barbarian federate forces inside the West Roman Empire consisted of hundreds of thousands of warriors, their principal threat was not a military one, because these barbarians were not united. The successful campaigns of Constantius III against them, while still a general, proves that West Rome still possessed adequate military strength to crush them when its forces were united under a single leader. It is here that lay the principal military problem for the West Romans. The position of the emperor was not strong enough to challenge the West Roman warlords who had managed to gain so strong a military position with the help of their personal retinues and personal wealth that they can really be considered to have been like true medieval feudal warlords. The West Roman Empire would have needed a warrior emperor who could have united all forces, but this was not to be because the ruler installed on the throne was a youth, and the warlords were not willing to crush the barbarian federates decisively because they could use their forces for their own personal advancement. In these circumstances, the principal threat posed by these barbarians was that living conditions under them seemed quite benevolent in contrast to those under the corrupt imperial authorities who fleeced the population mercilessly. Despite their moralizing tendencies the key texts that prove this are Salvian's *On the Government of God* (written ca. 440–451, esp. 5.4ff.), Paulinus of Pella's *Eucharisticus* (496ff.), and the texts of Libanius (*Orations* 2, dated ca. 380; *Orations 47*, dated to about 389–392) which refer to similar problems in the east. However, the East Roman Empire was far more successful in their fight for hearts and minds for three reasons: 1) The living conditions among the Huns and Persians were not attractive in comparison with the Roman Empire even with its corrupt authorities; 2) The Federate Goths were more firmly incorporated into the East Roman security apparatus until the reign of Leo I, which meant that the discontented could not seek safety among them; 3) The East Roman government appears to have curbed corruption especially among the military more successfully than the West Romans even if the evidence still shows that they could not suppress it entirely. The only thing that prevented the Roman populace going en masse to the barbarian side in the west was that the Visigoths were Arians and Franks pagans.[1]

In great contrast to the west under Honorius, the East Romans had managed to rebuild their military strength under Arcadius and the PP Anthemius to such an extent that they were able to defeat the Persians, Huns and West Romans. East Rome possessed a strong economy, a large army and a powerful navy, and its Gothic Federates were both loyal and effective after the Gainas affair. On top of this, the building of the so-called Theodosian Walls in Constantinople enabled the East Romans to weather out any storm even when the wars were not going as planned – a thing that proved very valuable when Attila the Hun stormed the Balkans.

Roman Society, Administration and Military in 425[2]

At the very top of Roman society stood the emperor with the title of *Augustus*. His designated successor bore the title *Caesar*. Actual power, however, could be in the hands of some other important person like a general or administrator or family member. There still existed senates in Rome and Constantinople which could be included in the decision making process when the emperor (or the power behind the throne) wanted to court the goodwill of the moneyed senators, but this was not usually necessary and could not be done when it was important to make decisions fast. Late Roman imperial administration was divided into three sections: 1) Military; 2) Palatine; 3) Imperial and Fiscal.

Late Roman armed forces consisted of the imperial bodyguards, praesental forces (central field armies), *comitatenses* (field armies), *limitanei* (frontier forces), *bucellarii* (private retainers), federates and temporary allies, in addition to civilian paramilitary forces. The strategic situation did not favour the Romans because they had enemies within the borders and outside. Basic tactics and military equipment remained much the same as it had been previously so that infantry tactics were based on variations of the phalanx with a clear preference for the use of the hollow square/oblong array while cavalry tactics were based on variations of cavalry formation with two lines. The Romans possessed a clear advantage over their enemies in siege and naval warfare, but this advantage lasted only as long as those enemies were unable to use Roman resources or Roman turncoats against them. A fuller discussion of strategy and tactics can be found in volumes 1–3.

As stated in Volume 3, the era from 395 until about 451 saw a massive increase in the size of a typical field army. This process had already started at the turn of the fifth century, but it assumed unprecedented proportions when the rise of Attila the Hun increased the sizes of the field armies even further, which he did by adding new tribes into his already massive force. The battle of the nations, the battle of the Catalaunian Fields in 451, saw the apogee of this development. In this battle, the West Romans assembled all the forces available in the west against all the forces available to Attila east of the Rhine. As I noted in volume 3, the figures recorded in the sources for this battle are actually not as outlandish as usually claimed by historians. We should remember that both armies consisted of masses of barbarian tribes and tribal confederacies each of which, even on their own, possessed massive armies. When one assesses this evidence one needs to remember that the Roman Empire and Eastern Europe up to the Urals possessed vast reserves of manpower that could be tapped by the commanders. We should also remember that

France was a heavily populated area which had once been one of the breadbaskets of the Empire, and that it could therefore support vast armies much akin to the armies of the Revolutionary or Napoleonic era France. Furthermore, it was quite feasible for the Romans and Germanic and nomadic tribal confederacies to march through even sparsely populated areas, because the sources clearly state that they always possessed vast numbers of ox-drawn carts and wagons to carry the necessary supplies whenever they invaded en masse. As noted in the previous volume, even Napoleon was able to campaign with 614,000 men in the vast expanses of sparsely populated early nineteenth century Russia. It was only thanks to skilful use of scorched earth tactics that the Russians were able to defeat the invaders.

Roman soldiers were equipped much as they had always been. The martial equipment of the heavy infantry consisted of spears and javelins of various lengths and types, *plumbatae*-darts, swords of various types, typically large round or oval shields (other types of shield were also used), armour (typically chainmail, but scale, plate and segmented armour was also used), and helmet (usually segmented or ridge, but single piece bowls were also used). Some of the heavy-armed were trained to use bows as well while all of them were trained to use slings. When the purpose was to fight in difficult terrain, the heavy infantry could go without armour (or were equipped with padded coats or leather armour) and helmets and be equipped with smaller and lighter shields, swords and javelins. The light infantry usually wore no armour and were equipped with swords, daggers, javelins, slings or bows. Heavy and light cavalries wore basically the same type of equipment as the heavy and light infantries, but some of their equipment had been

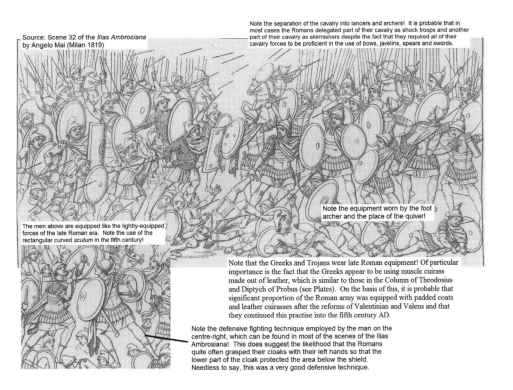

Source: Scene 32 of the *Ilias Ambrosiana* by Angelo Mai (Milan 1819)

Note the separation of the cavalry into lancers and archers! It is probable that in most cases the Romans delegated part of their cavalry as shock troops and another part of their cavalry as skirmishers despite the fact that they required all of their cavalry forces to be proficient in the use of bows, javelins, spears and swords.

Note the equipment worn by the foot archer and the place of the quiver!

The men above are equipped like the lightly-equipped forces of the late Roman era. Note the use of the rectangular curved *scutum* in the fifth century!

Note that the Greeks and Trojans wear late Roman equipment! Of particular importance is the fact that the Greeks appear to be using muscle cuirass made out of leather, which is similar to those in the Column of Theodosius and Diptych of Probus (see Plates). On the basis of this, it is probable that significant proportion of the Roman army was equipped with padded coats and leather cuirasses after the reforms of Valentinian and Valens and that they continued this practise into the fifth century AD.

Note the defensive fighting technique employed by the man on the centre-right, which can be found in most of the scenes of the Ilias Ambrosiana! This does suggest the likelihood that the Romans quite often grasped their cloaks with their left hands so that the lower part of the cloak protected the area below the shield. Needless to say, this was a very good defensive technique.

the standard infantry battle formations of the fifth and sixth centuries

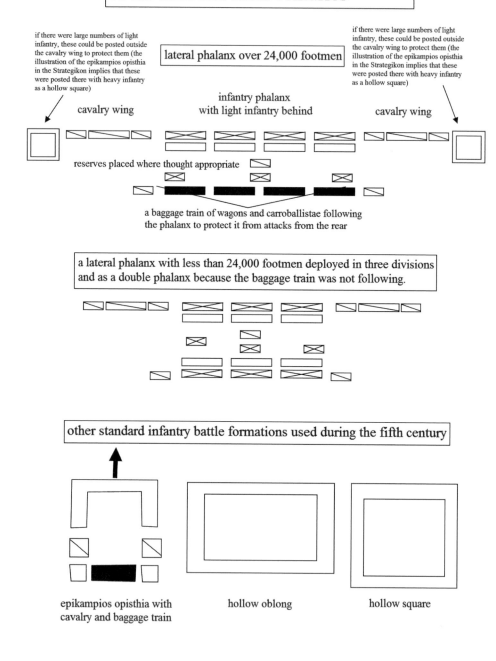

if there were large numbers of light infantry, these could be posted outside the cavalry wing to protect them (the illustration of the epikampios opisthia in the Strategikon implies that these were posted there with heavy infantry as a hollow square)

lateral phalanx over 24,000 footmen

if there were large numbers of light infantry, these could be posted outside the cavalry wing to protect them (the illustration of the epikampios opisthia in the Strategikon implies that these were posted there with heavy infantry as a hollow square)

cavalry wing

infantry phalanx with light infantry behind

cavalry wing

reserves placed where thought appropriate

a baggage train of wagons and carroballistae following the phalanx to protect it from attacks from the rear

a lateral phalanx with less than 24,000 footmen deployed in three divisions and as a double phalanx because the baggage train was not following.

other standard infantry battle formations used during the fifth century

epikampios opisthia with cavalry and baggage train

hollow oblong

hollow square

The following diagrams show the standard cavalry battle arrays of this era

The combat formation of a large cavalry army in excess of 10,000-15,000 men:

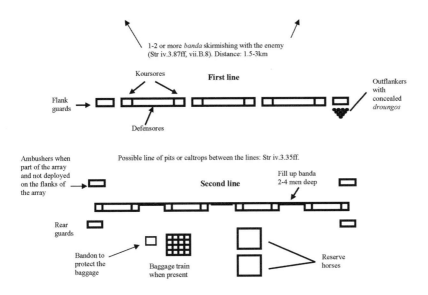

Super large battle array for cavalry armies in excess of ca. 50,000 men:

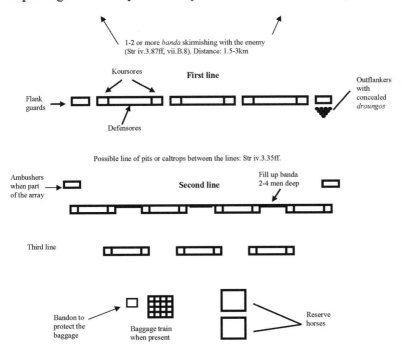

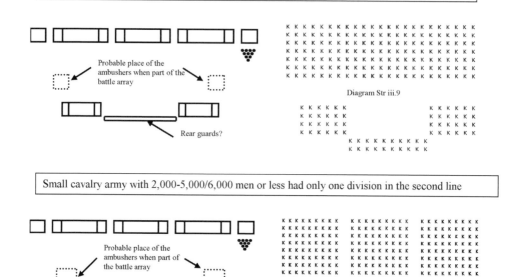

Medium sized cavalry army with less than 15,000/12,000/10,000 and more than 5,000/6,000 men

Probable place of the ambushers when part of the battle array

Rear guards?

Diagram Str iii.9

Small cavalry army with 2,000-5,000/6,000 men or less had only one division in the second line

Probable place of the ambushers when part of the battle array

Diagram Str. iii.10

modified to suit the needs of the cavalry battle. This concerns in particular the bow, which was weaker than the infantry counterpart. The equipment worn by rowers/sailors required to fight was also quite similar to the equipment of the land forces. The same is true for the equipment worn by the marines on board ships. The only real difference is that the shields used on board were required to be stronger and larger than typically on land. In addition to this, the armed forces possessed specialists for all sorts of needs, the most important of which were the siege specialists with their artillery pieces.

For equipment worn at this time, see the plates and the images of soldiers included in the text. The photos of the re-enactors in the plates are particularly valuable for their visual worth. The attached nineteenth century drawings of the images included in the *Ilias Ambrosiana* (fifth century or turn of the sixth century) give a good overall picture of what types of equipment were used by the Romans at this time. They include all the basic variants: the light infantry, foot archers, heavy infantry, cavalry lancers and mounted archers. This has already been included in previous volumes, but it is the best overall presentation of period equipment and is included for this reason.

The diagrams above show the standard land combat formations in use at this time. Those interested in analysis of this are advised to consult the previous volumes in this series and also subsequent volumes (together with my biography of the Emperor Gallienus for earlier instances) which analyse in greater detail the information provided by the *Strategikon*. See also Syvänne, 2004.

Naval combat formations were single line abreast with reserves, the double line/phalanx with reserves, convex to break through the enemy centre, crescent to outflank, and circle for defence. In advance of these there were two or three ships that acted as scouting ships, but which could also be used to break up the cohesion of the enemy array by leaving them exposed in front. Transport ships were usually placed behind the combat ships. The high quality of Roman seamen, rowers and marines together with better ship designs ensured the Romans naval superiority against any foe until the Vandals managed turn these advantages against them.

Chapter Two

Enemies and Allies

In 425 Rome's enemies were basically the same as before with the difference that now some were located inside the empire while Britain and Armorica were only nominally part of the Roman Empire as autonomous areas. The Picts and Irish threatened mainly the Britons, but the Saxons posed a threat to both Britons and Gaul. The Picts and the Irish possessed naval forces while their armies were usually lightly equipped but still capable of fighting in close order formations. Their siege skills were rudimentary. The Saxon navy was more formidable than the one used by the Picts, and their land armies were also more numerous and better at close quarters fighting. Their siege skills were slightly better than that of their neighbours, but still not on par with the Romans.

The Huns and Alans together with the Germanic Franks, Visigoths, Ostrogoths, Burgundians, Vandals, Suevi and other Germanic tribes, formed the principal threats for the Romans in continental Europe. With the exception of the Huns, some scattered Ostrogoths and some other Germanic tribes, most of these were now inside the Roman Empire. In other words, the principal problem posed by these enemies was strategic. The Romans no longer possessed clear geographical territories to defend. The tactical threat posed by them had remained the same. The Germanic peoples specialized in close quarters fighting with cavalry or infantry, but some of the tribes, like the Goths, were quite good at long distance fighting too. The Huns and other nomads used mainly mounted archers in combat, but were still prepared to fight at close quarters when needed. With the addition of siege skills borrowed from the Romans and footsoldiers drawn from their subjects, the Huns became a major threat in the 440s.

The principal threats in the east were the Sasanians, but the Caucasian peoples, Alans, Huns and Arabs could also cause trouble. The Sasanian Empire was a particularly fearsome enemy because the Persians possessed a very large and well organized empire with vast reserves of high quality cavalry and equally vast numbers of footmen usable as cannon fodder. Most importantly, the Sasanians possessed high expertise in siege warfare and were in some ways even more effective in that than the Romans. The Romans were therefore lucky that the Persians faced similar troubles with the nomads on their northern and Central Asian frontiers as the Romans. The basic components of Sasanian military methods remained the same as before, but Bahram V Gur introduced a number of reforms. These included the increased importance of mounted archery, the introduction of more powerful archery shooting techniques, the introduction of the arrow guide and possibly also the very small *siper*-shield to increase the length of the draw. He also increased the importance of the lancer charge. For these see my article of the reign of Bahram, available online at academia.edu, and the forthcoming analysis of fifth century military history of Iran by Katarzyna Maksymiuk and myself. The reign of Peroz saw further development in the general abandonment of the two-handed use of the lance in favour of the combination of shield and spear. The probable idea behind the use of the shield was that it gave better protection for its wielder against the arrows of the mounted archers of Central Asia that Peroz faced.

The enemies facing the Romans in the deserts of Arabia, Egypt and North Africa were also the same as before so that these and potential enemies consisted of the: Arabs, Yemenite Arabs, Nubians, Ethiopians and Berbers/Moors. At this time, these did not pose any major threats, until the naval losses suffered during the year 468, which enabled the Arabs and Yemenites to threaten the Romans in the Red Sea. In fact, the main threat to the Romans in North Africa was the Vandals, who crossed the Straits of Gibraltar with dire consequences for the Romans who now lost naval supremacy in the Western Mediterranean along with a major source of income and one of the breadbaskets of the Empire.

For a fuller discussion of the enemies of Rome and their tactics, see *MHLR* vols. 1–3. In the following narrative I do not always refer to the original sources when I include details of combat methods used by some particular enemy because I expect that readers are already familiar with these from previous volumes.

Chapter Three

The West in 425–429:
Three Mighty Men and a Lady

The Crowning

Theodosius II's representative the *Magister Officiorum* Helion placed the imperial robes upon the 6-year-old Valentinian III at Rome on 23 October 425 and thereby made him *Augustus*. So began the last period when the West Roman government still possessed the means to affect its own destiny. For developments before this see *Military History of Late Rome* volume 3. The actual government, however, was in the hands of Valentinian's mother *Augusta* Galla Placidia. *Comes* Flavius Constantius Felix was simultaneously made a *Magister Utriusque Militiae* and *Patricius* (Ann. Rav. a.425). Nothing is known of the exploits of this man before this date, which makes it probable that he had been one of the key players at Ravenna who had brought about the downfall of John. It is probable that Felix was a westerner because the new government needed to secure the loyalty of the forces based in Italy and also to reward the men responsible for the overthrow of John.[1] This meant that there now existed three competing military magnates in the West – Felix, Aetius and Bonifatius – and in order to be able to rule in the name of Valentinian, Galla Placidia had to perform a balancing act to keep these military men under her control and play each against the others.

The first policy statement of the new government was not to collect the Crown Gold donative (*aurum oblaticium*) from the populace of the city of Rome and the Senate in 426. The government clearly sought to endear themselves with the Senate in particular with this measure. Since the government felt that it needed to resort to such an extraordinary

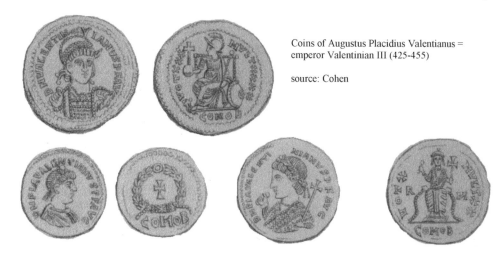

Coins of Augustus Placidius Valentinianus = emperor Valentinian III (425-455)

source: Cohen

measure, it seems probable that the city of Rome had not yet fully recovered from the sack of 410 and that the propertied classes had not fully recovered from the sack of their lands in Italy, Gaul and Spain.[2] In fact, it seems probable that the wealthier classes, many of whom had estates all over the Empire, had lost part of their revenue permanently thanks to the barbarian onslaught. The ability to forego this tax also means that the new government had at its disposal enough wealth to do so – most likely the Eastern government had given some sort of war chest for Galla Placidia to enable her to accomplish the task of retaking the West.

The surrender of Aetius and Castinus (see vol.3) had secured Italy and North Africa (with Mauretania Tingitana) for Valentinian, but the new caretaker government still needed to secure its position in Gaul, Britain and Spain. Hydatius states that the Vandals ravaged Spain and sacked Carthago Spartaria (Carthagena) and Hispalis in 425 in addition to which they raided the Balearic Islands and Mauretania. The pillaging of the Balearic Islands and Mauretania means that the Vandals had managed to capture ships from one of the coastal cities like for example the city of Carthagena as suggested by Ian Hughes (2012, 69). However, it is possible that Hydatius has condensed events of two to three years in Spain (424–5, or 425–6, or 424–6 or 425–7) all to take place in 425. The fact that the Western fleets were deployed against Bonifatius in 424–425 would of course have facilitated piratical raids. It is probable that these Vandal attacks were a continuation of the revolt that they had started in 419.

Aetius Pacifies the Visigoths

Prosper (a.425) and the Gallic Chronicle 452 (102, p.658 in Mommsen's ed. dated to the year 427) both state that the Visigoths were besieging the city of Arelate (Arles) and that it was relieved by Aetius, but Prosper dates the event to 425 and the Gallic Chronicle to 427. The former date is to be preferred. In my opinion, it is also probable that the Visigothic operations were simply a continuation of the revolt they had started in 422. However, if they or the above-mentioned Vandals had concluded a peace either under Honorius or John, then the death of either would have dissolved the treaty relationships – but it is improbable that these tribal confederacies would have been pacified as long as Castinus was the *MVM*.

Prosper's longer version states that the Visigoths retreated because of the imminent approach of Aetius, but did not go unpunished. Ian Hughes (Aetius, 63–66) interprets the evidence so that Aetius would not have received any forces from the armies posted in Italy because he was usurper John's former general as a result of which he would have been forced to go to Gaul (presumably to northern Gaul) to assemble an army to relieve the city of Arles. He suggests that the casualties that the Visigoths suffered resulted from the siege and not from any action by Aetius and that the relief of the city took place in 426 (a compromise between Prosper's 425 and CGall 452's 427). This in turn would have presumably caused the invasion of Franks in the North which Aetius crushed in 428. In my opinion this is unlikely because it is difficult to see why the West Roman government would not have used the forces they had in Italy for the relief of the city. The logistical support for the armies posted in the North went usually through the city of Arles so that it was of the utmost importance for the new government to relieve the administrative capital of Gaul (and its logistical hub) immediately as Prosper's dating suggests. It is also difficult to see why the Visigoths would have retreated unless threatened by a relief army.

When one combines the position of Arles on the eastern side of the Rhône (see the map in vol.3) with the statement of Prosper that the Visigoths suffered casualties during the retreat it becomes probable that Aetius had taken the most direct route from Italy to Arles so that he could bring relief as soon as possible and that Aetius's vanguard of cavalry, undoubtedly consisting of the Huns, had caught the retreating Visigoths when they were in the process of recrossing the Rhône. It is also likely that Aetius had been given an army by the new government because even if Aetius had retained 10,000–20,000 Huns in his own service, as is likely in light of his survival, this would not have sufficed against the Visigoths. It is in fact reasonable to think that the regular forces accompanying Aetius would have had a dual function: 1) to secure his loyalty with the order to kill him immediately if he attempted to form an alliance with the Visigoths (the army would probably have consisted of the East Romans); and 2) to provide Aetius with sufficient forces to relieve Arles and to convince the rebellious armies of Gaul to support the new legitimate government. In spite of having given part of the 'Western Army' to Aetius, Valentinian and Galla Placidia would still have been secured by three facts: most of the East Roman armies would have been retained in Italy; the commanders who had just ousted John were unlikely to rebel against their benefactor; and most of the surrendered western forces were securely held by Bonifatius, until shipped back to Italy.

We do not know what Aetius did during the rest of the year 425 and during the spring and summer of 426, but it seems probable that he would have continued operations against the Visigoths until they agreed to conclude a truce/treaty that satisfied the government of Ravenna. The reasons for this conclusion are that the sources do not mention any hostilities between the Visigoths and Romans before the year 430. It is improbable that Aetius would have left the war unfinished just as it would be improbable that Aetius would have been able to conduct a major campaign against the Franks in 428 if the Visigoths were still fighting against the Romans. Consequently, it is probable that Aetius continued his operations against the Visigoths during the spring and part of the summer of 426 until the Visigoths signed the peace treaty. It is probable (in spite of the silence of the sources) that the Vandals continued to raid Roman Spain while the Romans were fighting against other enemies. The revolt of the Franks is mentioned for the first time in the context of the events of the year 428, but it is possible that it had started well before that, for example in 425. It was in 425 that the famed Clodio took the kingship of the Salian Franks and it is probable that as a new ruler he needed to prove his military ability by conducting a series of successful military campaigns. However, the likeliest alternative is still that the Franks revolted only in 427, because it would be incomprehensible that Aetius would not have conducted any military operations against them in 426 if the Franks had already invaded in strength but it cannot be completely excluded either because it is possible that the Roman forces in the north of Gaul defended their territory effectively.

The fact that the *Patricius* Felix organized the murder of the Bishop of Arles, Patroclus, in 426 together with the assassination of Titus, a deacon of Rome, suggests that the new West Roman administration sought to exercise its rule over the people also through the Church hierarchy. In other words, the new administration sought to control the Church and through it the populace, which means that the Western Court had at its disposal three different channels to control the people: the armed forces, the civilian administration, and the Church. In some cases the religious and military functions were combined in the same man, the best example of which is the appointment of the *dux* Germanus as Bishop of Auxerre and his role in the pacification of Armorica and Britain.

Pannonian Campaign in 426/7

Aetius is attested to have been at Ravenna in about 426/7 where he supposedly initiated a scheme to destroy Bonifatius after the latter had returned to Africa (see below). The probable reason for Aetius' recall to Ravenna is that the East Roman army would have needed to start its retreat back into its own territory in 426/427 (see below), which would have made it necessary for Felix and Galla Placidia to remove some of the troops previously given to Aetius for two or three reasons: 1) to dimish the forces at Aetius' disposal; 2) to bolster the size of the army in Italy; and 3) if Aetius' force included East Romans they were due to leave Italy. It is in fact possible that Aetius had been given only Eastern forces with which he had relieved Arles because the Eastern forces would have definitely been loyal to the Theodosian House and would not have joined Aetius in any revolt. If this was the case, then Aetius brought back these forces after having secured the south of Gaul.

The Eastern Army appears to have returned to the East in about 426/7. The reason for this conclusion is that Marcellinus Comes records a Roman victory over the Huns for the year 1 September 426–31 August 427. Marcellinus and Jordanes (Get.166) state briefly that the Romans and Goths retook the Pannonian provinces which the Huns had held for fifty years. This has naturally caused plenty of speculation among historians.[3] My own interpretation is that the Western Government had been forced to hand Western Illyricum or at least part of Illyricum (Pannonia II and part of Dalmatia) to the Eastern Government in return for their support against the usurper John, and that the Germanic commanders of the East Roman forces resettled at least some of the Ostrogoths and Alans from this very same area in Thrace in 426/7 to bolster their own standing (Theophanes AM 5931). This treaty was put into effect after the Visigoths besieging Arles had been defeated and pacified, and Italy had been secured for Valentinian so that the Eastern field army could be withdrawn via Pannonia to Thrace. One of the aims of the war against the Pannonian Huns would have been to make it difficult for anyone to emulate Aetius' example and bring Huns to the West. Aetius' actions had clearly demonstrated the problem of having Huns on the Roman side of the river frontier. Consequently, when the Western Government had fulfilled its promise of handing over at least Pannonia and Dalmatia, the Eastern Government decided to push the Huns to the other side of the Danube. The best evidence for this comes from Jordanes' *Getica 166*. He states that in the 12th year of 'Vallia's' reign (415 + 12 = 427), the Romans and Goths drove out of Pannonia the Huns who had held it for fifty years. However, the next sentence suggests that Jordanes may have miscalculated the above figure by about one year. He states that after that Vallia (in truth Theoderic I) moved his army against the Vandals in the year when Ardaburius and Hierius became consuls in 427 with the implication that the expulsion of the Huns would probably have taken place before this in 426. In short, it is probable that the East Romans ousted the Huns from Pannonia as a follow-up for their Italian campaign so that they marched their army from Aquileia via Poetovio to Mursa and from there northwards to secure Pannonia II.

The consequences of this war were mixed. Firstly, it was the first stage in East Rome's strategy to fill up the hole in the defences in the north-west Balkans. Secondly, it appears to have resulted in the transferral of Goths from Pannonia to Thrace, which provided additional security for the capital while also creating a tribal grouping in the vicinity of the capital that ambitious men could exploit for their own purposes. It is more than likely that it was this group and the previous Goths settled in Thrace that subsequently became the Gothic group of Thrace commanded by Theoderic son of Triarius. I would suggest that the placing of the Goths and Alans in Thrace was part of the politics of the barbarian block in the military which consisted of Ardaburius and his son Aspar and of Plintha. Thirdly, the removal of Federate Goths from Pannonia II diminished the numbers of soldiers locally available against future incursions by the Huns. Fourthly, the expulsion of the Huns from Pannonia failed to secure the province in practice because (as we shall see) ambitious men could still call the Huns to assist them with the result that the defensive structures would prove futile. On the basis of the fact

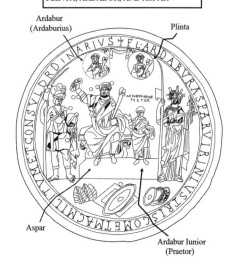

A PLATE DEPICTING THE EAST ROMAN BARBARIAN MILITARY ELITE: PLINTA, ARDABUR, AND ASPAR

Ardabur (Ardaburius)

Plinta

Aspar

Ardabur Iunior (Praetor)

The Plate above depicts the principal members of the East Roman barbarian block with Aspar's son Ardabur Jr. The slightly simplified drawing by Ilkka Syvänne. (© *Ilkka Syvänne 2014*)

Note the presence of the rectangular shield among the oval shields. These and other types of shields continued to be used well after their supposed abandonment in the third century.

that the Gepids subsequently fought the decisive battle against the Huns at Nedao in Pannonia in 453 it is possible that the East Romans settled the Gepids in the area when they evacuated the Goths and Alans to Thrace; but this is uncertain because it is possible that the Huns had settled the Gepids in the area after they had retaken the area from the Romans.

I would suggest that by 'fifty years' in both Marcellinus and Jordanes mean the *foedus* made by Gratian in 380 with Alatheus (Goths) and Saphrax (Alans). It is clear that their numbers included not only Goths and Alans but also Huns. It is also clear that the Huns of Pannonia did not control the provinces, because these had been under Western control previously, while in the light of Aetius' operations in the area it is obvious that the Huns still formed an independent entity within the Roman Empire that the ruler of the Huns north of the Danube could use to his own benefit. The East Romans wisely chose to divide the enemy by allying themselves with the Pannonian Goths. It is unfortunate that we do not know who the successful Roman general was. The likeliest candidates are the *MVM Praes.* Ardaburius, or his son Aspar, or the *MVM Praes.* Plintha (PLRE2 probably Aspar's father-in-law). This was a major victory. The Goths were transferred to Thrace (Theophanes AM 5931).[4] It seems probable that it was at the same time that the East

Romans forced at least some of the Rugii to become their Federates because the Rugii are attested to have been near the city of Viminacium as Roman Federates at some point in time between 434 and 441. See later.

Bonifatius' Revolt in 427

The extant sources give two completely different versions of how Bonifatius came to be suspected of having plotted against Galla Placidia and Valentinian, and two slightly different versions of how the Vandals were invited to North Africa.

Prosper (a.427) claims that Felix caused a war to be declared on Bonifatius because Bonifatius had refused to come to Italy. Prosper also mentions that Bonifatius' power and glory in Africa were increasing, which must have been as a result of Bonifatius' victories against the Moors mentioned by Augustinus. This in turn must have caused jealousy among his competitors Felix and Aetius. According to Procopius' version (*Wars* 3.3.14ff.), it was Aetius who brought about the war against his competitor Bonifatius. Procopius claims that Aetius slandered Bonifatius to Galla Placidia claiming that Bonifatius aimed at usurpring power. As a proof for this claim, Aetius stated that if she were to order Bonifatius to come to Rome he would not come. Placidia was convinced because Aetius had sweetened the lie by the supposedly clever means of testing Bonifatius' loyalty, but the witty Aetius forestalled this by writing a letter to Bonifatius in which he claimed that Galla Placidia was plotting against him and would summon him for no good reason to Rome so that he could be assassinated. Bonifatius believed the story, and when the summons came he refused to come.

The above-mentioned differences in the sources have unsurprisingly divided historians into two groups: those who put the blame of the breakup on Felix and those who blame Aetius. When assessing the evidence it should be kept in mind that despite being a contemporary Prosper was not necessarily right and it is possible that Procopius was better informed. On the basis of this it is impossible to be absolutely certain of what took place, but considering the cleverness of Aetius it would be more in keeping with his character that he was behind the whole scheme. It is in fact possible to reconcile the two accounts, if one supposes that Aetius had poisoned Felix's mind with the same lies or that Felix was convinced by Galla Placidia that Bonifatius must have been planning to revolt if he did not come when summoned. The caretaker government dispatched an expeditionary force under Mavortius, Gallio and Sanoeces against Bonifatius in 427 (Prosper a.427). The army appears to have consisted of regulars, Goths and Huns. Maenched-Helfen (p.419–20) suspects that Sanoeces was a Hunnic name, which would mean that he commanded the Huns.

Aetius vs. Franks in 428

While these forces were sent to North Africa, the Romans still faced the Vandals in Spain and the Franks in Gaul. We do not know what the Romans did regarding the Vandals in Spain, but we do know that Aetius was dispatched to Gaul to wrest control of the Rhine frontier back from the Franks which he accomplished in 428 (e.g. Prosper a.428). According to the Irish Annals (a.428) and other Irish sources, the High King of Ireland,

Niall, was killed by lightning at Sliabh Ealpa (the Alps) while besieging a town belonging to the Frankish king Faramund in Gaul (Bury, 354). This proves that the Romans were able to call into service even the Irish as their allies and use them as far away from home as the Alps.

The geographical details prove that when the Franks had conquered the Rhine frontier they must also have fought against the Federate Burgundians located in *Germania Prima* and whatever forces there were under *Dux provinciae Sequanici* (he is known to have commanded one *milites Latavienses*). This means that they had probably evicted the Burgundians and other forces southwards so that they would have regrouped somewhere in the Jura Mountains and/or in the area near Lugdunum. It is also probable that when Aetius marched against the Franks he bolstered the size of his army with these Burgundian fugitives and with the remnants of the regular forces from the north of Gaul which must have flocked southwards as well. Galla Placidia rewarded Aetius with the exalted position of *Magister Militum Praesentalis* in 429. The Romans fared less well in Spain, as we shall see.

Socrates' *Ecclesiastical History* includes a famous referral to the conversion of the Burgundians into the Catholic faith which is usually dated to the year 429/30. However, since the chapter is placed immediately after the appointment of Nestorius as Patriarch of Constantinople in 428, I prefer to date the conversion to 428/9. According to Socrates, the Huns had made continuous attacks against the Burgundians, most of whom earned their living as carpenters. When the Huns had killed large numbers of them, the Burgundians decided to seek help from the God of the Romans because He seemed to defend His followers. Consequently, they sent envoys to one of the cities of Gaul and asked the local bishop to baptize them. Having been fortified with faith, the Burgundians collected 3,000 men and surprised the Huns with a night attack in their encampment. The Huns were leaderless and therefore helpless because their king Uptaros/Octar had overeaten and died during the night. The Burgundians killed not less than 10,000 of their enemies, and from that date onwards were Catholic Christians. Previous research has established that the Burgundians in question were the transrhenian Burgundians on the eastern side of the Rhine. On the basis of Orosius' text, previous research has also established that the Burgundian Federates had already converted to the Catholic faith in the 410s, which means that the eastern Burgundians probably sought a bishop to convert them from the area occupied by the Federate Burgundians.[5]

I would connect this conversion with the events that had taken place in 426/7 and 428 in the west. The East Roman attack (with the approval of West Rome) against the Pannonian Huns in 426/7 had soured the relationship between the Huns and Romans with the result that Octar, the co-ruler of the Huns, had attacked Burgundians on the eastern side of the Rhine at the same time as the Franks were attacking the Federate Burgundians on the western side. It is quite probable that the Franks and Huns had formed an alliance and were simultaneously fighting against the Burgundians on both sides of the Rhine in late 427 and in 428. The Huns were acting prudently. Despite cooperating *de facto* with the Franks against the Romans and Burgundians, they had still not perpetrated *casus belli* because they had attacked only the East Burgundians who did not have any *foedus* with Rome. The West Romans were naturally not eager to make new enemies and ignored the fact. The Burgundian victory over the Huns made this also unnecessary. If the Hunnic attack against the Burgundians took place before the appointment of Aetius, it is possible that this had a role in Aetius' appointment. The victory achieved by Aetius with his Federate Catholic Burgundians against the Franks in 428 then demonstrated to the East Burgundians that the Roman God protected its followers, with the result that they dispatched their envoys to a city controlled by their brethren presumably either in 428 or early 429. The following East Burgundian victory over the Huns secured the Rhine frontier against the Huns for the next decade. If true, the death of Octar from overeating just before the attack was very fortunate; but it is of course possible that some Roman or Burgundian agent could have poisoned Octar's food (a typical Roman practice at the time as we shall see) or that Octar's death had resulted from the attack and not from the overeating.

The Alleluia Victory in about 429 (see also my *Britain in the Age of Arthur*)

The events associated with the activities of the Bishop Germanus suggest that Aetius' campaigns in the north of Gaul included the securing of Britain for the Empire through religious diplomacy rather than through force. According to *Vita S. Germani* (12ff. with Bede, Eccl. 19ff.; Prosper a.429), a deputation from Britain arrived in Gaul to ask help from the Catholic bishops against the Pelagian heretics. The bishops gathered a great synod to discuss the matter and decided to send Germanus (bishop of Autissiodorensis/Autessiodurum, mod. Auxerre) and Lupus (bishop of Tricasses/ Trecassina/ Augustobona, mod. Troyes) to Britain. According to Prosper, the bishops were sent by the pope Celestine, which can be reconciled with the above if one presumes that the synod was convened by the Pope. It seems likely that the Pope coordinated his activities with the earthly authorities. It is unlikely to be a coincidence that many of the bishops (like Germanus) were former military men or civil servants. The use of such bishops enabled the Roman government[6] to provide religious leadership in conjunction with administrative and military instructions.

Considering the distances involved it seems probable that the British ambassadors had arrived early in 429 (date given by Prosper for the arrival of the bishops in Britain) and that the bishops embarked on ships at Bononia late in 429, which would explain the storm their ship faced. The other alternative is that the envoys arrived in 428 and that it took until the spring of 429 for the bishops to begin their journey across the Channel.

The choice of these two bishops was particularly apt, for both were charismatic figures. Most importantly, Germanus had a military background, which made him particularly well-suited for the circumstances facing the bishops in Britain. Constantius (Vita 1–2) states that Germanus had risen to the rank of *Dux* of more than one province, which is likely to mean the rank of *Dux Tractus Armoricani et Nervicani* (M. E. Jones, 369–370), before election as bishop in about 418. It was at that date that the local populace effectively forced Germanus to become their bishop and protector against the imperial tax gatherers and officials. In short, Germanus sent his wife to a nunnery and became a bishop. The choice was a good one. Germanus had the presence of mind and the right connections to protect the populace. It is also important to understand that despite being a bishop Germanus still acted as a tool of the imperial authorities. He established a monastery to spread the Catholic faith among the barbarians (mainly Goths) settled in Aquitania (Vita 6ff.); and by acting as a mediator between the locals, imperial administration and church, he was able to help the Roman government maintain its grip on north-west Gaul and Britain (see also the events in 446–8). According to Constantius (9), Germanus performed his role as bishop as if he were still a *dux*. In fact, Germanus also acted as if he were a sort of police inspector and interrogator and cured many a thief (Const. 7).

The crossing of the Channel proved difficult because of the storm, but when the bishops reached Britain they were greeted by great crowds of people. Their arrival strengthened the standing of the Catholic Church immediately, but they still needed to prove their point in a public debate, which was probably held somewhere near Londinium (London). According to the hagiography, Germanus successfully refuted all the points put forward by the Pelagians. However, the decisive moment came when a tribune, his wife and blind 10-year-old daughter approached the bishops. Germanus performed a miracle and cured the girl's eyes with the result that the populace turned away from the false doctrine. It is obvious that the miracle had been staged for this purpose. The tribune in question had undoubtedly been ordered to perform this service and it is even possible that Germanus was his old commander. After the heresy had been refuted successfully, the bishops visited the shrine of St. Alban, which must have been located in modern St. Albans (Verulamium).

Then Germanus was retained in some unnamed place for a considerable period of time because he had suffered an injury and it was then that another 'miracle' took place. Several houses were burned in a fire, but the house in which the bishop stayed was 'miraculously' saved. It is possible that the fire was an arson committed by the Pelagonians in an effort to kill the bishop.

In the meantime, the Saxons and Picts had joined their forces and invaded with the result that the Britons had been forced to withdraw their army into their camp. Even though this is not mentioned, it is quite possible that the Pelagonians and the invaders cooperated. The British soldiers asked the bishops to help them, which does suggest that besides his spiritual abilities Germanus had also a reputation of being a gifted military commander. Germanus obliged and hastened to the scene of operations.

It is unfortunate that Constantius fails to mention the place where Germanus had rested and where the British camp was located. The traditional location for the subsequent battle is near Mold in Flintshire, but as Hoare (p.300) notes there are reasons to question this. It is possible that the St. Germanus of Auxerre has been confused with the St. Germanus of Man in the Celtic tradition (the Celtic name for Germanus being Garmon). It is also odd to find the Saxons cooperating with the Picts on the west coast. If the persons have been mixed up, then the subsequent battle would have taken place somewhere north of London, probably near Braughing. However, if the traditional place of the battle is correct, then the Picts would have formed an alliance with the Saxons in an effort to surprise the British defenders. The probable reason for such a plan would have been that the Saxons possessed bigger ships able to carry more men. The timing of the invasion would also have been a surprise, because it occurred early in the spring – it was Lent (in 429 or 430?). When the Saxons and Picts would then have disembarked their unusually large army in Wales, the local forces would have been hopelessly outnumbered, and it is not impossible that this is precisely what happened, and I have reconstructed the events according to this assumption. It is impossible to know for certain what the respective army sizes were, but one can make a rough estimate on the basis of the typical large invasion forces used by the Saxons and Picts (see Volume 1 for additional details) which suggest that a major invasion by both operating together could consist of about 10,000–15,000 footmen. The local Romans probably had no more than 6,000 to 7,000 regulars to oppose them unless they called reinforcements from the north and west, which was not an option they could use in the early spring. What is notable is that the traditional location of the battle was very close to the old legionary fortress of Deva (*Legio XX Valeria*) and I would suggest that this unit or its successor had remained there, and now, together with the local auxiliaries, engaged the invaders. It is possible that the locals had raised some sort of paramilitary forces to bolster their numbers, as implied by many sources, but we do not know whether these were present at this battle.

When the bishops arrived, British soldiers flocked to be baptized. A temporary church was built out of leafy branches inside the camp as befitted Easter Day. The soldiers clearly needed encouragement in the form of religious ceremonies to face the bloodthirsty barbarians. The enemy attempted to surprise the Britons by attacking them on Easter Day when the soldiers were supposedly disarmed. However, the scouts (*exploratores*) gave a timely warning and Germanus simply announced that he would take command of the army. He was clearly a man of some authority. Germanus chose some *expediti* troops (in this case probably lightly-equipped troops rather than men without baggage) and inspected the outworks and the likely direction of the enemy attack. He observed that the valley was enclosed by mountains. The traditional location for this valley is the River Alyn. Germanus stationed his *expediti* troops on the mountains in ambush. I would locate this place of ambush on the hill west of Mold/R. Alyn. I would also suggest that the Roman marching camp was located in the town centre of modern Mold and that the medieval church was built on the site of the Easter Church of St. Germanus.

Germanus ordered that all troops were to shout in unison the battle-cry Alleluia after he and Lupus did so. The purpose was to increase the effect of the ambush with the sudden shout. When the unsuspecting enemies had reached the vicinity Germanus and Lupus shouted the Alleluia three times and the whole Roman army repeated it in unison. The shout echoed loudly in the confined space with the result that the barbarians panicked thinking themselves surrounded – as they indeed were. According to Constantius, the barbarians threw away their weapons and ran, and some were drowned in the river they had just crossed. He also claims that the rout of the enemy had been achieved without any bloodshed, but as noted by M.E. Jones it is probable that this was just a way to exonerate the bishops of the guilt of having shed blood. It is clear that the Romans had ambushed the barbarians and pursued their advantage so ruthlessly that the panicked foes were forced to flee straight into the river. The victory was complete and the Romans were able to collect the booty scattered around the field at their leisure. According to Constantius, the victory achieved by Germanus had secured the wealthy island of Britain, and indeed this seems to have been the case, for Britain remained secure until the 440s.

As noted by M.E. Jones this story proves that Roman military organization, civil government, cities and Christianity had survived almost intact in Britain. I would go so far as to claim that Britain remained securely part of the Roman Empire and that several of the old Roman units like *Legio XX Valeria* or its successor still remained stationed in the island. The forces that were withdrawn by Stilicho and by Constantine III appear

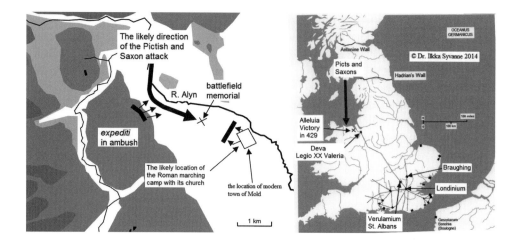

to have included only part of the army, which the Britons would then have replaced by local levies. Gildas' and Constantius' accounts (see later) make it clear that the Britons considered themselves part of the Roman Empire well into the 440s, and probably even beyond that, as the legend of Arthur proves.

Constantius' *Life of Germanus* (19ff) makes it clear that Germanus' role as protector of the people against the taxes was of paramount importance for the people of Gaul. The biographer constantly stresses the fact that Germanus was always conscientious of the fact that he and his retinue caused hardship to the people when he was travelling from one place to another and with this in mind he always took as small a retinue as possible. After all, it was his duty to act as consoler and protector of the taxpayers and had he himself been a cause of discomfort he could hardly have retained the trust of the people. The biography notes at least one instance in which Germanus travelled on behalf of the taxpayers to Arles to meet the *PP* of Gaul, Auxiliaris (435–9). It is to be presumed that Germanus' mission was a success. It is clear that Germanus had an important civic role to play in north-west Gaul and Britain.

Bonifatius Brings the Vandals to Africa

Procopius states that after Bonifatius had revolted, he immediately started to contemplate the possibility of forming an alliance with the Vandals because he knew that his own forces were insufficient to face the full might of the emperor's forces. Consequently he dispatched to Spain his most trusted friends to open negotiations with the Vandals with the promise that each of the sons of the previous king would obtain a third of Libya in return for their help against Galla Placidia and Valentinian. Power was in the hands of the legitimate son Gunderic (Gundericus/Gontharis), who was the king, and the illegitimate son Gaiseric, the cleverest of the bunch; the third brother was still a child. According to Prosper (a.427), both Bonifatius and the legitimate government vied to obtain the support of the Vandals with the result that the sea was opened up to the barbarians who had hitherto been ignorant of the management of ships. This has caused some researchers like Ian Hughes to suspect that the Vandals exploited the situation by taking the initiative themselves without actually having been invited by Bonifatius as claimed by Procopius. In my opinion, there is no need to whitewash Bonifatius' reputation on the basis of this. Strictly speaking Prosper's statement doesn't preclude an invitation and I would suggest that Procopius is correct in stating that Bonifatius' friends managed to convince all three brothers to join the African *Comes* and that in his distress Bonifatius had indeed invited the Vandals to Africa to the detriment of the Roman Empire.

The Vandal invasion, however, did not materialize as soon as Bonifatius had hoped, probably because the negotiations by the different parties took time to accomplish. Procopius' statement that the agreement was reached when all three brothers were still alive helps us to date the agreement to the year 428, because Hydatius states that Gunderic recaptured Hispalis in 428, but then incurred the wrath of God by pillaging a church with the result that he was seized by a demon and died. Procopius, however, provides two different versions. According to the first version Gaiseric killed his half-brother, and according to the version spread by the Vandals themselves Gunderic was captured in battle and then impaled by the Germans in Spain. If the last version is true then Gunderic was either defeated by the Suevi or by some Germanic Federates in Roman service, the first being more likely.

In the meantime however, and despite being heavily outnumbered, Bonifatius had managed to score a great success thanks to the fact that one of the enemy commanders, Sanoeces, had agreed to betray his fellow commanders, which happened when the army was besieging Bonifatius at Carthage. The fact that Bonifatius' wife was a member of the Visigothic royal house had undoubtedly a role in this desertion. Mavortius and Gallio were both killed and the survivors were presumably incorporated into Bonifatius' armed forces. This likely happened in late 427 or early 428 and was probably the reason why the Vandals agreed to ally themselves with Bonifatius rather than with the legitimate government. Most importantly Bonifatius' victory would have secured him most of the ships that had carried the enemy army and its supplies to Africa, and it is probable that Bonifatius subsequently dispatched this fleet to assist the Vandals in the crossing of the Straits of Gibraltar. The reason for this conclusion is that he lacked adequate numbers of ships to engage the Vandals later which must mean that he had dispatched his own ships to assist the Vandals. In other words, I would suggest that the Court of Ravenna had now lost a significant portion of its imperial sea-going fleet to Bonifatius. Ravenna's response was to dispatch a new army and fleet under the Gothic *Comes* Sigisvult (Sigisvultus) against Bonifatius which presumably happened in late 428 or early 429 despite the winter season because it is probable that his landing in Africa would have coincided with the absence of Bonifatius' fleet which would have been sent to assist the Vandals to cross the Straits.

The Vandal invasion of Africa was delayed presumably for two reasons: 1) the death of Gunderic resulted in a delay because Gaiseric needed to secure his position as the new king (it is also probable that Bonifatius' envoys had to renegotiate the treaty with Gaiseric); 2) the Suevi under their king, Heremigarius, exploited the withdrawal of Vandals to Baetica by pillaging the neighbouring provinces. It was thanks to the last-mentioned problem that Gaiseric was forced to abandon the crossing of the Straits from Baetica to Mauritania at the last minute and march his army back against the Suevi. Gaiseric shadowed the Suevi as they pillaged Lusitania and then slaughtered the enemy

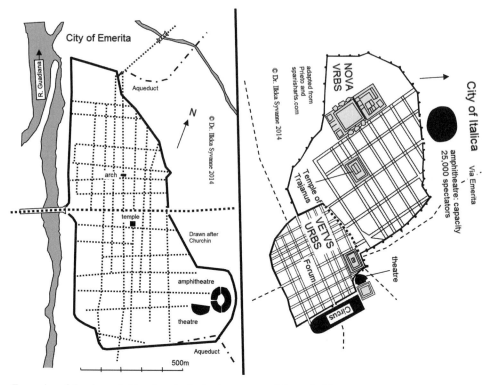

Examples of the sizes of cities that the barbarians captured from the Romans.

army near the city of Emerita. Heremigarius fled on horseback but was drowned in the river Ana. The defeat of the Suevi was facilitated by the fact that the Vandals attacked them after the Suevi had pillaged Emerita and were tired and laden with spoils of war. There are two possible reasons for the sudden arrival of the Suevi in the south: 1) the court of Ravenna had bought their services against the Vandals; 2) the Suevi just exploited the absence of Vandals by pillaging. The latter alternative is more likely because the Suevi were definitely in revolt the next year, 430.

After Gaiseric had crushed the Suevi, he marched his forces back to Baetica and then crossed the Straits at Gadira either to Tingis or Septem (mod. Ceuta) in May 429 (Hydat.; Isid. HRGVS 74). Gaiseric had apparently appointed at the beginning of his reign eighty *chiliarchoi* (commanders of 1,000) in charge of *lochoi* (units) to make it appear as if his army would have consisted of 80,000 active soldiers whereas in practice it consisted of 50,000 men (Procop. *Wars* 3.5.18–19), his purpose being to scare his enemies with inflated numbers. This actually represents the natural age division among the tribal societies so that when there were 80,000 fighters in the ranks only 50,000 were combat ready, the rest being too old or too young or injured (see Syvänne, 2004).[7] These latter were left to guard the families when the army fought. According to the eyewitness account of Possidius (28), this force consisted of Vandals and Alans mixed with one Gothic tribe and individuals of various nations. The Vandal navy must have consisted mainly of native Romans who were press-ganged into service. If we assume that the Vandals could ship across the Straits at least 20,000 men/women at a time, and assume that some of the ships would have been powered by sail rather than by oars, then one can assume that there would have been at least 15,000–20,000 oarsmen, sailors and marines, but the figure may have been even greater. As noted above, it is probable that Gaiseric's fleet also included ships dispatched by Bonifatius. We should not forget the non-combatants and families that both supported the soldiers and slowed down their progress. These must have numbered at least 80,000–120,000 women and children so that the overall number of people that Gaiseric needed to feed on the march would have been about 175,000–220,000. In addition to this, we need to include the horses for 80,000 warriors (after years of pillaging there could easily have been three horses per warrior!), and the horses and beasts of burden for the baggage train. Gaiseric was clearly a man of great ability to be able to move this massive migration of men and animals from Spain to Africa.

Even though the province of Tingitana belonged administratively to Spain, it still seems likely that Gaiseric did not meet any resistance on landing because it is probable that Bonifatius' friends would have secured the landing place in advance. However, this dating is contested by two other sources, the Annals of Ravenna, which places the crossing in May 428, and by Prosper who places the crossing to the year 427. The likeliest date is the commonly accepted May 429 for the reason that it tallies with the timetable required to complete the various operations conducted by the different parties. Procopius (*Wars* 3.3.26–7) notes aptly that the evacuation of Spain by the Vandals created a power vacuum which the Visigoths then filled later.

According to Procopius (*Wars* 3.3.27ff.), when Bonifatius declared revolt in 427, his friends were dumbfounded because such an action was entirely out of character for the man. They communicated this to Galla Placidia with the result that she dispatched them to meet Bonifatius at Carthage. When there, they heard the whole story and were shown Aetius' letter with the result that they were able to return to Rome to give a full and accurate report of the plot. Placidia was astonished, but did nothing because Aetius' position was too strong to be challenged and the Empire was already in too great a plight. Instead she told the friends of Bonifatius her side of the story, and asked them to persuade Bonifatius to agree to end the revolt so that the Empire would not fall under barbarian rule. In other words, the real reason for the sudden readiness of the empress to conclude a peace was the fact that the Vandals had now crossed into Africa and threatened the only unravaged area of West Rome which was also its breadbasket. When the envoys came Bonifatius agreed to end the revolt. It is not known whether Sigisvult then returned to Italy, but this is usually assumed. Bonifatius then sent envoys of his own to the Vandals with promises of great rewards if they would return to Spain, but to no avail. Gaiseric smelled blood – the rich provinces of Africa lay open to be pillaged and Bonifatius was forced to prepare for war. The Vandal masses moved inexorably towards Carthage. The towns, cities and forts along the way fell either because they were unwalled or the walls were in poor repair, because there were too few defenders, or because the defenders just fled. According to the eyewitness account of Posidius (28), the Vandals truly deserved their later fame as Vandals. This massive movement of people and animals also grew in size as deserters and slaves joined the Vandal trek and as the Vandals took locals as prisoners.

Bonifatius vs. Vandals

According to Procopius, Bonifatius deployed his army for combat against the Vandals somewhere in the neighbourhood of Hippone (Hippo Regius), but was defeated in battle and forced to flee to the safety of the walls of Hippone. Notably Bonifatius' army consisted solely of allied Goths (Posidius 28), which must therefore have consisted mostly of the followers of Bonifatius' Visigothic wife who belonged to the royal family plus the previous deserters. The city of Hippone was the home of the famous Saint Augustine who died just two months after the siege started on 28 August 430, but before his death he noted the great sufferings of the populace resulting from the siege. It is unfortunate that we do not know the size of the army Bonifatius deployed against the Vandals, but the odds are that even with the probable reinforcements left behind by Sigisvult he would have been both outnumbered and outclassed by the veteran forces of Gaiseric. Gaiseric probably also outgeneralled Bonifatius – he was one of the wiliest commanders the Germanic peoples ever produced. As noted by Ian Hughes (2012, 75), the government of Ravenna must have sent urgent calls for help to Constantinople soon after this for the East Roman help to arrive in 431. The situation was critical. Bonifatius was besieged at Hippone and the Vandals were therefore effectively in possession of the breadbasket of West Rome, and it is very probable that the city of Rome was once again facing famine.

Siege of Hippo Regius/Hippone ca. May/June 429–August/September 430[8]

The siege of Hippone proved difficult for both. The presence of the Vandal navy meant that they could blockade the city effectively on all sides. In addition to this, the location of the city slightly inland meant that the Vandals were also able to place their garrisons on the sea side. The reconstruction of the city of Hippone is based on the map produced by the French expedition to Algeria in 1846 and the book *Hippone*. However, the reconstruction of the likely location of the walls and moats is my own educated guess which is based on the extent of the city and the locations of the waterways because no traces of Roman walls have been found (Laporte, n. 10). As noted above, it is probable that Bonifatius had previously sent his own fleet and the captured imperial fleet to assist the Vandals in the crossing. This meant that Bonifatius and Ravenna lacked adequate naval forces to challenge the Vandal fleet in order to bring relief to Hippone. It is clear that the only good explanation for the inability of the West Roman government to challenge the Vandals is that the Vandals had gained possession of at least half of the naval resources previously possessed by West Rome. The contrast between the ability of Constantius III to blockade Visigoths and the inability of the West Romans now could not have been any greater.

The siege began at some point in time between 29 May and 27 June in 430, and lasted fourteen months. Eventually the Vandals exhausted their supplies because their provisioning was based on what could be obtained by pillage, and the concept of living off the land meant that the army had to be on the move. It was impossible to gather more supplies than the surrounding areas produced. Consequently, when the assaults

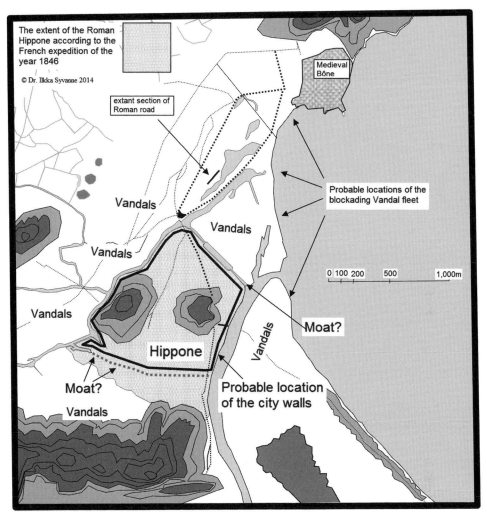

The Siege of Hippo Regius by the Vandals in 430–431.

had failed and the enemy had not surrendered, the starving Vandals were forced to move on to survive with the result that the blockade and siege was lifted in August/September 430.[9] When this happened, Bonifatius sallied out and marched to Carthage.

Coins of Galla Placidia (source: Cohen)

Chapter Four

The West: Two Mighty Men and a Lady 430–432[1]

Year 430: War on All Fronts

On the basis of Hydatius (a.430, 81–82), the defeat of the Suevi at the hands of the Vandals had not diminished their fighting spirit. According to Hydatius, the Suevi first released the hostages (!) and then attacked the central areas of Gallaecia, but this time they suffered a defeat probably owing to the casualties they had suffered in 429. The Suevi were forced to conclude a peace when some of their men were killed or captured by the people (*plebs*) who remained in the stronger forts (*castella*). This is one of those instances in which the fortifactions proved their great value against the Germanic peoples. It is notable how honourably the Suevi behaved in this instance. They did not try any surprise attack, but released the hostages they were holding and declared war. This text also proves that the defence of central Gallaecia was conducted primarily by the local common people, the plebs, but I would not preclude the presence of some remnants of local garrisons among their ranks because the likely stronger forts were the cities of Leon (Legio) and Lugo (Lucus Augusti) both of which were former garrison

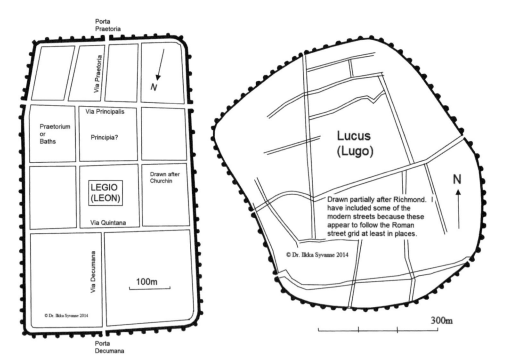

The two best fortified cities of central Gallaecia.

towns. See accompanying maps. However, what is clear is that whatever military forces there were left, these were now under local civilian command.

Gaul was also facing renewed revolt of the Visigoths or a splinter group of Visigoths, because Hydatius (a.430, 82) states that the *comes* Aetius wiped out a band of Visigoths near Arles after the capture of one of their chiefs called Anaulfus. See also the year 438. On the basis of this there is no way of knowing for certain whether the Visigoths in question were acting independently or with the approval of Theoderic I, but the fact that the Visigoths sent an envoy called Vetto to Gallaecia to negotiate with the Suevi suggests rather the latter. It seems probable that this defeat forced the Visigoths to renew their treaty with the Romans or even more likely that the campaign was continued in 431 (see below), because it seems probable that Aetius was unable to complete the campaign, the reason for this being that the Iuthungi had been invited into Noricum by the Nori. The revolt of the Nori, who must be the inhabitants of Noricum, typifies the problems the West Romans faced. The corrupt imperial administration oppressed the people with harsh taxes and provided nothing in return, which made the people all too eager to call the barbarians to assist them.

After Aetius had learnt of the troubles in Noricum, he acted with the celerity so typical of him and defeated both the Iuthungi and the Nori after which he marched back to Ravenna (Hydat. a.430, 83–84). Notably, the future emperor Avitus was one of the commanders accompanying Aetius. The Nori, however, had not yet been subdued. The probable reason for Aetius' recall to Ravenna, before the revolts were fully quelled, was that West and East Rome had collected a powerful force to be dispatched to Africa to help Bonifatius against the Vandals. The West Roman force must have consisted primarily of the men stationed in Italy under Felix.

There are two different versions of what happened when Aetius reached Ravenna. The first is that Felix, his wife Padusia and deacon Grunitus were plotting against Aetius, and when Aetius found this out he killed them all. According to the second version, provided by Hydatius, Felix was killed in a mutiny of soldiers. Ian Hughes (2012, 78–79) has pointed out that there is not necessarily any disagreement in these versions. It is entirely plausible that Aetius could have incited the troops to kill Felix, Padusia and Grunitus by stating that they were plotting against him. However, in my opinion the likely reason for Aetius' ability to convince the troops would not be that he was a Westerner and Felix an Easterner as suggested by Hughes, but rather the probability that when Aetius came to Ravenna he brought back those Praesental forces that were under him to replace Felix's men that had already been dispatched to join the East Roman fleet and army. On the basis of this, I would suggest that it is improbable that Felix had actually plotted against Aetius, but that it was Aetius who just exploited the absence of Felix's troops by inciting the remaining men into a mutiny.

The lack of resources forced the West Romans to move their few existing military assests continually from one front to another with the result that they were unable to provide permanent solutions to any of their troublespots. At the end of the year 430, the Vandals were still roaming free in Africa; the Suevi had been only temporarily pacified; the Visigoths had either been pacified or continued their revolt; the Iuthungi and Nori were defeated but the latter had not been subdued; and the Picts and Saxons were attacking Britain. The West Roman military forces were stretched so thinly that the Spaniards and

Britons were largely left to deal with their problems by themselves – the Spaniards were given occasional military assistance, but the Britons who were furthest away received only spiritual help in the form of the bishop Germanus. It is no wonder that the West Romans were forced to seek help from the East. The extant chronicles give such sparse details of events that it is actually possible that the Franks renewed their revolt in 430 because Aetius was conducting a campaign in Gaul in 431 rather than in 432 (see below) or that the 431 campaign in Gaul was still fought against the Visigoths.

The Year 431: Defeats and Victories

The reinforcements despatched jointly by Ravenna and Constantinople arrived probably either in late 430 or early in 431. The East Roman fleet and army were commanded by the *MVM* Aspar. Bonifatius and Aspar decided to engage Gaiseric, but were so completely defeated in battle that it was each man for himself. The captured men included Aspar's *domesticus* Marcian (Marcianus), the future emperor. According to the legend spread later, Gaiseric saw the shadow of an eagle land on Marcian with the result that Gaiseric thought that it was not right to kill the man. Gaiseric then demanded Marcian swear an oath that he would never attack the Vandals if he were to be become a king, and so it happened. The story is usually considered a later embellishment to explain why Marcian never attacked the Vandals, but one cannot entirely rule it out because many fifth-century Romans were quite superstitious. If there is any basis in truth for the story, it is possible that the cunning Gaiseric could have used such a psychological ploy to convince (the possibly superstitious) Marcian of his fate just before his release.

The remnants of the defeated army were apparently regrouped in Carthage which the Vandals were unable to threaten, thanks to the presence of the fleet that had transported the East and West Roman forces. It is probable that the vast majority of the ships consisted of those dispatched by the Eastern Court. The fact that the Vandals were unable to blockade Carthage from the sea proves that the fleet the Easterners had dispatched was very considerable, perhaps as large as 150–200 liburnae/dromons plus the transport ships. Eventually the situation stabilized so that neither side was able to defeat the other. However, before this happened, the Vandals were able to exploit their victory by conquering several places, the most important of which was the city of Hippo Regius/Hippone which became Gaiseric's HQ.

Meanwhile, Aetius had apparently been forced to return to Noricum to finish the job. This time he defeated the Nori so decisively that we hear of no similar troubles for the rest of the century. It is unfortunate that Hydatius (a.431, 85) gives no details of what had taken place or how the revolt was crushed. It leaves many unanswered questions. Did Aetius reorganize the administration and the defences at this time, or did he leave these things to the local loyalist magnates? In my opinion, it is more likely that Aetius reorganized the province in 431 because there still remained regular units in existence in the area as late as the 470s.

The Suevi were dissatisfied with the peace treaty they had signed and renewed their hostilities in 431 and this time they had greater success, because the chronicler bishop Hydatius was dispatched as ambassador to Aetius to seek his help (Hydat., a.431, 86). The successes achieved by the Suevi seem to have encouraged the Visigoths to seek their help, but their envoy Vetto returned empty-handed. Hydatius mentions that Aetius was fighting in Gaul when Hydatius was dispatched to seek his help. It is usually thought that Aetius must have been fighting against the Franks whom he defeated in 432, but since Aetius' previous campaign against the Visigoths had been cut short by the invasion of the Iuthungi and because the Visigoths had sent an envoy to the Suevi in 431, it seems preferable to think that Aetius continued his interrupted campaign against Theoderic I during the summer of 431. This time the campaign proved a success and the Visigoths were forced to conclude a peace. However, I would still suggest that Aetius had been forced to find a quick solution rather than a satisfactory result, because it is probable that the Franks also invaded in 431 making it necessary for Aetius to continue his campaign in the north of Gaul.

We also know that at some point in time before 442 the Visigoths and Vandals formed an alliance which was sealed with a marriage between Theoderic's daughter and Gaiseric's son Huneric, but we do not know the exact date. There are two probable dates for this, which are the year 431 or the years 435–7. In 431 Theoderic is attested to have been seeking allies. On the other hand, it is possible that Theoderic followed the same policy later. It is possible that Theoderic concluded an alliance with the Vandals just before revolting in 435 or during the revolt in 436–7 because the Vandals are attested to have started their own revolt against the Romans in 437. The likeliest year is 436 because if the treaty was concluded then, the successes of the Visigoths in 436 would have encouraged the Vandals to start their own revolt in 437. However, one cannot entirely rule out the possibility that the alliance was already concluded in 431.

The Year 432: The Showdown between Aetius and Bonifatius

Aetius appears to have defeated the Franks decisively either during the winter of 431/2 or in the spring of 432 (Hydat. a.432, 88) because it would otherwise be difficult to see how he could have accomplished the other things he did in 432. After his defeat, Clodio seems to have transferred his target of attack to the areas east of the Rhine where he managed to subdue the Thuringians by about 439 (Thuringian subjects of the Salian Franks: FRMG 594, 596, 598, 612). After the Franks had been forced to conclude a peace, Aetius dispatched the *comes* Censorius as an envoy to the Suevi in the company of the bishop Hydatius. The lacuna in the relevant part of Hydatius' text prevents certainty, but it appears probable that Censorius was accompanied by some forces which he was to use to force the Suevi to conclude a peace. We do not know what he achieved with these, but since a peace was signed in 433 Censorius cannot have been entirely unsuccessful. See below.

Galla Placidia was apparently very unsatisfied with the murder of Felix and usurpation of Aetius, and when Aetius and his forces were fighting in Gaul she decided to exploit Aetius' absence by recalling Bonifatius to Italy and by deposing Aetius. It is practically certain that Bonifatius took with him his *bucellarii* and probably also some of his other forces, because the aim was nothing less than to defeat Aetius and his veteran army. Bonifatius sailed to Portus and from there marched to Rome where he was nominated as the *MVM Praes.* and *Patricius*. This also implies that Bonifatius took with him the West Roman fleet that had transported the recent reinforcements. The fact that Aspar was

The accompanying images show the Greeks fighting against the Trojans in the so-called *Ilias Ambrosiana* (drawings by Mai 1819). The manuscript is usually dated to the fifth century, or alternatively to the reign of Anastasius at the turn of the sixth century. The soldiers wear late Roman equipment and can therefore be considered to be roughly representative of Roman forces engaging each other in a civil war, as happened when the forces of Aetius and Bonifatius engaged each other. Note also the continued use of the rectangular scutum. This is definitely not a case of the artist copying earlier works of art because he clearly depicts period equipment elsewhere and if one accepts these to be representative of period equipment, then one should also accept the rest as I am doing. However, the artist has still made one compromise, which is that he (purposely) represented the Trojans (usually but not always) with Phrygian hats and the Greeks with helmets so that the audience could see which side was which. Please note however that the type of combat that is being depicted in these illustrations would have only represented such places on the battlefield or phases in combat in which the orderly battle lines consisting of ranks and files would have already broken, for example as a result of some bold individuals fighting their way through the enemy array. This is the Hollywood-style presentation which forgets the stage in which the fighting was more orderly and which also forgets that some of the units retained their order throughout the battle and pursuit.

able to stalemate Gaiseric's huge army, with the forces that he had left, stands as a proof of Aspar's skills as a commander. He was probably not among the greatest commanders of all ages because he suffered so many serious defeats (none of which, however, was decisive), but he appears to have been still a competent general because it was not a mean feat to stalemate the crafty Gaiseric and his Vandals. Before reaching the neighbourhood of Carthage, the Vandals had taken several well-fortified cities that had stronger defences than the city of Carthage so it was not the walls of that city that kept the Vandals at bay but the skill with which Aspar defended them and the neighbouring areas. The key for his success must have been the naval superiority provided by the Eastern Fleet.

When Aetius learnt the bad news, he marched his army back from Gaul at the double and managed to intercept Bonifatius' army at Ariminum (Rimini) before it was able to reach Ravenna. According to Marcellinus Comes (a.432), the day before the battle Aetius had ordered a spear to be made for him which would be longer than the spear wielded by Bonifatius. This proves two things. Firstly, it proves that there was a standard length for the cavalry spear which Aetius now wanted to surpass. This detail also makes it likely that the spear was the *contus* wielded with a two-handed grip. See my artistic reconstruction of this duel in the Plates and the accompanying image from the Column of Arcadius. Secondly, he knew the heroic bent of Bonifatius, which meant that Bonifatius would be prepared to fight duels when challenged. It is in fact quite possible that Bonifatius had previously wounded the Visigothic king Athaulf in a similar duel fought between the commanders in the midst of other fighting (see vol.3). It is a pity that the sources do not give any details of the ensuing battle, except that Bonifatius won and that Aetius delivered a fatal wound on Bonifatius with his longer spear. This last piece of evidence suggests that the commanders fought a duel, but we do not know whether it happened before the battle, during it, or after Aetius had already lost. The commanders also appear to have made some sort of gentlemen's agreement that the loser would be allowed to retire to

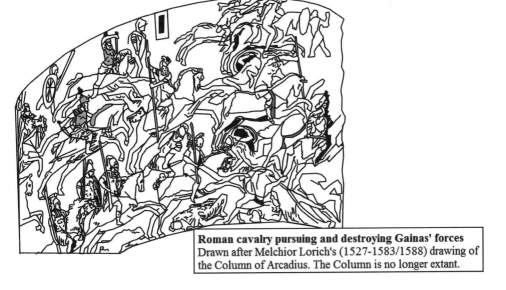

Roman cavalry pursuing and destroying Gainas' forces
Drawn after Melchior Lorich's (1527-1583/1588) drawing of the Column of Arcadius. The Column is no longer extant.

his estates, because after the battle Aetius did so. The sources state that Bonifatius died within a few days (the wound being the immediate cause of death) or after three months (gangrene) from the wound he had received, or that he died of illness (this presumably would refer to the gangrene). Bonifatius' son-in-law Sebastianus was nominated as his successor and it is probable that he was behind the assassination attempt of Aetius in his home. Aetius survived the attack and fled to Rome presumably in an attempt to gather support, and when this was not forthcoming he continued his flight to Dalmatia and from there through the 'Pannonias' to the Huns.

The fall of Aetius meant the dismissal of many of his men, which must have included *comes* Censorius who was recalled to Ravenna. When he left, the Gallaeci resorted to the use of Episcopal mediation, which brought tangible results. The king of the Suevi, Hermericus, agreed to conclude a peace in 433, which was sealed with the exchange of hostages.

Chapter Five

Aetius is back 433–440[1]

Aetius's Hunnic Helpers: 433–434

Ruga/Rua (Rugila), the ruler of the Huns, received his old acquaintance with open arms and promised to help Aetius in return for some unspecified payment, which on the basis of Priscus' fragment 11.1 is usually considered to have been part of Pannonia bordering the River Save/Sava. Blockley (1983, p.243) translates the relevant part as follows: 'Orestes, a Roman by origin who lived in the part of Pannonia close to the river Save which became subject to the barbarian by treaty with Aetius, the general of the western Romans.' This interpretation has been challenged by Maenchen-Helfen (89–90), but in my opinion needlessly. There is no need to suspect the traditional interpretation for two reasons: 1) the Greek text can be translated this way (as it usually is); 2) the traditional interpretation is also supported by the circumstantial evidence. It was thereafter that the East Romans, who had previously held the upper hand against the Huns, were compelled to start paying tribute (350 lbs of gold per year to Rua) to the Huns. Most importantly, the Huns still had East Roman prisoners at the time of Rua's death. Aetius would not have felt any compulsion if his treaty with the Huns caused troubles for the East Romans, because the East Roman faction was clearly in power in the West. Furthermore, Aetius was an exile whose life was under threat. It is probable that the portion of 'Pannonia' that Aetius had given to the Huns consisted of parts of Valeria, Pannonia II and Savia. It is quite possible or even probable that these were the former Federate lands of the Pannonian Huns from which they had been evicted by the East Romans in 427.

The sources do not state how the Huns helped Aetius to regain his position, but they do state that the West Romans, presumably Sebastianus, called the Visigoths to help them which does suggest a real military threat. In my opinion it is clear that the help provided by the Huns involved military operations in which they crossed the Danube and marched to Italy (possibly already under Attila) because it is very improbable that the West Roman government would have conceded a defeat to Aetius without any credible military threat. Furthermore, Aetius' campaign against Galla Placidia clearly coincides with the timing of the war between the Huns and East Romans. It is also clear that Sebastianus was not liked. The officers and the rank-and-file both appear to have felt admiration towards their former commander Aetius.[2] Therefore, Sebastianus had to go. Aetius was reinstated while Sebastianus fled to Constantinople.

The fact that the Huns had East Roman captives and that the East Romans were paying a tribute of 350 lbs of gold per year to Rua/Ruga in 434/5 proves that the Huns had inflicted a defeat on the East Roman forces close to the scene of operations when they assisted Aetius. After this the Eastern government made the situation even worse by making the mistake of admitting within their own borders refugees from the Hunnic realm in 433/4 with the result that Rua issued an ultimatum for the East Romans to return the refugees. Rua prepared for war in 435, but died before that.

Aetius was now the unchallenged master of West Rome and could start to make his plans for the future. These included the marriage with Pelagia, the widow of Bonifatius, which secured for Aetius Bonifatius's extensive wealth and *bucellarii*. According to the legend, Bonifatius had told Pelagia to marry Aetius after his death. This means that Aetius' first wife had died before 432. Pelagia belonged to the royal house of the Visigoths, which either helped or hindered Aetius in his dealings with the Visigoths. The most important wedding gift of Pelagia was her vast army of Visigothic followers, the *bucellarii* of Bonifatius.

The exact division of the provinces in the Balkans between East and West Rome after Aetius's campaign is problematic because we know that the East Romans were in possession of Dalmatia and Pannonia with Valeria (or the whole of Western Illyricum) after 427, but had ceded them to the West Romans by 454 (Proc., *Wars* 3.6.7). This means that it is possible that the East Romans were forced to cede Dalmatia (without Praevalentina) back to the West when Aetius's Huns defeated them, or that they handed them over as a dowry when the marriage between Valentinian III and Licinia Eudoxia took place in Constantinople on 29 October 437. The fact that Marcellinus subsequently revolted when Aetius was murdered in 454 proves that he was West Roman commander, but this leaves open the question of when the East Roman government had returned Dalmatia (and possibly Pannonia I, Noricum) to the Western Government. On the basis of the fact that West Rome and Attila maintained peace during the years 446–451, and Attila did not pillage Dalmatia in 447, it appears probable that this must have happened before that date.[3]

If the restoration of the city walls of Salona were not started immediately after 425, then the project was definitely started after 434 as suggested by Lawrence (184). The treaty between Aetius and Rua, which had brought the Huns to within striking distance of Salona, would have made this necessary. The new projecting towers were small by East Roman standards and were located close to each other to compensate for this. Lawrence (p.184) considers this to be a prime example of the revolutionary character of Theodosian fortification principles followed in the East in comparison with those followed in the West, but at the same time one needs to remember that the towers may have been added at a time when the East Romans ruled Salona. Therefore, one can perhaps make the educated guess that the construction project followed local preferences. It is in fact quite possible that one of the reasons for the longevity of East Rome was its adoption of more sophisticated fortification methods. See the map in Volume 3. Regardless of Lawrence's criticism, the reinforced defences of Salona were still so strong that they enabled the birth of an independent political entity under Marcellinus in 454 and then under Julius Nepos. Therefore the reinforced fortifications were more than adequate for the task.

Aspar the Western Consul

We do not know what exactly happened in North Africa during the years 433–4, but we do know that the Western government nominated Aspar as their consul for the year 434, which suggests that he had either inflicted a very serious defeat on the Vandals and/or that he had immediately recognized Aetius as the de facto ruler of the West after the latter's arrival in Italy. The situation in the Balkans, however, was acute (see above and below) so that it was in the interest of East Rome to recall Aspar together with his forces. As a result of this the West and East Roman governments negotiated a peace settlement with the Vandals in 435 in which the Vandals were recognized as Federates and granted land in Numidia, Proconsularis and Sitifensis (see the map). The Vandals were also required to pay a yearly tribute to the Romans in return for their right to live in those territories. The peace made it possible for Aspar and his forces to return home where their presence was urgently needed in Pannonia.

The Dark Year 435: Revolts

Even though the Romans managed to find a satisfactory conclusion for the war against the Vandals in 435, West Rome still faced daunting problems. According to the chronicles West Rome faced two simultaneous revolts in 435: 1) The Armoricans revolted as 'Bacaudae' against the imperial authorities under the charismatic leader Tibatto; 2) The Burgundians revolted in *Germania I* and invaded the neighbouring *Belgica*. The reasons for this sudden outbreak are not known, but one may make some educated guesses. It is probable that the Armoricans had once again felt that the imperial authorities oppressed them with heavy taxes and gave them nothing in return. The Burgundian Federates may have felt genuine anger over the favouritism shown by Aetius towards his Hunnic benefactors, when the very same Huns were oppressing their brethren on the other side of the Rhine. It is also possible that the favourable treaty negotiated by Gaiseric with the Romans had caused envy among the other Federates who therefore also wanted to renegotiate their treaties through violence.

Aetius decided to resort to a two-pronged offensive against the rebels. He dispatched the *comes* Litorius with the Hun cavalry (Aetius clearly retained for his own use very significant numbers of Huns after 433) against the Bacaudae of Armorica while he himself marched against the Burgundians. We do not know the numbers involved, but one may make the educated guess that Litorius' army consisted of at least 30,000–40,000 men to enable him to handle the situation against the Bacaudae and later against the Visigoths (see below), while Aetius must have led an army of at least 50,000–60,000 men for him to be able to face the Burgundian army of 50,000–80,000 men. It is improbable that Aetius could have collected more men than this because he still needed to leave men behind to secure both Italy and south of Gaul, because in light of the events recorded for the next year it is improbable that the Visigoths would have sent reinforcements for Aetius. However, it is possible that the strength of Aetius' army would have been bolstered by Frankish Federates that would have attacked the Burgundians from the North while Aetius would have attacked from the South. Aetius, who was also accompanied by the future emperor Avitus, crushed Burgundians with the result that they were forced to sign a humiliating peace treaty. This success proved emphemeral because the Burgundians revolted again almost immediately after Aetius had left the scene. Litorius was also successful against the Bacaudae, but the rooting out of the many pockets of resistance took him full two years. When Aetius reached Italy, he was rewarded with the title *Patricius*. Galla Placidia and Valentinian, who was now officially a fully grown man, could do little else but attempt to flatter the generalissimos.

The 436: Difficulties Accumulate

The year 436 proved even worse than the previous one. When Litorius was still fighting against the Bacaudae, the Burgundians revolted again. It is probable that the Burgundians had been incited to do this by the Visigoths who also revolted at the same time (Hughes 2012, 94). The Visigoths captured several neighbouring towns and then besieged Narbonne. This means that the Visigoths had overrun the Alan forces that protected the city. In addition to this, the Suevi appear to have revolted in Gallaecia in 436 even if the first clear referrals to this are in 437 and 438. We do not know whether the Suevi had finally agreed to join the Visigoths or whether the successes achieved by the Visigoths caused the Suevi to join the common Germanic uprising.

As noted by Ian Hughes (2012, 96–97), Aetius appears to have been forced to assume the defensive stance for most of the year 436. I agree with Ian Hughes that it is also probable that in this situation Aetius was forced to hire more Huns, but I do not agree with his suggestion that Aetius would then have ceded the territories in Pannonia to the Huns. This happened already in 432/3. It seems probable that the Huns were quite eager to exact vengeance against the Burgundians for the killing of Octar when given the chance. It is in fact possible or even probable that the Hun mercenaries arrived under their new king Attila (see also Chapter 7) just like Uldin had previously arrived to support Stilicho.

The Year 437: Aetius Strikes Back with Hunnic Help

The return of the East Roman army and especially its fleet in 435 had created a power vacuum in the western Mediterranean which the Vandals were not slow to exploit at the first opportunity. As noted above, Theoderic and Gaiseric seem to have formed an alliance at some point during the 430s and the year 436 is the likeliest date for this because the Vandals (or rather barbarian federates) are attested to have started piratical raids in 437.[4] It is possible that the Vandal fleet blockaded the city of Narbonne from the seaside in 437 (or perhaps already in 436, because the chronicles date the events rather haphazardly) while the Visigoths blockaded it from the landside, because it is otherwise difficult to understand why the Romans did not attempt to bring any assistance or provisions to the city by sea. This appears to be the likeliest reason for Prosper's statement that barbarian federates had become pirates in 437, but it seems probable that the Visigoths were also assisted by the remnants of the West Roman Imperial Fleet that had turned into pirates under the leadership of Sebastianus.

According to Hydatius (a.444–5, 449), Sebastianus, the son of Bonifatius, had been forced to flee from Constantinople in 444. He sought a place of refuge from Theoderic I, but was declared an outlaw with the result that he fled to Barcelona, and continued his flight from Barcelona to the Vandals in 445 where he was killed in 449. Hydatius's information can be connected with the revolt of the Bacaudae in Tarraconensis that occurred at the same time. See later. According to Marcellinus Comes, Sebastianus had fled from Constantinople to Africa in 435 where he was killed. Priscus (fr. 4) states that the reason for Sebastianus' flight from Constantinople was that his retainers had become pirates and harassed the Hellespont and Propontis. This last piece of evidence suggests that when Sebastianus had fled from Italy in 433/4 he had also taken part of the Imperial Fleet with him and that his retainers used this fleet for piracy. This in its turn suggests that Sebastianus and his followers fled in ships from the East to the Visigoths in 435 and then supported the Visigoths during their siege of Narbonne in 436–7. However, this does not preclude the simultaneous participation of the Vandals because they can be attested to have formed an alliance with Theoderic I at about this time because Huneric had married Theoderic's daughter (see above). Prosper (a.440) claims that Sebastianus fled from Spain to Africa in 440 at the time when Gaiseric was pillaging Sicily with the result that Gaiseric returned to Carthage on the double because he feared that Sebastianus would be attempting to retake Carthage. Sebatianus's plan however was to ally himself with the Vandals, but things turned out contrary to his wishes. Sebastianus's flight from Spain in 440 can be connected with the peace between the Visigoths and Romans. See later.

It is more difficult to establish a date for the expulsion of Sebastianus from Gothia, because the evidence is contradictory. If Prosper is correct, then Sebastianus had sailed to North Africa already in 440, but if Hydatius is correct then Sebastianus sailed to North Africa only in about 444/5. It is impossible to be certain, because both authors were contemporaries, but one can reconcile Prosper's and Hydatius's accounts if one combines both so that Sebastianus sailed from Spain to North Africa in 440 as claimed by Prosper, but then returned and spent the following years either as a fugitive in the Visigothic realm and/or as a pirate, and then fled from Gothia to Barcelona in 444 and from there to North Africa in 445 as claimed by Hydatius. All of the extant evidence suggests that Sebatianus possessed a sizable pirate fleet which was so powerful that even Gaiseric feared it. Notably Marcellinus Comes also mentions in the context of the year 437/8 that the pirate Contradis together with his pirates was captured and killed. Marcellinus fails to elaborate further, which makes it impossible to know the exact context – we do not even know where he was captured, East being likelier – but it is possible to speculate that Contradis may have been one of Sebastianus' followers.

Conspicuously and typically for the period, the behaviour of some bigoted Catholic bishops contributed to the willingness of Gaiseric to resume hostilities. These bishops had foolishly disturbed the Arians in the midst of their church service. Gaiseric not unnaturally punished the culprits and exiled or killed those Romans whose loyalty he suspected before launching a full-scale war. In this context it should be noted that Gaiseric, who was an illegitimate son of the previous ruler, seems to have faced several real conspiracies which made him paranoid with the result that he suspected everyone, even his own sons. Gaiseric launched several witch-hunts against his enemies or supposed enemies which included both Romans and Vandals. This was just one of the many persecutions that he launched in the course of his long career.

I would suggest that Aetius remained in and around Arles in a defensive position with his Praesental and Federate armies against possible Visigoth attack while he waited for the arrival of reinforcements. After Aetius had received the reinforcements either in late 436 or early 437, he left a suitable force behind to protect the south of Gaul and marched north against the Burgundians. It is probable that Aetius also waited for the arrival of

Litorius who had in the meantime managed to capture Tibatto, and when the head of the snake had been cut off the revolt collapsed. He may also have waited for the arrival of Avitus. Litorius was ordered to relieve the city of Narbonne while Aetius marched against the Burgundians. En route Litorius proved unable to control all the Huns with the result that some of his Hunnic mercenaries deserted and started to pillage the Auvergne region. Litorius wisely disregarded this and marched on against the Visigoths to achieve operational surprise while the *MVM per Gallias* (?) Avitus moved against the Huns.

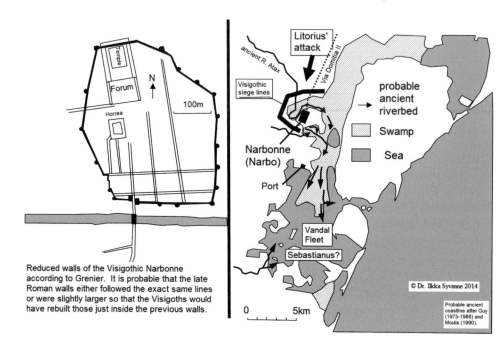

Reduced walls of the Visigothic Narbonne according to Grenier. It is probable that the late Roman walls either followed the exact same lines or were slightly larger so that the Visigoths would have rebuilt those just inside the previous walls.

© Dr. Ilkka Syvänne 2014

Probable ancient coastline after Guy (1973-1988) and Moulis (1990).

According to Sidonius (Pan. Av., 240ff.), when the news of the killing of Avitus' servant and other atrocities committed by the Huns reached the ears of Avitus in Clermont, he armed (scale armour, greaves, gleaming helmet with gold-crest, *contus/pilum/hasta*-spear, *ensis/gladius*-sword) himself and mounted his horse, after which he charged out against the Huns. He charged into the fray with his spear, and then used his sword to kill the enemy around. It was in the midst of the combat that Avitus recognized the enemy leader and challenged him to single combat. This proves that the actual fighting had become a prolonged cavalry battle in which the different units advanced and retreated each in turn which then enabled the persons opposite each other to issue challenges. The champions advanced against each other three times and on the fourth charge Avitus managed to transfix his opponent with his spear so that it passed through him. Sidonius fails to tell what happened next, but it seems probable that the Huns acknowledged Avitus as their leader, after which Avitus joined his men with Litorius's army before the latter had reached the neighbourhood of Narbo/Narbonne. It was then that Avitus famously negotiated with Theoderic who then agreed to abandon the siege of Narbo (PLRE2; Sid. Pan. Av. 475–80). It was thanks to this that Avitus was able to join Aetius on his campaign against the Burgundians (PLRE2; Sid. Pan. Av. 234–5).[5]

The peace negotiated by Avitus appears to have proved temporary because on the basis of Prosper the Visigoths seem to have renewed their siege very soon after Avitus' departure. This time Litorius surprised the besieging Visigoths and routed them. Each of Litorius' horsemen had been ordered to carry two measures of corn (*modii*, sing. *modius*) which were now given to the starving population. As noted above, the fact that the Romans did not attempt to bring supplies via the sea suggests the presence of the Vandal navy and Sebastianus somewhere nearby.[6]

Aetius also appears to have ordered Litorius to dispatch a detachment of soldiers against the Suevi after the relief of Narbo because Hydatius (a.437–438) states that Censorius and Fretimund were dispatched as ambassadors to the Suevi in 437 with the result that the Suevi were forced to sign a peace treaty in 438 with those Gallaeci with whom they had fought. The peace, however, proved ephemeral once again.

In the meantime, Aetius had inflicted a crushing defeat on the Burgundians. According to Hydatius, 20,000 Burgundians were slaughtered by the *Dux* and *Magister Militum* Aetius in 437. The king Gundahar/Gundicaire and the whole royal house were wiped out. The likely reason for the later legends that Attila had killed the royal house of the Burgundians is that he accompanied Aetius on this campaign. Notably, Avitus was one of the commanders of Aetius during this campaign as well (Sid. *Pan. Av.* 234–5).[7]

The crushing of the Burgundians seems to have taken place relatively early in 437, because it is probable that Aetius accompanied Valentinian and Galla Placidia when Valentinian travelled to Constantinople to marry Theodosius' daughter Licinia Eudocia. The marriage was celebrated on 29 October 437. The relationship between the eastern and western halves of the Empire could not have been better and as a sign of this concord both consuls for the year 438, Aetius and Sigisvult, were nominated by the West.[8]

The Year 438: Old Wars Continue and New Wars Break Out

As noted above, the Suevi signed a peace treaty in 438, but then broke it almost immediately. The real reason for the signing appears to have been the poor health of the king Hermericus rather than Roman military action, because once Hermericus had handed over his power to his son Rechila, the Suevi attacked and defeated Andevotus in pitched battle near the Singilis River in Baetica. Hermericus died four years later after a long illness. Rechila's attack was a great success because he captured Andevotus' great treasure of gold and silver at the same time – had he been bringing the salaries of the Roman army serving under Censorinus (see below)? Contrary to prevailing opinion (e.g. in PLRE2), it is probable that Andevotus was a barbarian in Roman service rather than an independent Vandal chieftain left behind by Gaiseric. The best evidence for this is the operations Rechila conducted in the next two years. The fact that Rechila was operating in Baetica and Lusitania during this and subsequent years proves that he had adopted a new and wiser strategy than his father. He avoided the strong Roman defensive positions in Gallaecia and concentrated his attack against the less well defended portions of the Peninsula. As we shall see this change of strategy paid off and eventually enabled the Suevi to also challenge the Romans in Gallaecia.

As noted above, the Vandals appear to have allied themselves with the Visigoths in 436 and may have supported the latter with their fleet during the siege of Narbo. The Vandals are attested to have raided several islands including Sicily in 438 and I would suggest it is probable that the raiders in question consisted of the fleet that had returned from Narbo. The referral to the islands might mean the Balearic Islands and/or Corsica and Sardinia. The West Romans were clearly quite impotent on the sea without East Roman help. As discussed above, this if anything proves that the Vandals must have been in possession of a significant portion of the former West Roman Praesental fleets.

The defeat in front of the city of Narbo had not crushed the hopes of the Visigoths and the war was resumed in the spring. The *MVM per Gallias* Avitus was promoted to the position of *PPG*. This appointment had three probable goals: 1) it rewarded Avitus with the highest position in the administration; 2) it placed a Gallic senator in charge of the Gallic administration, which ensured the goodwill of the local magnates so necessary for obtaining logistical support; 3) it placed a local man with extensive military knowledge in charge of supplying the armies operating in Gaul. Avitus' successor as *MVM per Gallias* appears to have been Litorius who therefore must have acted as Aetius' second-in-command (*hypostrategos*) during this campaign season. According to Hydatius, the *dux* Aetius slaughtered 8,000 Goths during this campaign season. As noted by Hughes (2012, 99) and Clover (41), it is quite probable that we should connect this with the Battle of Mons Colubrarius mentioned by Merobaudes' panegyric. The other possible date for this fragment would be the year 430 when Aetius also wiped out a division of Visigoths.

To make an analysis of Aetius' strategy and tactics at this time it is worth quoting Merobaudes' fragment (*Pan.* 1.10ff., tr. by Clover with comments added in italics):

When I came down to the winding, majestic shore, where the rushing sea flows in as far as Salonae … I met someone who related that he had participated in your recent campaigns. 'All the forces of the Goths,' he exclaimed, 'had sallied forth with their king [*Theoderic I*] to ravage Roman territory. When our leader learned of this … no longer did I wait for him to say, 'He went forth and joined in conflict,' for I did not doubt that this was done by you; I asked immediately where, how, and how many you had put to flight. 'At the mountain,' he then replied, 'which the ancients as if by premonition called Snake Mountain [*Mons Colubrarius*] (for here the poisons of the state have now been destroyed), he surprised – as is his custom – and killed the greatest part of the enemy [*this suggests that Aetius specialized in the use of cavalry which he used to deliver surprise attacks and ambushes; i.e. he used nomadic style guerrilla warfare as befitted a student of the Huns*]; once the infantry units, which were very numerous, were routed, he himself followed hard on the scattering cavalry troops [*this suggests a sequence in which Aetius had first surprised and defeated the Visigothic cavalry which he had followed up to the infantry, after which he engaged and defeated the infantry before following after the fleeing cavalry*] and overwhelmed those standing fast with his might [*i.e. with a massed cavalry charge*], and those fleeing with his eager rapidity [*i.e. Aetius probably possessed light cavalry which was mounted on swift horses*]. Not long afterwards the king himself was on hand with the remainder of his forces [*this suggests that Aetius had defeated the front section of the Visigothic marching column along a snaking road and was gone with his cavalry before the Visigothic reserves under the king were able to reach the scene of carnage*], and stupefied with sudden horror near the trampled bodies. … a lacuna.

The above quote is important for the reason that it demonstrates how Aetius used his cavalry forces, which probably included very significant numbers of Huns, to great effect in guerrilla campaigns against the Visigoths. Aetius' aim was to force the enemy to submit with a minimum effort and risk to his own precious forces.[9] However, we still should not make the mistake of concluding that Aetius would have resorted to this tactic alone, for Merobaudes' panegyrics prove that Aetius used infantry and siege engineers when he judged it advantageous. It was just that in this case Aetius considered it wiser not to risk a pitched battle. In fact, Merobaudes' *Panegyric I* (frg. 1B) proves that Aetius prepared himself for fighting whenever there was respite from fighting. He surveyed the locations of the cities, mountain passes, fields, river crossings, distances between places, to find out which places were better suited for infantry and/or cavalry, which better for attack, which better for defence, and which places could be provisioned easily. This knowledge proved useful, for example during the war against the Huns. The *Panegyric 3* (144ff.) proves that Aetius was also expert in siege warfare (see later). In sum, before Aetius decided on his modus operandi, he always analysed the situation and the locale where the fight was to take place and planned and operated accordingly. Most importantly, since Aetius was forced to fight a series of defensive wars, he planned well in advance how to use the terrain to his own advantage. There is no doubt that Aetius was a superb military commander.

Military Catastrophes in 439–440

In late 438 or early 439 Aetius decided that the Visigoths had been sufficiently weakened for him to be able to leave the conduct of the war in the hands of the *MVM per Gallias* Litorius which gave him chance to return to Italy. As noted by Hughes (2012, 102), this made it easier for Aetius to provide strategic direction for all parts of the Empire, but then two massive disasters upset Aetius' plans.

Litorius led his army, consisting mostly of Huns, against the weakened Visigoths. Initial progress was impressive and the Visigoths were forced to retreat into their 'capital city' Toulouse. Litorius intended to crush the Visigoths once and for all and sought a decisive battle. Unfortunately for the Romans, Litorius' previous successes had made him overconfident. According to Prosper, Litorius also wanted to outstrip Aetius' achievements and asked the advice of soothsayers. This last piece of evidence may suggest that Litorius was one of those late Roman fools with a pagan bent who trusted in the advice of soothsayers, or alternatively that he was a wise commander who wanted to encourage his mostly Hunnish warriors through religious mumbo jumbo – the latter alternative is more likely. Whatever the truth, Litorius led in person an impetuous cavalry charge against the Visigoths and was himself captured after his Huns had been annihilated or imprisoned. The latter were put to death a few days later. Despite the fact that Litorius had inflicted many casualties to the Visigoths before his capture (Prosper a.439), this was a huge disaster for the Romans because it not only resulted in the death of an able commander, but most of all it resulted in the annihilation of a veteran force of Hunnish auxiliaries that would have been sorely needed in the coming years.

Aetius was forced to return to Gaul together with reinforcements drawn from the Praesental forces. We do not know what Aetius did, but we know that after this the Romans and Visigoths signed a peace, which does suggest that Aetius had forced the Visigoths on the defensive. Prosper's cryptic statement that in 439 Vitericus proved loyal to the state and became renowned for his skills in war, which is followed up by the signing of the peace with the Visigoths after the inconclusive war, suggests that Vitericus (presumably a Visigoth) had inflicted a defeat or a series of defeats on his fellow Visigoths on behalf of Aetius, which made it possible for Aetius to conclude the peace without significant loss of face. It is possible that Vitericus belonged to Aetius's *bucellarii* which consisted mostly of Visigoths and Huns.

Aetius chose as his peace negotiator Avitus because he had a good personal relationship with Theoderic and the Visigoths. According to Sidonius, it was largely thanks to Avitus that the two sides were able to bury their hatchets. The resulting peace treaty was unsatisfactory from the Roman point of view, but appears to have satisfied the Visigoths because they maintained peace until about 452/3. It is possible that the Romans for the first time recognized Theoderic as king,[10] and it is probable that one of the terms of peace had been the transferral of the Alans, who had previously deserted the Visigoths, away from the area. In fact, it is possible that the presence of these Alans right next to the Visigoths had been the principal cause of the fighting. Hydatius and Prosper date this peace to the year 439. The precise date would probably have been very late in 439 (or early 440), because Aetius returned to Italy only in 440 (CGall. 452). It is very probable that Aetius was forced to conclude the peace with the Visigoths only because he needed to transfer his forces against the Vandals who had in the meantime captured Carthage. Aetius had once again been forced to leave a war unfinished so that he would be able to march his armies against another enemy. The West possessed too few men and even fewer able commanders.

The situation in Spain was also turning from bad to worse. Rechila continued his operations in Lusitania and Baetica and captured the city of Emerita in 439 (Hyd. a.439). It was necessary to end at least one of the wars somehow. After Aetius had concluded peace with the Visigoths, he sought to secure strategically important Arles and south of Gaul by settling the Alans under their king Sambida (Sangiban?) in the deserted rural regions of Valence. It is probable that these Alans were the Alans who had previously been settled north-east of Narbonne as suggested by Bachrach. The strategic purposes of this settlement were to keep the Alans happy with better lands, to protect the area against the Visigoths, to control the Bacaudae movements in the south of Gaul, and to protect the approaches to the Alps and Italy. Some Alans may have remained behind north-west of Narbonne because the place names still reflect their presence in the area. The settlement of Alans caused a quarrel between the *PPG* Albinus and Aetius, which not unnaturally ended in the defeat of the former – he lacked the military resources at Aetius' disposal.[11]

As noted above, the Vandals had inflicted a huge disaster for the West Roman Empire. The Vandals marched against Carthage in October and captured it through a stratagem on 19 October 439. Carthage was pillaged in organized fashion so that the inhabitants were forced to hand over their valuables to the Vandals while chosen properties were also confiscated/stolen for the Vandals. With one blow Gaiseric had secured for himself the merchant and military fleets of the city and the corn and other taxes of Roman North Africa. It is probable that the West Romans had also posted a naval detachment of their Praesental Fleet to Carthage for its protection and the loss of this naval force weakened the already weakened West Roman Fleet almost beyond recovery. To secure his own position Gaiseric started an immediate persecution of the Catholic clergy and Roman nobility. The Catholic churches were confiscated and then given to the Arian clergy, and the properties of the Roman aristocrats were confiscated for the Vandals. Gaiseric's followers were therefore rewarded with massive booty while the staunchest supporters of Roman rule were effectively eliminated. Most of the Catholic clergy and nobles were either exiled or chose to flee to Italy.

Salvian's moralizing account (7.8ff.) gives additional reasons for the fall of Carthage and for the persecution of local Roman nobility by the Vandals. According to him, the churchmen of Africa were worthless and morally corrupt. He accused the Africans and the Carthagians in particular of complete moral corruption, by stating that some of them practised homosexual behaviour publicly with the full approval of the magistrates and the rest of the population. For him the city of Carthage was 'a sinkpot of lust and fornication' with harlots and homosexuals. In particular, he (7.20–21) accused the local Roman nobility and soldiers of being effeminate and the real cause of the Roman disasters. His account suggests that one of the reasons for the conflict between the Vandals and Romans were the cultural differences. On the basis of Salvian's account it seems probable that the Arian Vandals saw the Roman Africans as a morally corrupt and despicable lot that were ripe for the taking and in need of straightening, and when one remembers that there were also similarly thinking men among the Romans (e.g. Salvian) it is not surprising that this 'moral' minority or majority welcomed such actions. It is also probable that the Visigothic Federates who served in Africa had similar views, which certainly did not help the defence of Africa. Salvian's account also suggests that openly gay behaviour was not accepted in Gaul or Spain even if adultery (though forbidden by law) and drunkenness were. It is clear that Roman society was badly divided from within.

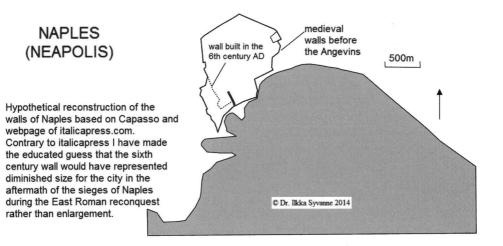

NAPLES (NEAPOLIS)

wall built in the 6th century AD

medieval walls before the Angevins

500m

Hypothetical reconstruction of the walls of Naples based on Capasso and webpage of italicapress.com. Contrary to italicapress I have made the educated guess that the sixth century wall would have represented diminished size for the city in the aftermath of the sieges of Naples during the East Roman reconquest rather than enlargement.

© Dr. Ilkka Syvänne 2014

The loss of North of Africa was a massive blow to the West Romans. They had lost their most important source of corn for Rome and Italy and also a very important source of tax income, and this at a time when their tax base had already been severely hurt by the previous pillaging of Italy, Illyricum, Gaul and Spain. On top of that, tax income from Spain was now under threat from the Suevi and local desertions. The piratical attacks of the Vandals against Sicily and other islands had effectively cut off trade and thereby the income produced by trade. The immediate reaction of the government was probably the conclusion of peace with the Visigoths (see above) and the recall of Aetius to Italy together with the order for the *magister militum praesentalis* Sigisvult to station soldiers and Federate troops along the coasts and cities for their protection (see below), and Valentinian rebuilt and strengthened the walls of Rome and other cities like Naples and Terracina (Jacobsen 117) in preparation for the Vandal invasion and dispatched an urgent plea for help to Constantinople, which the eastern government answered in the affirmative – after all, power was in the hands of the same family and the loss of Carthage was also a severe blow to the interests of East Rome. The security of the western borders of East Rome depended on the ability of West Rome to defend her own territory. The Eastern government also recognized the naval threat posed by the Vandals and Theodosius II ordered that the Sea Walls of the Theodosian Walls of Constantinople were either to be strengthened and repaired, or repaired because long sections of the walls had been destroyed in the recent earthquake (see above and later). The Easterners also recognized that the Vandal navy posed a threat to the other coastal areas and in particular to the Egyptian grain supply.

The financial and military disaster required some desperate measures. Valentinian enacted a series of *Novellae* in 440 and 441 to increase tax income and to improve defences. In January 440, the emperor annulled all special tax exemptions and tax reductions. The law issued in March 441 stated that all imperial lands that had been rented with tax privileges and church properties were to be taxed at the regular rate. At the same time the special privileges that had been granted to high dignitaries were taken away so that everyone was required to contribute to the building and repair of military roads, manufacture of arms, restoration of city walls, provisions-in-kind, and all other public works. Additional pieces of legislation followed in June. The civilians, who had in 364 been forbidden to carry arms without special permission, were now granted complete freedom to carry whatever weapons they could obtain to enable them to protect their land, lives and property against piratical Vandals – the *Novella* recognized the impossibility of protecting the entire length of the coastline with soldiers and Federates. The two *Novellae* enacted in March 440 recognized the pressing need to bolster the size of the army with new conscripts, and the latter reinstated the punishments to those who harboured deserters or failed to fulfil their quota of recruits for the armed forces. The loss of African corn resulted in the easing of trade restrictions so that the East Roman merchants were allowed to bring merchandise and corn freely to the West – the principal reason for this decision being the urgent need to feed the population of the city of Rome. On 4 June 440 the government enacted a *Novella* which aimed to put a stop to the abuses of tax collectors by transferring the judgment of complaints away from the counts of the treasuries to the Praetorian Prefect. The aim was to protect already hard pressed taxpayers from corruption and abuse, but this ran contrary to the interests of the corrupt senators and their cronies. According to Ian Hughes, this caused a rift between Aetius and a court faction that continued until Aetius' death. The *Novella* was repealed by the new *PPI* Paterius on 27 September 442.[12]

The Suevi continued their campaign in the south of Spain in 440. They besieged the *comes* Censorius, who had once again been dispatched as an envoy, in Myrtilis/

Martylis (Mertola). Censorius surrendered on terms after which he spent his remaining years as a prisoner until he was killed by the Vandals at Hispalis in 449. The fact that no reinforcements were forthcoming from Gaul or Italy meant that the Suevi could besiege and take the major Spanish cities one city at a time. The accompanying illustration[13] gives a good example of how difficult it would have been to take the cities with assault, but now it sufficed just to blockade them. In the absence of a united command structure, the Spanish cities (city councils and magnates) were unable to unite their citizen militias for a common defence. The lack of military protection caused the citizens of Tarraconensis to revolt as Bacaudae in late 440, which meant that the Western Government had lost control of almost the whole of Spain. The response was not slow in coming. Astyrius was appointed as *MVM* and dispatched to Spain to quell the Bacaudae in 441. The Roman government always took revolts, mutinies and threats to the social order more seriously than the foreign invasions and this was one of those instances. It is possible that the leader of the revolt was none other than Sebastianus, son-in-law of Bonifatius, whose presence in Barcelona is attested for the year 444 by Hydatius. The reason for this suggestion is that Hydatius has clearly misplaced the time of Sebastianus' departure from the East (attested to be 435 by Marcellinus) which means that he may also have misplaced the other dates regarding Sebastianus' career. However, since Hydatius was contemporary to the events, it is still probable that he has dated the arrival of Sebastianus in Spain correctly even if he has misdated the other portions of Sebastianus' carreer. On the basis of this it is probable that events progressed as noted for the years 435/7 and for the years 444/5. See above and below. The exact title of Astyrius is not known. He may have been *MVM* of Gaul or Spain or honorary *MVM* with military duties.

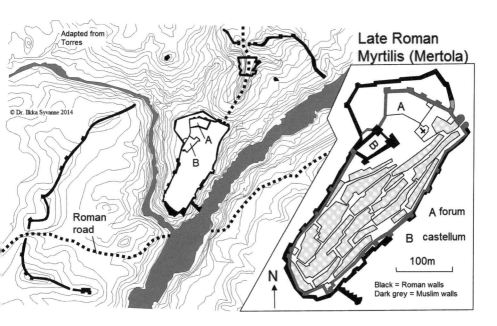

Adapted from Torres

© Dr. Ikka Syvanne 2014

Late Roman Myrtilis (Mertola)

A

B

A

B

Roman road

A forum

B castellum

100m

N

Black = Roman walls
Dark grey = Muslim walls

Hypothetical reconstruction of the city of Lilybaeum (Marsala) based on Freeman and ZZG.

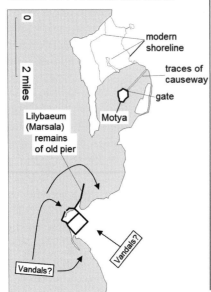

Hypothetical reconstruction of the defences of the city of Panormus (Palermo) based on the location of ancient shoreline.

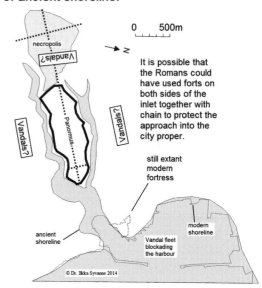

The Western government spent the whole of 440 making preparations for the defence of Italy and in the launching of a campaign against the Vandals with the East Romans once their forces arrived. The Vandals exploited the absence of any active measures against them by striking first. Gaiseric directed his forces against Sicily, which together with Sardinia was one of the few remaining producers of corn for Rome. Gaiseric's forces pillaged Lilybaeum and other towns of Sicily while his main army put the city of Panormus under siege. One of his detachments also crossed the Straits of Messina and raided the mainland. This put additional pressure on the Western Court. Panormus, however, resisted successfully as did the local forces in Bruttium.

Chapter Six

The West 441–450[1]

Then reading the following chapters, the reader is advised to take into account that the sequence and dating of the events between 441 and 450 is very uncertain, as a result of which any reconstruction is bound to be uncertain. I have based my own reconstruction mainly on the various degrees of probability that different scenarios present and have included a number of caveats.

The Empire Strikes Back in 441/2

On the basis of the timing of the Hunnic and Persian offensives against East Rome, the Eastern Fleet appears to have sailed to Italy in May or June of 441. The departure had been delayed by the Persian surprise attack in the spring of 441. According to Theophanes, the fleet consisted of 1,100 cargo ships plus warships. This implies a land army of at least 40,000–45,000 men, but may also mean an army of about 100,000 men as was the case with the similar number of ships in 468. In addition to this we should include the army dispatched by the Western Government, which may mean that the land forces numbered 60,000–65,000 or more, maybe up to 120,000 men.

The expeditionary forces were commanded by the *strategoi* Areobindus/Ariobindus (*MVM Praes.*), Ansila (*MVM Vacans?*), Germanus (*MVM Vacans?*), Inobindus (*comes or dux or MVM?*), and Arintheus (*comes or dux or MVM?*). The badly frightened Gaiseric withdrew his forces before the Eastern Fleet arrived, with the result that when the Eastern Fleet arrived in Sicily presumably in the late spring 441 it settled on playing a waiting game, probably because it was then that the eastern commanders learnt of the news that the Huns had invaded the Balkans and the Persians the East. The other reason for Gaiseric's quick withdrawal was the unexpected arrival of Sebastianus in North Africa in 440. Gaiseric assessed the odds to be against him and immediately dispatched envoys to seek peace from the Romans. In this situation it was not wise to endanger his forces needlessly. Since the negotiations involved both Roman governments, they took time. Consequently the East Romans became a heavy burden to the Sicilians. The East Romans apparently forced the West Romans to accept a negotiated settlement, because they needed to transfer their forces back to the Balkans against the Huns because the East Romans had only managed to conclude a year-long truce with Attila. See later.

The treaty was concluded in 442 and its terms required Gaiseric to hand his son Huneric/Honoric as hostage and pay yearly tribute to the western government. This last term presumably meant yearly grain and olive oil shipments to Rome and possibly some other taxes too. That Gaiseric was ready to agree to such terms suggests strongly that the East Romans had collected a truly sizable force. It is also possible that Gaiseric had previously suffered a serious defeat at the hands of Aspar (see before) so that he feared the capabilities of the Eastern forces. The terms of the peace however appear still to have been satisfactory for Gaiseric because he abided by them until about 448. The terms were also satisfactory enough for the West Romans, because they could not hope for better terms in the absence of eastern help. The western government was also forced to intervene on behalf of African refugees who had been asked to pay their taxes in spite of their situation. The exiles were given tax relief and financial aid, the collection of interest on their loans was forbidden, and they did not have to pay their loans until they had become financially solvent. In addition, the western government appears to have negotiated with the Vandals a settlement according to which some of the refugees were allowed to return.[2]

Novellae 6.2, 13, 34 and other sources prove that the Empire regained control over the three Mauritanias (Tingitana, Sitifensis and Caesariensis) and the west of Numidia, but had lost control of the provinces of Africa and Byzacena to the Vandals. *Novella* 13 defines the military duties of the *Limitanei* in the Mauritanias so that those who had homes in the interior were allowed a leave of one month per year to visit them. The same *Novella* also states that the *dux* was to make certain that there were no armed men who could harass the locals with the exception of those who had promised their own retinues (*bucellarii*) for use against the enemy. These *bucellarii* were granted the right to take as war booty everything else except the valuables that the locals could prove to have lost. These forces were apparently quite adequate for use against the Moors, but naturally not against the Vandals so their continued existence depended on a cordial relationship between Rome and Carthage.

Meanwhile, the Suevi had continued their operations in Spain. Rechila captured Hispalis (it is probable that he would have captured Italica on the opposite side of the river before this) after which he gained control of the provinces of Baetica and Carthaginiensis in 441 presumably because the local magnates decided to negotiate a peace settlement with the Suevi so that they could retain their estates untouched. This meant that the only areas left unconquered by the Suevi were parts of Gallaecia and Tarraconensis. It was in the latter area that the Romans achieved their only military successes. Asturius slaughtered the Bacaudae mercilessly in 441, but could not defeat them yet. The revolt persisted and fighting continued in 442. As long as this situation persisted, the western government could not expect any taxes from Spain. Asturius was replaced by his son-in-law Merobaudes in 443 who crushed the Bacaudae of Aracelli, but was then recalled thanks to some court intrigue. Consequently the problem was not solved.

Gaul and Britain and Bishop Germanus in 441–443

The exact sequence of events between 441 and 445 is clouded in mystery and many different reconstructions are possible. The sources lack reliable dates. It is usually presumed that the Bacaudae of Armorica had once again started to show signs of independence in about 441/2 because the CGall 452 states that the *Patricius* Aetius settled Alans in ulterior Gallia which can be demonstrated to mean Armorica in the area from Orléans (Aureliani) to the Baie de la Seine. It is usually assumed that the settlement of the Alans only aggravated the situation so that the Armoricans revolted with the result that Aetius ordered the Alans to crush the revolt. This in turn is usually connected with the Armorican plea to the Bishop Germanus to help them. Germanus' mediation failed because he died in Ravenna either in 445 or 448. For additional information, see below. The Armorican rebels were so successful that they attacked Aetius' lieutenant Majorian (Maiorianus) at Tours. Majorian, however, defeated them. The revolt was then supposedly squashed primarily by the Alans in about 445.[3]

I propose alternative sequences for the events that took place in 441–445. The exact sequence of events depends on how one dates the exploits of Bishop Germanus, and the date of the settlement of Alans in ulterior Gaul. According to the CGall 452, the Alans were settled in 442, but it can be demonstrated that the dates in the CGall are unreliable (e.g. the Vandals supposedly captured only Carthage in 444), which means that its date of the settlement of the Alans in Armorica is also unreliable. Regardless of this, I have accepted that the Alans were settled by the *Patricius* Aetius in ulterior Gallia in 442 which can be demonstrated to mean Armorica in the area from Orléans (Aureliani) to the Baie de la Seine.

There are three possible ways to date Germanus' actions in Britain, Armorica and Ravenna on the basis of Germanus' ability to travel through Armorica and the apparent absence of Aetius from Gaul and Ravenna: 1) In 441/2 when Aetius would have in all probability been in the south of Italy to coordinate the joint operations against the Vandals followed by peace negotiations; 2) In 444 and early 445 when Aetius would have been absent from Gaul and Italy to direct the campaign against the Huns; 3) In 448 when the Bacaudae revolted again and when Aetius may have been in Illyricum to negotiate with the Huns. The last of the three can be dismissed if Gildas's claim that the Britons sent a plea for help to Aetius in 446 is dated accurately.

This leaves the first two alternatives. If the CGall 452 has dated the settlement of the Alans correctly to the year 442, then Germanus' trip to Britain can be dated to 441. The fact that he appears to have travelled through Armorica suggests that the Salian king Clodio had already conquered territory at least up to Tournai or Cambrai so that the shortest route to Britain was closed. Germanus's ability to travel was also affected by the fact that the territory between Boulogne and Rouen was in Saxon hands just like the territory of Calvados around Bayeux in Normandy and the islands of the Loire. According to Gregory of Tours (2.19 with Clover 43), Clodio, the ancestor of Clovis, lived at Dispargum in Thuringia (usually identified as Duisburg, Germany). He captured first Tournai (Turnacum) at some undated occasion, after which Clodio sent spies to the town of Cambrai (Camaracum). When Clodio had learnt what he wanted, he followed in their footsteps, crushed the Romans and captured the town. He then lived there for a short time (i.e. he died soon after this, see below) and captured the territory up to the Somme. Merovech, the father of Childeric, was his son (FRMG 594, 596). In other words, these conquests must have taken place before Germanus sailed to Britain but before Trier was sacked by the Ripuarian Franks. The Franks would have exploited the absence of Aetius's field army, which would have been in the south of Italy during 440–442. It is also possible that the settlements of Alans should be connected with the invasion of the Salian Franks and/or Ripuarian Franks rather than with the Armorican revolt. This brings up the second alternative dating, the year 444/5 (which would mean that we should date the settlement of Alans to ulterior Gaul also to the year 444/5). This last version is supported by three facts: 1) Aetius was absent from Gaul and Italy during the Hunnic trouble; 2) Aetius was at Trier in 445 and probably also in 446 which suggests that the Ripuarian problem resurfaced in 443/4 when Aetius's main army was in Illyricum; 3) Sidonius' referral to the siege of Tours suggests that it happened soon before the battle of Vicus Helena (see below).

Germanus, Britain and Armorica in 441/2 or 444/5

Therefore it was in about 441/2 or 444/5 that the Bishop of Autessiodurum (Auxerre), Germanus, was once again called to Britain to restore order upset by the resurgent Pelagians (Constantius 25ff.). Germanus together with Severus (the Bishop of Treves, mod. Trier from 426 to 476) sailed to the island. This suggests that the city of Trier was not threatened by the Ripuarian Franks at the time. It should be noted that the bishops travelled via Armorica because the road to Boulogne was controlled by the Salian Franks. On arrival they were greeted by Elafius, one of the leading men of the country, who had brought with him his crippled son. The bishops and Elafius once again staged a show for the crowds that had gathered to witness the arrival of the holy men, and Germanus duly healed the son. The people were once again impressed by the staged miracle after which the bishops held sermons against heresy. The Pelagian preachers were rounded up and then escorted to the continent with the result that Pelagian heresy was uprooted so thoroughly that Britain remained staunchly Catholic at the time when Constantius wrote his hagiography in the 480s. What is notable about this story is that the British upper class maintained control over the populace through Catholic religion, and when the Pelagians challenged Catholic doctrine they challenged the whole Roman administration of the island. The role of the bishops in the upkeep of the order was clearly of the utmost importance. The fact that Germanus and British aristocracy exiled the heretics to the continent proves that Britain and Gaul were still part of the same Empire. However, it also proves that the contacts between Britain and Rome were now conducted not by imperial administrators but by the clergy. This means that Britain was effectively autonomous and that taxes were spent locally. Regardless, one can still consider Britain to be part of the Roman Empire at this date just like Noricum Ripense can be considered to have been part of the Roman Empire under its local leaders, the most important of which was the bishop St. Severinus, until Noricum Ripense was completely abandoned in 488. The heretics who were exiled in Gaul were presumably relocated to Brittany where additional refugees followed soon after this. The fact that the exiles consisted of Pelagians made them readier to turn to brigandage as Bacaudae and may have contributed to the rise of revolts in 442 and 448.

When the bishops returned to Gaul, Germanus was immediately greeted by a delegation of Armoricans who begged his help in an effort to avert a war. This suggests that Germanus travelled through Armorica which would have been impossible if it had already revolted. The shorter road through the area controlled by the Salian Franks to the city of Boulogne would not have been secure. Armoricans had evidently once again refused to pay their taxes. The result was that Aetius the Magnificent had ordered Goar the 'savage' King of the Alans to march to Armorica to teach them a lesson they would not forget while Aetius himself, after having pacified the Salian Franks, marched to Italy to make preparations against the threatening Hunnic war.

Germanus, the old campaigner, acted boldly and went to block the advance of the iron-clad cavalry forces of the tribes. He rode to meet the king who was surrounded by his *catervae* of cavalry. At first Germanus requested the king to desist from the invasion through an interpreter, but when Goar disregarded this, Germanus reprimanded him and then finally seized Goar's bridle and thereby halted him and the army. This was a truly bold gesture and it upset Goar's self-confidence to such an extent that he dismounted, encamped his army and submitted to the bishop's will on condition that Germanus obtained a pardon for the Armoricans from the emperor or Aetius. Goar promised to wait until Germanus obtained the pardon.

Germanus set out for Italy in secret. There are two possible reasons for the secrecy: Firstly, it is possible that Germanus did not expect to be able to convince Aetius who must therefore have been in Gaul; second, that Germanus wanted to avoid the type of attention he got in Italy when he was recognized and because Aetius was not in Gaul but in Noricum/Pannonia/Illyricum negotiating with the Huns. The latter alternative is more likely.

When Germanus reached Milan, presumably in 442 or 445, he was recognized with the result that he was from then on required to heal the sick. When Germanus reached Ravenna he was greeted by the Emperor Valentinian III, Empress Galla Placidia, the Bishop of Ravenna Peter, and other notables. Germanus' healing duties continued. He healed the son of Volusianus, the *cancellarius* of the Patrician Sigisvult/Segisvultus (consul in 437 and *MVM* in 437–448), and he also successfully exorcised the adopted son of the *PSC* Acolus. It is therefore not hard to believe that Constantius is right in claiming that Germanus would have obtained a pardon for the Armoricans had the latter just not been foolish enough to revolt again under Tibatto. However, the healing of the sick had come with a high price: the old man contracted an illness from one of them and died on 31 July 442 or 445,[4] but I prefer the former (see below).

The fame of the saint was such that the Empress, Bishop Peter and other prelates all took pieces of Germanus's clothing as relics. No expense was spared in the funeral, the corpse was escorted back to Gaul, and the revolt of the Armorican Bacaudae was duly crushed by Goar.

So ended the life of a very significant man who had twice ensured that Britain would remain part of the Roman Empire and who had also been so bold as to halt the attack of the king of the Alans who was acting on behalf of the de facto ruler of the Roman Empire. The people of north-west Gaul and Britain would have sorely needed his services in the future.

Reconstruction of the Events in Gaul in 441–443

It is impossible to be certain of the sequence, but if we accept the dating of the Gallic Chronicle for the settlement of Alans in ulterior Gallia to the year 442, then it appears probable that when Aetius withdrew the forces from Gaul to fight against the Vandals in 440, the Salian Franks exploited the situation by pushing as far as Cambrai in 440/1 with the result that the Roman government required the Armoricans to contribute more to the defence of north-west Gaul in 441/2. Since Armorica seems to have been an autonomous area, this seems to have meant the levy of its manpower against the Franks, which the Armoricans opposed. The only mobile forces close to the Salian Franks and the Armoricans were the Alans of Goar, which meant that Aetius was forced to order Goar to attack the Armoricans. The Roman regulars south of the Loire (note the presence of Majorian at Tours, see below) were needed to separate the Visigoths and Armoricans.

It was then that Germanus returned from Britain and attempted to mediate but Tibatto's attack against Tours, which was ably defended by Majorian in the summer of 442, resulted in all-out war. The transferral of part of the Alans against the Bacaudae then enabled the Salian Franks to push their frontier as far as the Somme. The following map is based on Bachrach's (1973) reconstruction of the places granted to the Alans. Kouznetsov and Lebedynsky (106ff.) suggest that there may have also been settlements of Alans further west. The local nobility opposed this and was duly crushed alongside the Bacaudae.

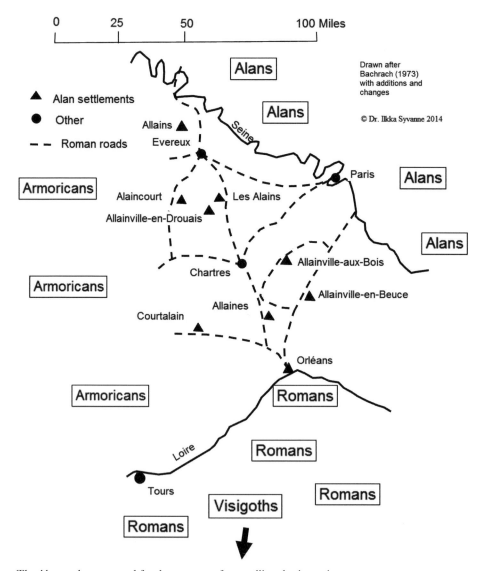

The Alan settlements used for the purpose of controlling the Armoricans.

The Ripuarian Franks also exploited the situation by attacking Cologne and Trier in 441 after the Bishop of Trier had travelled to Britain. The fact that the Ripuarian Franks were able to conquer Trier means that they had also defeated the Burgundian Federates to get there. If the Bishop had been present during the fourth siege, one would expect that the Christian sources would have said so. Instead of this we have Salvian's account of the siege of Trier in which he accused the nobility of Trier of moral corruption. He states that after the third siege and destruction of the city, presumably in about 428–432, the few surviving local nobles demanded the restoration of the circuses from the emperor. He (6.13–18) rightly accused the local citizens of unbelievable stupidity. Instead of spending the money on defences, the people yearned for entertainment and drunkenness. According to Salvian (6.13), when he was present at Trier as an eyewitness (presumably during the third pillage), the leaders of the city were in the midst of drunken revelry (drink, dice, rape, play, carelessness) when the barbarians took the city by surprise attack. In short, he claimed that the leading citizens and drunkards neglected all safety measures against the barbarians and even after the third destruction continued to do so with the result that the city was pillaged for the fourth time. This is a very strong statement against the avaricious magnates of Trier, and Salvian accuses the other decurions of Gaul of the same idiocy – they did not take any measures to protect themselves against the barbarians in their midst, but concentrated on fleecing the citizens while enjoying themselves in a depraved manner. On the basis of the imperial legislation, this accusation seems valid. But there is also a good psychological basis to explain such behaviour: when everything seems to be falling apart, people often live as if every day is their last.

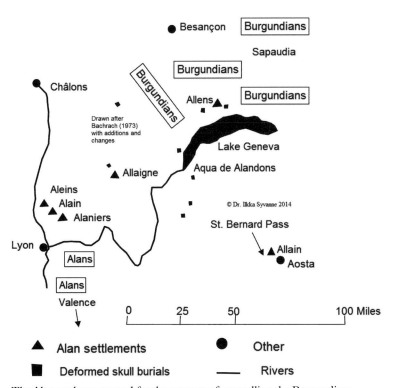

The Alan settlements used for the purpose of controlling the Burgundians.

The peace agreement with the Vandals enabled Aetius to transfer his army against the Ripuarian Franks in late 442. Aetius' operations in Gaul were halted prematurely when the Huns under their new leaders Bleda and Attila turned their attention to the West in 443/4 after they had defeated the East Romans. It was then that Aetius recognized that he would not be able to crush the Ripuarian Franks during the campaign season of 443. Consequently Aetius formed a new defensive line to the south of the previous settlements by settling the Burgundians in Sapaudia (Savoy) in 443. For a fuller discussion of the various theories of the extent of ancient Sapaudia, see Escher. Bachrach's (1973, 68–71) analysis of place names in the neighbourhood of Lake Geneva suggests that there were settlements of Alans around the Burgundians so that the Alans protected the city of Lyon and protected the road to Italy (the St. Bernard Pass). The Alans in question probably consisted of detachments posted in the neighbourhood of Valence. I would suggest that Aetius once again used the trustworthy Alans as a safeguard against possible duplicity of the Burgundians just as he used the Alans against the Visigoths, Armoricans, and Bacaudae. The placing of the Alans in all key positions in Gaul proves that Aetius' defensive plans were entirely dependent on their tested loyalty and effectiveness.

Aetius vs. Bleda and Attila in 443/4

The Huns appear to have turned their attention West almost immediately after they had defeated the East Romans in 442/3, because the Western Government sought to increase the size of the army through a levy of soldiers on 25 May 443, which was then repeated on 14 July 444. The first of these (NVal 6.2) stated that the senators and all landholders were to present the required number of recruits for service. According to the second (NVal 6.3), thanks to imminent expenses (Pharr's note 10: For the war against the Huns) for which the treasury was insufficient it was necessary to force the inactive *illustres* (illustrious men) together with most administrators to provide money for recruits. In other words, the first *Novella* increased the size of the armed forces in 443 and the latter provided additional money for it. *Novella 15*, however, proves that the state was still unable to pay and supply the enlarged army that had been assembled against the Huns.

Valentinian's *Novella 15* (NVal 15) issued between 11 September 444 and 18 January 445 is very important for a number of reasons,[5] but the most important of these is the referral to the need to possess a numerous army. Therefore, it is worth quoting (NVal 15.1, tr. by Pharr, with comments added in parentheses):

We do not doubt that it occurs to the thoughts of all men, that nothing is so necessary as that the strength of a numerous army should be prepared for the exhausted circumstances and the afflicted condition of the State [*this piece of text proves beyond doubt that the period conflicts required large armed forces*]. But neither have We been able, through various kinds of expeditures to effect the arrangement of a matter so salutary for all, nor has any person been found who will regulate this matter by his own efforts. And thus by experience itself, neither for those who are bound by new oaths of military service [*new recruits*], nor even for the veteran army can those supplies seem to suffice that are delivered with the greatest difficulty by the exhausted taxpayers, and it seems that from that source the supplies that are necessary for food and clothing cannot be furnished [*the economic situation was clearly desperate and the state was unable to provision and pay its armed forces*]. Unless the soldiers should be supported by trading [*NVal 15.1ff. all transactions between buyer and seller taxed; unsurprisingly, it did not take long for black markets to emerge and the government was forced to legislate against this on 25 April 447 (NVal 24)*], which is unworthy and shameful for an armed man, they can scarcely be vindicated from the peril of hunger or from the destruction of cold. ... For if We require these expenses from the landholder, in addition to the other things which he furnishes, such an exaction of taxes would extinguish his last tenuous resources [*the state was too weak to force the rich to bear the expenses when civil servants were corrupt and the poorer people had already been fleeced too much*].

The above makes it abundantly clear that the Romans needed to possess a large army to face the simultaneous threats on all frontiers. This was not any small-scale affair. The text proves the desperate state of the economy after the loss of income from Britain, and parts of Gaul, Spain, Africa, Pannonia and from the ravaged areas. The simultaneous collapse of trade networks cannot have helped. It also proves that the government was unable to meet even its present obligations to the soldiers. The only obvious solution would have been to convert the army into a conscript citizen army and/or Federate army or that all new recruits would have belonged to a citizen army which would have been supported through payments in kind. However, this option was not viable because the Emperor and the upper classes needed a professional army to control the citizens. It would have been suicidal for the Emperor to create a conscript army of citizens in a situation in which the poorer classes were already taking arms against the Emperor, as the Bacaudae for example in Gaul and Spain. Consequently the West Roman government lacked good alternatives. The raising of taxes was necessary even if it hurt the economy and thereby lowered the tax yield even further. In contrast to the Roman regular army, the Germanic Federates were cheaper to maintain, which meant that the relative position of the Germanic tribal forces only improved over time as the regular Roman armies were falling apart.

It is unfortunate that we have only two very meagre sources for the war between Aetius and the Huns of Bleda and Attila. The first of these is Merobaudes' *Panegyric 2* and the other is an inscription on a lost tombstone. Both of these have been analyzed in detail by Maenchen-Helfen. It is worthwhile to quote sections from both:

Here the glory of Italy is buried, the hero Constantius, who was the shield of his country, its walls and weapons. Invisible in war, lover of true peace, though pierced with wounds, he was victorious everywhere [*this suggests that he defeated the enemy even in the battle in which he fell*]. He subdued the race that crossed the middle of the sea [*Vandals*] and likewise the land refused to give aid to the vanquished [*possibly a referral to war against the Visigoths*]. He was sober [*quite exceptional during late antiquity*], mighty in battle, chaste, a powerful commander, first in judgment, first in war. ... he was bringing terror to the Pannonian tribes [*the Huns*]. In war he sought honours for himself and his sons, to the nobles he gave as gifts the cut-off heads. In the midst of his sons the father lies stabbed; the grievous mother does not know whom to lament, overwhelmed by her sorrow. Worse is the misfortune of Rome, robbed of so great a senator; … The saddened armies are standing still [*in other words, the armies were not destroyed at the same time as Constantius fell*], after their great commander has been taken away, with whom Rome was powerful, without whom she is lying prostrate [*implies that the Romans were forced to negotiate*]. (Inscription, tr. by Maenchen-Helfen, p.102; analysis 102–3)

He [*Aetius*] returned with the Danube at peace, and has stripped the Tanais of madness [*Huns*]; he orders the lands, glowing-hot with blackened upper air, to be free of their habitual warfare. The Caucasus has granted repose to the sword, and its savage kings [*Bleda and Attila*] renounce combat. (Merobaudes, Panegyric 2.1–5, presented on Aetius' Third Consulship on 1 January 446, tr. by Clover, 13)

In my view Maenchen-Helfen's analysis of the above is accurate. There has to have been combat between the Romans under Aetius and the Huns under Bleda and Attila, which had ended in favour of Aetius. However, I do not accept Maenchen-Helfen's view that the war would have been limited. In light of the Roman victory celebrations (Aetius was given third consulship in 446 and a statue) and the subsequent murder of Bleda, it seems very probable that Aetius had achieved a major success.

Gaul and Spain in 443–446

The absence of Roman field armies in 443/4 meant that the still extant garrisons, Federates, *Laeti* and citizens of Gaul and Spain were forced on the defensive for the years 443 and 444. I would suggest that we should connect Sebastianus's exploits in Spain with this situation. Hydatius states that Sebastianus was at Barcelona in 444. It seems probable that the Visigoths had either expelled him (as stated by Hydatius) because he was a liability, or that Theoderic had sent him to Barcelona to create confusion among the Romans. It seems probable that Sebastianus and his retainers marched to Barcelona immediately after Merobaudes had left in 443 and attempted to hold it until they were forced to flee as a result of Roman counter-offensive after the Hunnic war had ended. Hydatius doesn't mention any Suevic military activity for 443 to 445 which probably means that the Suevi were consolidating their position in the areas they had conquered.

At about the same time as Aetius defeated the Huns, he or Valentinian made a diplomatic coup with the betrothal of Gaiseric's son Huneric with Valentinian's daughter. Huneric was forced to divorce his first wife, the daughter of Theoderic. This in its turn meant that the alliance between the Vandals and Visigoths came to an end.

On top of this, the subsequent brutality shown by the paranoid Gaiseric made any reconciliation impossible in the future. According to Jordanes (*Getica* 184), after the divorce of Huneric and the daughter of Theoderic, Gaiseric, who treated even his own children cruelly, started to fear that Theoderic's daughter could attempt to poison him. He cut off her nose and ears and dispatched her back to his father – cruel even by barbarian standards. Ian Hughes (136–7 after Halsall) is surely correct that this resulted in the sending of the Vandal navy against the Suevi (see below).

We do not know what happened in Gaul between 443 and 444, but one may guess that the defensive arrangements of Aetius had done their job with the result that the Franks had been unable to advance any further while the Alans of Goar had crushed the Bacaudae of Armorica.

The inevitable Roman counter-attack came in 445. Aetius dispatched one army under the *MVM* Vitus to reconquer Spain, while he himself took charge of the campaigns against the Franks. Hydatius records Vitus' campaign to the year 446, but since Sebastianus fled from Barcelona to the Vandals in 445, it is clear that some Roman army must have already advanced to Tarraconensis in 445. According to Hydatius (a.449), Sebastianus was killed shortly after his arrival on Gaiseric's orders. If Sebastianus fled to the Vandals already in 445 this was not soon after his arrival which means that Hydatius may have condensed his account considerably. On the basis of this it is possible that Sebastianus had spent the life of a pirate during the years 445 to 449 by moving from one place to another until he reached Vandal territory. Aetius had given Vitus a sizable force clearly with the intention that the Bacaudae and Suevi would now be crushed once and for all. Not unnaturally, considering the locale, Vitus's army included large numbers of Visigoths.

Vitus' advance in Tarraconensis was accompanied by a naval raid by Vandals against the Suevi in Gallecia, because Hydatius states that the Vandals raided Turonium in Gallaecia (Hughes 2012, 136–7). The apparent purpose was to distract the Suevi so that Vitus could advance into Tarraconensis. According to Hydatius, Vitus did indeed achieve considerable success initially and harassed the inhabitants of Carthagiensis and Baetica in 446. The inhabitants in question must have been those Spaniards who had allied themselves with the Suevi. It was then that the King of the Suevi attacked Vitus. When the Visigoths were defeated in battle, Vitus panicked and fled. Had the Visigoths provided the cavalry and the Romans the infantry contingent so that Vitus retreated with the latter? The Suevi exploited their victory by pillaging the provinces. This was a huge disaster which meant that the Romans were in no position to contemplate any recovery of Spain for years. In my opinion, there are strong grounds to suspect Visigothic duplicity, because every time they were led by Roman commanders (Castinus and Vitus) they were defeated and whenever they were led by their own kings they defeated the Suevi with ease.

Meanwhile Aetius had shown his usual vigor by defeating the Ripuarian Franks in 445. The date for this is secure because *Novella* 17 issued in Rome on 8 June 445 proves that Aetius was at the time in Gaul. It states that Aetius was to make sure that Bishop Hilary of Arles would follow the dictates of the Pope. The bishops that Hilary had ordained illegally were to be removed from office. The *Novella* also reinstated the need for all bishops to follow the will of the Pope. This proves that the state considered it to be of the utmost importance that the Church would be centrally governed so that it could be the better used as a tool of control towards the population. The fact that the regulation of Church matters was placed in the hands of the military commander, here and in other *novellae*, proves the close cooperation between these two state organizations, both of which were hierarchically organized parts of the same state apparatus. It is no coincidence that many of the bishops were former military commanders. When the state structures then collapsed, the Church was left in control.

I would suggest that we should connect the ending of Merobaudes's *Panegyric II* (2.144ff.) with the final stages of the conflict between Aetius and the Ripuarian Franks. The ending of the poem is usually connected with the end of the Visigothic war in 440/1 (e.g. Clover, 58–9), but the placing of the extant fragment at the end of the poem rather suggests that it was the last event just before Aetius's consulship in 446. According to this fragment, Aetius defeated the Teutonic enemy, which combined East and West, in Gaul. The Teutonic enemy which combined East and West is likely to be the Franks because they claimed to have come from Pannonia. Moreover, Merobaudes calls the Visigoths 'Getae' and not 'Teutons' in the same poem. It should be noted that the identity of the enemy is not known with any certainty, and I have included a summary of the ending only to demonstrate that Aetius also knew how to besiege and take fortified places. He was not a Hunnic cavalry general, but a Roman general who knew how to employ all his assets in the best possible way.

The fragment describes a situation in which Aetius had overcome the enemy and forced them to seek shelter in a fortified camp on a hill. Before this, Aetius had reconquered the fortresses (Trier, Cologne?) taken by the enemy. This implies that Aetius had defeated the enemy at least twice, either in pitched battles and/or in ambushes, before the described situation. Firstly, for Aetius to have been able to retake the fortresses, he would have needed to defeat the Frankish field army either in ambush or battle. Secondly, it is clear that Aetius must have defeated the Franks again for him to force them inside their fortified camp – this second force would have consisted of the regrouped Frankish field army which would also have been reinforced by levies. The defences of the Frankish camp consisted of the turreted hill, ramparts of piled earth, and of a shield-wall of spear- and sword-wielding men and bowmen. This was not typical of the Visigothic fortified camps which usually used moving wagon laagers, hence my suggestion that the enemies were the Franks. The fact that the enemy forces are described as infantry also suggests that they must have been the Franks. The Romans used wooden siege towers to overtop the walls, and also ramps, arrows, spears and fire. When the Romans had burned the walls, the defenders panicked, some fled, others were killed, and still others asked for pardon.

After Aetius had crushed the Ripuarian Franks, he marched north to engage the Salian Franks. This time however, there would be no major engagements because Aetius had learnt from his spies that it would be possible to eliminate the enemy leadership with a surgical commando strike.

The Commando Attack at Vicus Helena in 445

According to Sidonius's *Panegyric of Majorian* (213ff.), Aetius launched a surgical surprise attack against the wedding party of the Salian King Clodio at a place called Vicus Helena. The location is unknown, many different places being suggested, but the poem gives enough details for one to be able to reconstruct the principal features of the attack and where it took place. It is worthwhile to quote the poem for the many interesting details it provides (tr. by Anderson, 71ff.). The quote describes the accusation of Aetius's wife against Majorian.

> [*Aetius's wife*], already jealous [*she belonged to the royal house of the Visigoths*]. ... What realm shall I win for my son, ..., if ..., our little Gaudentius is trodden underfoot by this youth's destiny? [*Oost is surely right that this must refer to Valentinian III's plan to marry his daughter to Majorian, which would have precluded marriage with Gaudentius when the other daughter was betrothed to Huneric.*] Already Gaul and Europe sound his praises. ... When he [*Majorian*] defended the Turoni [*defence of Tours presumably against the Bacaudae*], ..., thou [*Aetius*] wast not there; but a little later ye fought together where Cloio [*Clodio*] the Frank had overrun the

helpless lands of the Atrebates [*these were the conquests described by Gregory of Tours*]. There was a narrow passage at the junction of two ways, and a road crossed both the village of Helena, which was within bowshot, and the river, where that long but narrow path was supported by [*a bridge*]. ... [*Aetius*] wert posted at the cross-roads, while Majorian warred as a mounted man close to the bridge itself. ... amid Scythian dance [*was the bride a Visigoth?*] and chorus a yellow-haired bridegroom was wedding a young bride of like colour. ... these revellers, ... he [*Majorian*] laid low [*may imply that Clodio was among the killed*]. ... [*Majorian's*] helmet rang with blows, and his hauberk with its protecting scales [*thorax squamis = scale armour*] kept off the thrusts of spears [*hastae*], until the enemy was forced to turn and flee. ... the victor snatches their chariots and carries off the bride ... [*Frankish*] faces are shaven all round, and instead of beards they have thin moustaches ... Close-fitting garments confine the tall limbs of the men; they are drawn up high so as to expose the knees [*like the traditional legionary trousers!*], and a broad belt supports their narrow middle. It is their sport to send axes [*the axe is the two-bladed bibennis but presumably means the francisca*] hurtling ... to whirl their shields, to outstrip with leaps and bounds the spears [*hastae*] they have hurled and reach the enemy first [*this presumably describes the same tactic as the sixth century Agathias namely that the Franks threw first the harpoon/pilum-like angon-javelin which hit the enemy shield with the result that the Frank who threw the javelin stepped on it and brought down the enemy's shield*]. Even in boyhood's years the love of fighting is full-grown. Should they chance to be sore pressed by numbers or by the luck of the ground, death may overwhelm them, but not fear, ... [*i.e. the Franks preferred to fight to the death just like the other Germanic peoples, which also suggests that Clodio and his retinue died fighting*]. Such men did he put to flight [*this suggests that some fled to be butchered by Aetius' men*]. ... All thine exploits he shares, many more he performs without thee. All men fight for their emperor; I [*Aetius' Gothic wife*] fear ... [*Majorian*] ... now fights for himself [*the wife accused Majorian of having plans to overthrow Aetius with the result that Aetius sacked Majorian in the sentence left out of this quote*]

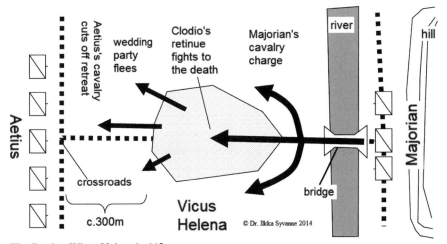

The Battle of Vicus Helena in 445.

The quote vividly describes a situation in which Aetius's spies had managed to collect truly important information on the whereabouts of the enemy king which Aetius knew how to exploit. He appears to have maintained tight control over the information flow because he was able to achieve complete surprise over the enemy. The success was clearly achieved by marching a cavalry force unobserved to the site, which was at some point divided into two divisions, one under Aetius himself who took a blocking position behind the enemy at the crossroads, while Majorian led another portion of the army to the bridge and then over it against the wedding party. The enemy was put between hammer and anvil, completely surprised and annihilated. Aetius had defeated the Franks with one well-aimed surgical strike against their king and military leadership most of whom appear to have been eliminated in the attack.

Contrary to what Ian Hughes (2012, 136) states, this battle does not prove that the warfare of the period would have been a small-scale affair. This goes against all extant evidence which has usually been dismissed by modern historians as unreliable because they claim large-scale encounters. In short, most modern historians have a preconceived opinion that all large figures in the sources are to be dismissed as unreliable while the very few instances of small numbers are used as evidence for this. This is folly. I have already criticized this strongly in *The Age of Hippotoxotai* (2004) and will repeat it again. One has to analyze the operations in their right context. The surprise attack at Vicus Helena was a surgical commando strike against the enemy leadership which does not prove that other larger operations would not have been undertaken by all parties. The fact that the Roman cities of Gaul possessed tens of thousands of inhabitants behind walled cities required that their enemies would have to use large armies to conquer them. It would have been impossible for a force of a few hundreds or at most thousands to challenge the still extant Roman garrisons and federates and to conquer the cities; if the Franks had attempted to conquer a town with a force of a few hundred men, it would have been easily destroyed even by the local citizen militia. Thanks to the fact that the sources for East Rome are more detailed, we actually possess detailed evidence of how effective these paramilitary citizens could be during sieges against Huns or against professional Persian cavalry. We also possess evidence for similarly large numbers of urban militias for the Roman cities of Gaul for the sixth century (see e.g. *The Age of Hippotoxotai*), which makes the claim of small-scale affairs ridiculous. Period warfare consisted of raiding, banditry and major operations just like it always has.

Sidonius's account proves that very soon after the great victory at Vicus Helena (definitely before ca. 450/451), Valentinian III had come up with a plan to marry his daughter Placidia with Majorian while the other daughter Eudocia was to be married with the Vandal prince Huneric. The plan was to preclude marriage between Gaudentius and Placidia, which would have secured the Western Empire for Aetius' family. Aetius' wife learned of the plan and apparently warned her husband of the threat. She demanded the killing of Majorian, but Aetius opposed this. He merely dismissed Majorian. Aetius' purpose was to demonstrate how inconsequential the young Majorian really was. There was no need to kill him.[6]

The death of Clodio together with most of the tribal leadership appears to have resulted in the conclusion of peace so that the Franks once again acknowledged Roman supremacy. The likeliest successor for Clodio is his kinsman or son Merovech (FRMG 594, 596), the father of Childeric I. It is even possible that Merovech could have been Aetius' source of information regarding the location of the wedding ceremony at Vicus Helena. Aetius celebrated his victories over the Franks by issuing coins struck in the mint of Trier in 445/6. On 1 January 446 he was in Rome to celebrate his third consulship.

It was also at about this time that the West Romans (Valentinian III's government) made a momentuous decision which was to have far reaching consequences in the future as it strengthened the Pope's position among the bishops. According to Bury (St. Patrick p.46), *Novella 16* dated to 445 gave the Pope 'Sovran powers' over the provinces still under West Roman rule. This decision however was necessary because the West Romans needed to use the only well-functioning administration at their disposal to control the populace in those areas that had barbarian Federates. All central governments naturally have centralizing tendencies and it is therefore not surprising that the West Romans adopted this solution. It must have seemed like a good solution because the government must have thought that it would be a lot easier to control the Pope in Rome than the various different bishops separately in their bishoprics. The strengthening of the position of the Pope also gave the central government stronger control over the Church apparatus in these areas and thanks to the fact that the native population consisted mostly of Catholics it was possible to widen the rift between the natives on the one hand and the Arian Goths and pagan Franks on the other.

The Years before the Storm 446–450

Aetius' victory over the Huns in 443/4 did not put an end to the problem. On the contrary, it only led to further troubles. Attila killed his brother Bleda either in 444, 445 or 446, after which he secured his own standing among the many tribes encompassing the Hunnic Conderederacy by conducting extensive campaigns on the steppes. After this Attila was ready to launch an attack against the Romans. The first object was of course West Rome, because Attila had previously been defeated by them.

Aetius dispatched an embassy to negotiate with Attila, which is described in Cassiodorus's letter. This letter had been analyzed by Maenchen-Helfen (105–6). In this letter Cassiodorus describes how his grandfather, who was accompanied by Aetius's son Carpilio, met Attila. Attila was angry over some unnamed matters which would have provided him with a pretext to start war. Cassiodorus's grandfather performed his diplomatic mission so well that not only did he manage to pacify Attila but also made him eager to seek Aetius's favour. This seems to be a slight overstatement since Carpilio was left behind as a hostage. Still, it is clear that some sort of mutually beneficial agreement was reached. It is probable that it was then that Attila was made an honorary *MVM*, a position which entitled him to receive a substantial salary, and that he also received an educated Italian, Constantius, to serve as his *notarius*. The diplomatic negotiations must be placed to the year 446 because it is clear that Aetius' inaction during Attila's East Roman campaign in 447 was caused by the fact that his son was Attila's hostage. Attila in his turn appears to have released the son after this campaign, because Carpilio was no longer in Attila's court in 449. Attila's purpose had clearly been to neutralize the West Romans in preparation for his eastern war, which he achieved when Aetius had handed over his own son as hostage. At the same time as Attila concluded his treaty with Aetius, he also handed over to Aetius, as a gesture of his 'goodwill', Aspar's dwarf Zercon, who had been captured by the Huns in about 442/3. After his capture Zercon had become a favourite of Bleda, which appears to have been frowned upon by Attila. Aetius duly restored the dwarf back to Aspar. It is not known what Aetius thought of this gift.

The sources record Vandal piratical raids against Italian and East Roman coastal areas (Rhodes mentioned specifically) after Attila had defeated the East Romans in 447 (Priscus fr. 10). On the basis of this, it seems probable that Gaiseric exploited Roman weakness and allied himself with Attila as the events of 451 prove. The West Romans could no longer use Huneric as a hostage because they had foolishly released him in about 445/6. In addition to this, the western government seems to have decided to postpone the marriage contract between Huneric and Eudocia which Gaiseric would have interpreted as a hostile action. It is in fact possible that the Vandal-Hunnic alliance predates Attila's 447 invasion of the Balkans so that Gaiseric's Vandals distracted part of the East Roman army and navy from coastal defence duties at the same time as Attila invaded. The initiation of hostilities by the Vandals meant that they also cut off Rome's corn supply so that by 450 the Italians were suffering from famine. It is also probable that at the same time as Gaiseric did these things he also conquered the Mauretanias from the Romans and then secured these conquests by demolishing all city walls except those of Septem, Caesarea, Hippone, and Carthage. The purpose was to ensure that rebels would not be able to hide inside the walls, but on the downside this also meant that henceforth the civilian settlements would be more vulnerable to Berber raiders.[7]

In 449 the relationship between Attila and the West soured once again at the same time as the Eastern Government also faced the prospect of renewed war with the Huns. Attila appears to have threatened both halves of the Empire by using various kinds of grievances as his excuses. In the case of West Rome, Attila complained that he had been defrauded by the West Romans. Constantius the Gaul (sent by Aetius previously) who had acted as Attila's *notarius* had in the course of the earlier campaign been given golden bowls by the Bishop of Sirmium which were to be used to ransom prisoners. When the city was sacked and the bishop killed, Constantius had kept the bowls and had taken them to Rome where he had pawned them. When Constantius then returned with 'pockets full of cash', Attila grew suspicious and had him executed. After this, he demanded that the bowls were to be returned to him together with the banker Silvanus who had accepted the stolen goods. Aetius dispatched an embassy to calm down the situation with instructions to promise gold (the bowls had been sold by the banker) but not to hand over the innocent banker. The ambassadors may also have tried to direct Attila's attention towards the Persian Empire, which supposedly was ripe for the taking despite the re-fortification of the Derbend Pass. It is not known how the situation was solved, but we do know that peace prevailed until 450.[8] The fact that the Huns could be expected to attack through the Caucasus proves that Attila's Empire encompassed the area from the Rhine (Burgundians were Attila's clients) up to the Caspian Sea.

The threat posed by Attila seems to have kept Aetius in Italy during the years 447–50 because we hear of no Roman counter-offensive in Spain or Gaul. According to Hydatius, Rechila, king of the Suevi, died as a pagan in Emerita in August 448 and was succeeded by his son Rechiarius, a Catholic. Rechiarius secured his own position by raiding the farthest reaches of Gallaecia so that his followers would obtain booty, which proved that

Rechiarius was an able commander of the armies. This seems to suggest that most of Gallaecia was in Roman hands while the bulk of the Suevic forces were concentrated in Lusitania. In 449 Agiulfus assassinated Censorius in Hispalis, which suggests that the Suevi had now decided to wage total war against the remaining pockets of Roman resistance. Rechiarius concluded an alliance with Theoderic which was sealed by the betrothal of Rechiarius with Theoderic's daughter. Theoderic was more than willing to ally himself with the Suevi against the Romans after Valentinian had allied himself with the Vandals, especially so because Gaiseric had also mutilated Theoderic's daughter. In February 449 Rechiarius pillaged the Vasconiae while he was en route to the Visigoths to marry his bride, the daughter of Theoderic. At about the same time as this happened, the Spanish Bacaudae under Basilius killed the Federate troops posted at Turiaso (Tyriasso) clearly in conjunction with the Suevic campaign in the same area. Rechiarius continued his march to Aquitania in July 449 where the marriage ceremony between the two royal houses cemented their alliance. After this, Rechiarius returned and together with Basilius pillaged the neighbourhood of Caesaraugusta (Zaragosa) and captured the city of Ilerda through trickery. The Romans had now effectively lost also control of the western part of Tarracona so that their terriories were now restricted to parts of Gallaecia and eastern Tarracona and possibly to some individual cities and areas elsewhere.

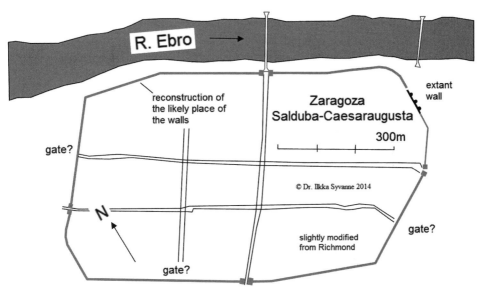

The defences of this city proved too much for Rechiarius.

The Gallic Chronicle mentions for the year 448 the flight of the physician Eudoxius to the Huns. He is claimed to have had perverse talents as Bacaudae leader. This made him an ideal refugee from the Hunnish viewpoint because Attila was already making plans for a campaign in the west. Attila had crushed the East Roman armies and defences in the Balkans in 447 with the result that he had once again started to cast his eyes towards West Rome. Attila undoubtedly entertained the possibility of using Eudoxius for the purpose of causing desertions among the Armorican citizen militia.

Further north in Britain the situation was even worse. The Gallic Chronicle 452 dates the beginning of the Saxon dominance of Britain to the year 441/2. This date is acceptable if it is to be taken to refer to the start of the invasion because the conquest of Britain starting from the area just south of Hadrian's Wall down to the south of Britain could easily have taken years to accomplish before the Britons sent their plea for help (described by Gildas) to Aetius in late 445 or in 446. According to Gildas 19, before the beginning of 446, the Picts and Scots had once again invaded Britain with great determination and had landed their force in the area just south of Hadrian's Wall. There on the Wall was a garrison (which must mean collectively all of the garrisons) manned by a useless bunch of cowards according to Gildas. The Britons were consequently forced to abandon the Wall and cities and to disperse as best they could, but their enemies pursued them relentlessly. On top of this, the Britons started to fight against each other, which made their enemies' job even easier. It was then that the remaining defenders decided to seek help from Aetius (Gildas 20–23, tr. by Giles):

Again, therefore, the wretched remnant [*remnants of Briton/Roman forces in Britain*], send to Aetius, a powerful Roman citizen, [*envoys who*] address him as follows: – 'To Aetius now Consul for the third time [*i.e. in 446*]: the groans of the Britons.' … 'The Barbarians drive us to the sea; the sea throws us back on the barbarians: thus two modes of death await us, we are either slain or drowned.' The Romans, however, could not assist them, and in the meantime the discomfited people, wandering in the woods, began to feel the effects of a severe famine, which compelled many of them without delay to yield themselves up to their cruel persecutors, to obtain subsistence; other of them, however, lying hid in mountains, caves and woods, continually sallied out from thence to renew the war. And then it was, for the first time, that they overthrew their enemies, who for so many years had been living in their country [*it is not known with any certainty how many years this means*], for their trust was not in man, but in God; … The boldness of the enemy was for a while checked, but not the wickedness of our countrymen: the enemy left our people, but the people did not leave their sins. … The audacious invaders therefore return to their winter quarters, determined before long again to return and plunder. And they too, the Picts for the first time seated themselves at the extreminity of the island, where they afterwards continued, occasionally plundering and wasting our country. During these truces, the wounds of the distressed people are healed, but another sore, still more venomous, broke out. No sooner were the ravages of the enemy checked, than the island was deluged with … every kind of luxury and licentiousness. … Kings were anointed, not according to God's ordinance, but such as showed themselves more cruel than the rest; and soon after, they were put to death by those who had elected them, without any inquiry into their merits, but because others still more cruel were chosen to succeed them. … For a council was called to settle what was best and most expedient to be done, in order to repel such frequent and fatal irruptions and plunderings of the above named nations [*this would be the famous Round Table, which would have been modelled after the older provincial council*]. Then all councillors, together with that proud tyrant Gurthrigern [*Vortigern*], the British king, were so blinded, that, as a protection to their country, they sealed its doom by inviting in among them (*like wolves into the sheep-fold*) the fierce and impious Saxons, a race hateful both to God and men, to repel the invasions of the northern nations.

The above quote makes it clear that the Romans abandoned the Britons to their own devices in 446 and that some of the Britons were eventually able to overthrow the invaders. Those Britons who considered the living conditions on the island intolerable fled to the continent in such numbers that part of Armorica came to be called Brittany/Bretagne. This is the point where the legend of Arthur begins, which I have analyzed in a separate monograph. I occasionally refer to this book in the text.

In 449 Aetius rewarded his supporters so that Astyrius was nominated as consul, Firminus as PPI and Opilio as PVR. This ensured Aetius full control of the imperial finances which were in a mess.

Salvian and the Troubled Roman Society in ca. 449–450

Salvian's *On the Government of God* which was written some time between 440 and 451 provides an important analysis of Roman society at this time and is worth quoting at length (5.4ff. tr. by Sanford):

> But as for the way of life among the Goths and Vandals, in what single respect can we consider ourselves superior to them, or even worthy of comparison? Let me speak first of their affection and charity. ... Now almost all barbarians, at least those who belong to one tribe, under one king's rule, love one another, whereas almost all the Romans are at strife with one another. What citizen does not envy his fellows? Who knows complete charity to his neighbours? ... not even relations preserve bonds of kinship. ... for the many are proscribed by the few, who use public levies for their individual gain, and convert the bills of indebtedness to the public treasury to their private profit. Nor is it only the highest officials who do this, but the least too in almost equal measure, not only the judges, but their obedient underlings as well. For what cities are there, or even municipalities and villages, in which there are not as many tyrants as curials? ... Therefore not one of them is safe, indeed scarcely any are safe, except the very greatest, from the plunder and ruin of this universal brigandage other than those who are a match for the brigands themselves. Matters have come to such an evil pass, to such a criminal condition, that only the wicked man may count himself secure. ...Meanwhile the poor are being robbed, widows groan, orphans are trodden down, so that many, even persons of good birth who have enjoyed a liberal education, seek refuge with the enemy to escape death under the trials of general persecution. ... So you find men passing over everywhere, now to the Goths, now to the Bagaudae, or whatever other barbarians have established their power anywhere, and they do not repent of their expatriation, for they would rather live as free men, ... The result is that even those who do not take refuge with the barbarians are yet compelled to be barbarians themselves, for this is the case with the greater part of the Spaniards, no small proportion of the Gauls, and, in fine all those throughout the Roman world whose Roman citizenship has been brought to nothing by Roman extortion. I must now speak of the Bagaudae, who

despoiled, afflicted and murdered by wicked and bloodthirsty magistrates after they had lost the rights of Roman citizens, forfeited also the honour of the Roman name. We transform their misfortunes into crime, we brand them with a name that recalls their losses, with a name that we ourselves have forced into crime. For by what other causes were they made Bagaudae save by our unjust acts, wicked decisions of the magistrates, the proscription and extortion of those who have turned the public exactions to the increase of their private fortunes and made the tax indictions their opportunity for plunder? ... The rich themselves from time to time make additions to the amount of taxation demanded from the poor. ... Take the Franks, they are ignorant of this wrong; the Huns are immune to it; there is nothing of the sort among the Vandals, nothing among the Goths. For in the Gothic country the barbarians are so far from tolerating this sort of oppression that not even Romans who live among them have to bear it. Hence all the Romans in that region have but one desire, that they may never have to return to the Roman jurisdiction. It is the unanimous prayer of the Roman people in that district that they may be permitted to continue to lead their present life among the barbarians. Yet we are surprised that the Goths are not conquered by our resistance, when the Romans would rather live among them than at home. ...I could find occasion to wonder why all the poor and needy taxpayers do not follow their example, except for the one factor that hinders them, namely that they cannot transfer their poor possessions and homes and their household. ...Therefore some of those of whom I speak, who are either shrewder than the rest or have been sharpened by necessity, have lost their homes and farms by such enroachments, or have fled before the taxgatherers, because they cannot hold their property, and seek out the farms of the rich and great, to become their coloni. Those who are driven by the terror of the enemy flee to the forts, and those who have lost their immunity as free men take refuge in some asylum out of sheer desperation. So also these men, ..., subject themselves to their lowly yoke of serfdom.

The above quote makes it absolutely clear why the West Romans failed to defeat the barbarians who lived amongst them. The principal reason in the west was the massive corruption of the magnates and curial class both of whom robbed the poorer classes. The flight of the people either to the relative safety provided by barbarians, Bacaudae, rich patrons, or forts meant that the taxes for all the rest were raised even higher because both the state and the rich needed to make up for the lost revenue. Salvian also provides an explanation for why most of the poor were still forced to stay under Roman rule: it was impossible to move property to barbarian territory, hence the migration of the relatively wealthy who could carry most of their property in monetary form.

Salvian (books 7–8) also claims that there was a moral dimension to the Roman troubles. He claims that the Roman upper classes were morally corrupt, that all Africans were evil, the African nobility effeminate, and that other Romans still had some good left in them despite being adulterous, lovers of prostitutes, circuses, wine and gluttony. In contrast he considered the barbarians 'chaste' and 'pure'. Salvian stated that the Goths were treacherous but chaste; Alans chaste but not treacherous; Franks treacherous but hospitable; Saxons cruel savages, but chaste. This means that all who thought like Salvian saw the barbarians as liberators from moral corruption. It is probable that the barbarians also considered the Romans to be amoral and despicable which naturally influenced their views and policies. This cultural contrast did not bode well for the Romans.

Salvian's account regarding the greed of the Roman upper classes is confirmed by Paulinus and imperial legislation (NVal 1, 4, 6.3, 7.1–3, 10), but in such a way that most imperial legislation was directed against the abuses of its own personnel rather than against the curials. The probable reason for this is that the imperial administration attempted to correct the abuses of the curials by using its own personnel for tax gathering. Valentinian's *Novella* 7, which was issued as a result of the report given by the *PPI* Maximus on 4 June 440, gives a good indication of how the palatines also misused their powers. According to the report the palatines exacted so much money into their own pockets that the ability of the landholders and tradesmen to pay their taxes was in danger. *Novella* 1.3, issued simultaneously on 14 March 450 to the consuls, praetors, tribunes and Senate, proves that the problems persisted and that the government recognized the severity of the situation and did its best to correct the abuses. It is clear that the Western Government recognized that it too had to fight for the hearts and minds of the people if it hoped to be able to overcome the barbarians. This *Novella* proves that corrupt tax investigators were in the habit of seeking the assistance of provincial staff, scholarians, and other officials with which they terrorized landholders with imaginary tax arrears, and exacted harsh punishments (imprisonment, torture and hanging) on those who could not pay. The result was that landholders were forced to buy postponements or were ruined. The government sought to solve the situation by remitting all tax arrears up to the year 448, the only exception being the province of Sardinia where some corrupt persons had stolen the money. Furthermore, the choosing of the tax investigators was taken away from one judge (who could be corrupted) and placed collectively in the hands of the praetorian prefect and *Patricius*, the latter probably meaning Aetius. In other words, Aetius attempted to put a stop to the corruption of the civilian authorities, which the civil service undoubtedly saw as an infringement into their territory. As noted, the legislation issued by the state dealing with the tax inspectors and palatines suggests that the Emperor had attempted to correct the abuse of the taxpayers by the curials by using imperial administrators to ensure that the state received its taxes. The *novellae* in their turn prove that this was not entirely successful and Majorian's *Novella* 2 from the year 458 proves that the attempt to correct the situation only worsened it.

One can summarize the situation in 450 as follows: the state did not obtain the necessary taxes for the upkeep of the army thanks to corruption; taxpayers saw the barbarians as liberators; and the administrative structure was falling apart. All this proves that the West Roman state was losing its fight for hearts and minds while its state structures were falling apart.

Novella 28 (11 Sept. 449) which deals with the *principes* of the *agentes in rebus* is important for the reason that it acknowledges the importance of the *agentes in rebus* for the West Roman Empire in the year 449. The Emperor followed the recommendation made by *Mag. Off.* Opilio regarding the privileges, subsistence allowances and emoluments due to *principes* of the organization so that the men in question would be protected against the avarice of the judges (presumably governors). Their services were sorely needed for the 'public needs'. The contents of the *Novella* suggest that even the members of the 'secret service' could be fleeced and that this was to be stopped immediately. One can imagine that the *agentes in rebus* were ever more important for the internal security of the West Roman Empire in a situation in which the barbarian enemies were located inside its borders. Therefore it is clear that the importance of traditional military intelligence against the barbarians by the *Limitanei* had diminished in comparison with the organization devoted to internal security especially because the Roman state failed to create internal borders against their barbarian allies.

Chapter Seven

East from 425 until 450[1]

Eudocia and Theodosius

As noted in the volume 3, it is clear that Empress Eudocia was behind the rise of those who were either tolerant towards pagans, Jews and Samaritans or were themselves pagans or closet-pagans, and who preferred the policy of détente with Persia. The leading person of this group between ca. 423 and 425 was the new *PPO* Asclepiodotus, Eudocia's maternal uncle. He so robustly enforced the new pieces of legislation which granted protection for Jews and pagans against persecution by Christian fanatics that St. Simeon addressed a letter to Theodosius II in which he accused him of being a friend, comrade and protector of the faithless Jews, with the result that Theodosius felt compelled to sack Asclepiodotus. Despite this, in practice the authorities seem not to have increased their persecution of the minorities. It should also be stressed that the fall of Asclepiodotus did not mean that the Empress's influence would have waned. On the contrary, she was still able to influence her husband while her competitor Pulcheria was forced out of the immediate circle of the Emperor.

In the field of foreign policy the most important decision reached by the supporters of Eudocia between 423 and 440 was the granting of a place of asylum for Galla Placidia and Valentinian in early 423 and then their restoration back to power in 424/5 so that the two halves of the imperial house were united. This was sealed by the betrothal of Theodosius' daughter Licinia Eudoxia with Valentinian. The marriage ceremony took place on 29 October 437. For further details, see above and below.

It has also been suggested that Eudocia's influence was behind the reorganization and enlargement of the so-called University of Constantinople to act as a competitor for the universities of Antioch, Alexandria and Athens which had a pagan background. The University of Constantinople now received imperial patronage and protection and had a distinctly Christian character in contrast to the other universities. This had far reaching consequences because the University of Constantinople taught several generations of learned men who came to occupy high positions in the imperial administration. The combination of classical learning with Christian doctrine was important from the point of view of making classical Hellenic science and culture more acceptable for the Christians which ensured its survival in the East. The new constitution of the University was important for another reason. The fact that the Greek language section had slightly more professors than the Latin meant that the first stage in the direction of the eventual dominance of the Greek language in the East had now been taken, which would eventually lead to the emergence of separate identities in the East and West.

The Birth of the Nestorian Heresy in 428–435[2]

Theodosius' choice of Nestorius as the new Patriarch of Constantinople in 428 proved particularly disastrous for the future as he proved to be a divisive personality. In a very short time Nestorius managed to alienate and anger: the Arians (the Germanic military leadership, imperial bodyguards and the Praesental armies) in the capital by attacking their church just four days after his inauguration; the monks by forcing them inside cloisters; the populace by suppressing the circus, theatre, games, and dancers; Pulcheria and her sisters and friends by accusing Pulcheria of having slept with many men (Pulcheria was accused of lusting after *Mag.Off.* Paulinus) and by refusing to grant Pulcheria the privileges she had become used to; the various heretical sects by making the Emperor issue harsh legislation against them; Cyril the Bishop of Alexandria by failing to grant him the customary courtesies; and most importantly, the clergy, the populace, and Pulcheria and her friends by refusing to call Mary *Theotokos* (Mother of God) and demanding that she should be called *Christotokos* (Mother of Christ). Thereby Nestorius claimed that Mary had given birth to a man and not to a God. Nestorius' opponents claimed that he had divided Jesus Christ into two people, one human and one divine, while Nestorius protested that his Christ was a single person with divine and human natures.

Pope Celestine condemned Nestorius at a Council held in Rome in 430, and next year, with the support of Pulcheria, Cyril of Alexandria organized a counter-movement against Nestorius and also obtained the Pope's support for this purpose. The Emperor and Eudocia supported Nestorius almost to the end and convened a Church Council at Ephesus in 431 to discuss the supposed heretical views of Nestorius. To ensure Nestorius would come out on top, the emperor dispatched *Comes Domesticorum* Candidianus with the *Domestici* to act as his representatives for the purpose of putting pressure on the participants. Nestorius' entourage included his friend *Comes* Irenaeus, who certainly came with his own *bucellarii*, and we should not forget that Nestorius was also accompanied by his thugs, the *Zeuxippitai* (the bath attendants of the Baths of Zeuxippos). Cyril, however, arrived with his own Egyptian thugs (rustics, monks, clergy, sailors, bath attendants, ruffians), which were transported to the scene on Egyptian grain ships. The Bishop of the city of Ephesus was Memnon who was Nestorius' opponent. In the background was also the clever Pulcheria who pulled the strings like a puppet master. Memnon used his own supporters and Cyril's thugs to intimidate Nestorius' supporters and then tricked Candidianus into reading the wrong text. They then drove him and the other bishops away, declared Nestorius heretic, excommunicated him, and deposed him. Nestorius' supporters, the military forces included, proved powerless to oppose. It was then that John the Bishop of Antioch arrived with his supporters. John organized a counter-synod, which in its turn deposed Cyril and Memnon.

Candidianus had informed the Emperor of the condemnation of Nestorius but still tried to control the movement of information in order to manipulate the situation by posting soldiers at all land and sea exits of Ephesus while their supporters in Constantinople attempted to stop any messengers dispatched by Cyril. All precautions proved futile. In the end Pulcheria's clever manipulation of the situation proved too much. She organized massive demonstrations in Constantinople against Nestorius with the result that many of the leading men of the government had a change of heart. These men included the praetorian prefects, the city prefect, the Master of Offices, *magistri militum* and the Palace eunuch Scholasticus. In the end, the Emperor decided to abandon Nestorius to avoid greater harm. Nestorius was exiled and Maximianus was appointed the new Patriarch. Pulcheria had won.

The cost of this religious squabble proved great for the Roman Empire for it eventually resulted in the separation of the Persian Church from the Roman Church when the rulers of Persia decided to back the Nestorians. This effectively cut off the information flow from the Christians of the East and weakened the support the Roman armies could expect to obtain from the Christian population in Persia.

At about the same time as Pulcheria managed to force Theodosius to abandon Nestorius she also managed to restore her own standing as the person who took care of the administration of the empire while Eudocia cared for the offspring. At the same time as Pulcheria once again became the principal political advisor of the Emperor, the Emperor abandoned marital relations with his wife Eudocia. We do not know why this was, but it resulted in a change of policy once again. Pulcheria instigated a policy of unification of the Church. The bishops who refused to abandon Nestorius were deposed. Dorotheus of Marcianopolis refused to step down with the result that *MVM Praes.* Plintha was sent to install his successor by force. The most important part of the project however was to force the Antiochian party (supporters of Nestorius) and Alexandrian party to find some common ground. Tribune and notary Aristolaus was dispatched to shuttle between Antioch and Alexandria in 432 while the *MVM per Orientem* was ordered to assist if necessary. Cyril of Alexandria attempted to ensure that he would succeed by bribing Pulcheria's staff and many others in Constantinople, but in the end the compromise position prevailed. In March 433 John of Antioch agreed to abandon Nestorius, and the Monophysite Cyril of Alexandria accepted that Christ had two natures: human and godly. Those who did not accept this compromise were persecuted. In the East the mission was given to *MVM* Dionysius and his vicar Titus, the *Com.Dom.* The *Comes* Irenaeus lost his rank and property and was exiled to the Egyptian desert. Nestorius followed in his footsteps in 435.

Theodosius' Legal Reform 429–438

In March 429 Theodosius initiated a project to reform the existing legal codes by setting up a commission to review, update and rearrange all existing law codes from the late third century onwards. The first edition was completed in 435, but was not published presumably because the Emperor, who took personal interest in the process, was not satisfied with the result. The Emperor appointed a new commission led by Antiochian lawyer Antiochus Chuzon (PPO in 448). The results were published to great acclaim as the *Codex Theodosianus* in 438. The personal interest of Theodosius is also in evidence in the great rash of new legislation that he issued as *Novellae* immediately after the publication of the *Codex*. Most of these were issued immediately in 438–39, but additional *Novellae* were also added later so that the last of these date from 444.[3]

The creation of the new legal code was important for several reasons. It created a comprehensive law system that was to be followed in both halves of the Empire, and one by which the legal codes of both halves of the Empire could be implemented over the whole of it. It created a legal system to which additions could be made by new emperors, and was the basis for Justinian's legal reforms (*Codex* and *Institutes*) and for the *Lex Visigothorum* of Alaric II in 507.[4]

The Preface to *Novella* 16 (NTh 16) is particularly important from the military point of view and it is therefore worthwhile to include Pharr's translation (p.501) of the relevant portion of the text: 'It will profit the barbarian nations to be delivered to the sovereignty of Our Divinity, Our victories will appear to be fruitful to those who obey Us, only if the advantages of peace are established by regulation of the laws.'

The legislation of the religiously motivated Theodosius was particularly harsh towards the Samaritans and Jews. In 438 he prohibited them from all *dignitates* (temporary direct appointments by Emperor) and *militiae* (permanent military and administrative positions) while not relieving them from the duty of service of the *cohortali/cohortales* (hereditary provincial officials) or from the *curia* (the city council in which the decurions/curiales served with financial handicaps). This discrimination alienated both groups, eventually leading them to revolts and mutinies and to side with the Persians. It was thanks to the anti-Semitism of the bigoted Christians that the Samaritans and Jews, at the time loyal to the Empire, were turned against it. In short, it was now that the Eastern Government committed the same mistake as had been committed by Honorius in the West.[5]

Theodosius considered the establishment of law and order throughout the Empire to be of the utmost importance for its capacity to attract barbarian nations to submit to Roman rule. He was not entirely mistaken in his beliefs, as the barbarians did eventually seek to establish similar laws in their own kingdoms.

It is probable that East Rome was more successful in implementing Theodosius' programme of law and order, despite its rampant corruption, and was therefore able to contrast itself favourably with the Persians and Huns. Despite the legislation put in place against the Jews, Samaritans, pagans and other religions, the Roman Imperial Administration usually sought to defend these against the Christian fanatics and sought to establish law and order even for the downtrodden. In contrast, when the Persians persecuted religious minorities it was the administration headed by the magi (who also acted as prosecutors, judges and executioners) that killed the unfortunate victims often by subjecting them to prolonged cruel torture. Their only place of refuge lay in the Roman Empire. The Huns must have had some sort of laws based on ancient tribal customs and practices, but they did not provide the same kind of protection as the Roman laws, not to mention the fact that the harsh nomadic lifestyle was not particularly attractive for the average peasant, artisan or tradesman. The Hunnic rulers were also bad masters to the tribes they had subjected to their authority as the constant string of fugitives fleeing to Roman territory proves.

Wars in 431–439

As noted above, the victory of the Vandals over Bonifatius brought about a joint response by the two halves of the Empire in 430/431. The Vandals defeated both Bonifatius and Aspar, and the defence of Carthage was left in Aspar's hands after Bonifatius sailed to Italy against Aetius in 432. Aspar was able to keep the Vandals at bay. This may imply that he had received reinforcements from the East. The war between Aetius and Bonifatius resulted in disaster when, after the death of Bonifatius, the ousted Aetius sought help from the Huns of Rua/Ruga in 433. In return for their help Aetius promised them the territories that they had lost to the East Romans in 427. These territories lay between the Danube and Italy and were therefore the natural first object of the Hunnic invasion in 433. The East Romans were defeated and forced to cede the territories in question, to hand over deserters from the Hunnic realm and to pay a yearly tribute of 350 lbs of gold. The East Romans lacked resources to make a proper response because they had dispatched all of their available reserves to Carthage under Aspar and against the Yemenites in Arabia (see the reign of Marcian).[6]

In about 434/5 a number of tribes bordering the Danube (the Amilzuri, Itimari, Tounsoures, Boisci and others) fled to the Roman side of the border with the result that Rua dispatched his trusted diplomat Eslas to inform the Romans that he intended to punish these tribes. The Romans wanted to defuse the situation by sending an embassy before Rua had a chance to launch his attack. The *magistri* and former consuls, the Gothic Plinta (Plintas/Plinthas) and Thracian Dionysius, competed for the post. Plinta attempted to gain the position with Hunnic help, but Rua/Ruga died and was succeeded by Attila and Bleda before Plinta's retainer Sengilach could achieve his object. Consequently, Plinta resorted to the use of the Roman Senate, which recommended (undoubtedly because of bribery) that the Emperor would send Plinta. The Emperor confirmed this. Plinta requested that the *magister scriniorum* Epigenes would accompany him as ambassador. The Emperor accepted this. The two sides met each other outside the city of Margus. The resulting agreement granted to the Huns what they wished: 1) The Romans agreed to hand over the fugitives and not to receive any fugitives in the future; 2) The Romans agreed to return all those prisoners-of-war that had managed to flee back to the Roman side unless each of them paid a ransom of eight *solidi*; 3) The Romans promised not to make any alliances against the Huns; 4) The Romans granted markets with equal rights; 5) And the Romans agreed to pay 700 lbs of gold each year to the Hunnic kings. The fugitives that the Romans handed back included members of the royal house, who were duly executed by the Huns. As a result of this agreement, Attila and Bleda were able to concentrate their attention towards the tribes of Scythia, which included the Sorosgi, and the Romans were able to bring back their forces from Carthage after the peace between Valentinian III and Gaiseric had been signed in 435.[7]

Some time between 435 and 440 the Rugi revolted against the East Romans under Valips and captured Noviodunum (Priscus fr. 5). Valips' intention was to invade Illyricum and Thrace, but the Romans forestalled him and besieged him. Valips' position was desperate because he faced a numerically superior Roman army bent on taking the city. His solution was to post the children of the prisoners on the walls, with the result that the Roman soldiers stopped their attack. To save the children, the Romans agreed to end the siege on terms.

It is probable that it was in about 434–7 that one Qusayy conducted, with the support of the Roman 'Caesar', a campaign against the city of Mecca. This Qusayy was an ancestor of the Prophet Muhammad. He was born in Mecca, and his father died soon after. His mother remarried a man from the tribe of Udra. As a result of this, Qusayy spent his youth among the Udra near the Roman border. According to the Arabic tradition, Qusayy marched to Mecca and fought against the southern Arabic tribe of the Khuzaa, and with the assistance of Caesar overthrew them. After this he gathered together the clans of Quraysh and settled them in and around Mecca, restored the 'religion of Abraham', and rebuilt the Kaba thereby assuring the supremacy of Mecca as a place of worship. Since it is known that Qusayy was a contemporary of al-Mundhir, it is clear that this event could have taken place at any time between about 405 and 434/7, but the likeliest dates would be the years 434–7. It is also possible that this campaign was conducted as a joint operation with the Persian ruler Bahram, but it is equally possible that it was conducted against Bahram's allies in the region. The exact circumstances of the events on the Red Sea and Horn of Africa are not known beyond the fact that Bahram appears to have conducted a naval campaign in the area during the 430s and that the Aksumites were probably clients of Persia by about 457.[8]

Marriage of Valentinian III and Licinia Eudoxia

On 29 October 437 a marriage ceremony took place in Constantinople between Valentinian and Licinia Eudoxia which sealed the union between the eastern and western halves of the Empire. One of the organizers was Volusianus who was still a pagan. He was duly converted by his niece St. Melania the Younger. Melania was an impressive person and befriended the Empresses. Eudocia, who had now handed over her daughter to Valentinian, was in need of consolation and decided to make a pilgrimage to Jerusalem where Volusianus could meet Melania again. The trip may also have had another motivation which was to impress the highly religious Theodosius II with the piety of his wife so that Eudocia could regain her husband's trust.[9]

Eudocia's Pilgrimage and Consolidation of the Defences in 438–440

When Eudocia arrived at Antioch, the city of her ancestors, she delivered a celebrated imperial address to the city's senate. She showered wealth on the city and the city fathers duly erected statues of her to celebrate their benefactor. Evagrius (1.20) mentions that Theodosius II enlarged the city walls of Antioch to the suburb of Daphne as a result of the

A nineteenth century photo of a diptych of Felix now in Paris.

Hattenroth's (1891) impression of how Aetius might have looked.

image in San Maria Maggiore, Ravenna, ca. 500. (*Public domain*). Note the use of large shields and two spears with the implication that the soldier was expected to throw at least one of the spears before making contact with the enemy.

A possible bust of Theodosius II, which Bernoulli identifies with Eugenius.

Berkasovo II helmet. Reconstruction by Vicus Ultimus. (© *Vicus Ultimus*)

A coin of Theodosius II. British Museum. (*Photo by author*)

A coin of Eudoxia, a daughter of Theodosius II and wife of Valentinian III. British Museum. (*Photo by author*)

A coin of Valentinian III (Valentinianus III). British Museum. (*Photo by author*)

A coin of Galla Placidia, mother of Valentinian III. British Museum. (*Photo by author*)

A Gothic village – Masłomęcz, Poland. Reconstruction by Vicus Ultimus. The Gothic *foederati* in Roman service could be housed in similar villages on Roman territory. (© *Vicus Ultimus*)

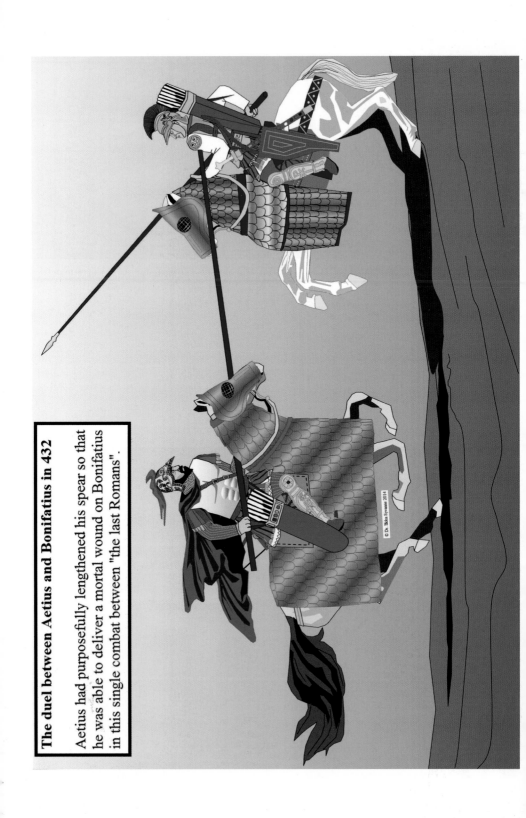

The duel between Aetius and Bonifatius in 432

Aetius had purposefully lengthened his spear so that he was able to deliver a mortal wound on Bonifatius in this single combat between "the last Romans".

© Dr. Ilkka Syvänne 2014

A Gothic village – Masłomęcz, Poland. Reconstruction by Vicus Ultimus. The Gothic *foederati* in Roman service could be housed in similar villages on Roman territory. (© *Vicus Ultimus*)

Hejmstead, Romo – North Sea coast. Reconstructions by Vicus Ultimus. (© *Vicus Ultimus*).

A reconstruction of Carnuntum. A wedding party. (© *Vicus Ultimus*)

Musée Parc archéologique des Temps Barbares. Note the helmets and other equipment in display. (© *Vicus Ultimus*)

A modern reconstruction of Carnuntum with tents and other military equipment. (© *Vicus Ultimus*)

Draco-standard. Reconstruction by Vicus Ultimus. (© *Vicus Ultimus*)

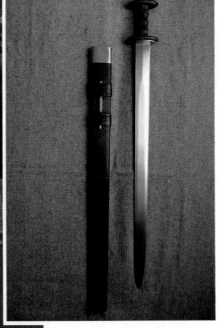

Reconstruction of 'Ejsbol-Sarry' subtype 2, variant 2 spatha by Vicus Ultimus. (© *Vicus Ultimus*)

Gothic village – Masłomęcz, Poland. The Gothic *foederati* in Roman service could be housed in similar villages on Roman territory. Reconstruction by Vicus Ultimus. (© *Vicus Ultimus*)

'Lenticular shields'. Reconstruction by Vicus Ultimus. (© *Vicus Ultimus*)

Hejmstead, Romø – North Sea coast. Reconstructions by Vicus Ultimus. (© *Vicus Ultimus*)

Vicus Ultimus re-enactors at Hejmstead, Romo – North Sea coast. (© *Vicus Ultimus*)

A member of the Vicus Ultimus re-enactors with a draco-standard at Hejmstead, Romo – North Sea coast. (© *Vicus Ultimus*)

ejmstead, Romo – North Sea coast. Note the protective cover for the spearhead and the great variety of elmets and equipment in use at this time. Reconstructions by Vicus Ultimus. (© *Vicus Ultimus*)

Left: Christies – helmet. *Centre:* Augsburg II – helmet. *Right:* Burgh Castle – helmet. Reconstructions b
Vicus Ultimus. (© *Vicus Ultimus*)

Top: Christies – helmet.
Second from top: Berkasovo – helmet.
Second from below: Christies – helmet.
Below: Deurne – helmet.

Nydam-Kragehul – Subtype 2 spatha.
Reconstructions by Vicus Ultimus.
(© *Vicus Ultimus*)

Members of the Vicus Ultimus near the reconstructed Gothic village – Masłomęcz, Poland. (© *Vicus Ultimus*).

Nydam-Kragehul spatha.

A spatha, 'Ejsbol-Sarry' subtype 2, variant 2. Reconstructions by Vicus Ultimus. (© *Vicus Ultimus*)

Members of the Vicus Ultimus near the reconstructed Gothic village – Masłomęcz, Poland. (© *Vicus Ultimus*

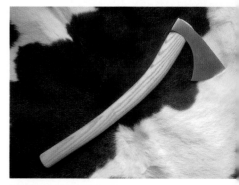

Burgh Castle francisca.

Nydam-Kragehul – Subtype 2 spatha.
Reconstructions by Vicus Ultimus. (© *Vicus Ultimus*

Spatha – Snipstat – Illerup.

A Gothic village – Masłomęcz, Poland. Reconstruction by Vicus Ultimus. The Gothic *foederati* in Roman service could be housed in similar villages on Roman territory. (© *Vicus Ultimus*)

Re-enactors from the Polish Group Vicus Ultimus at Heimstead, Romo – North Sea coast. Note the protective cover for the spearhead, draco-standard and the great variety of helmets and equipment in use at this time. (© *Vicus Ultimus*)

entreaties of Eudocia, but then states that some historians claimed that the enlargement of the walls took place under Theodosius I. Modern historians have usually accepted this, but connect it with the statement of Malalas (13.40) that the wall was built when Antiochus Chouzon the Elder was *PPO*. Malalas dates the event to the reign of Theodosius I, but it is usually suspected that he has confused the two Theodosii. According to Malalas, the purpose was to enclose the houses outside the wall so that the new wall ran from the Gate of Philonauta to the place known as Rhodion so that it enclosed the mountain as far as Tiberius's Wall. The new wall was extended as far as the stream Phyrminos, which ran down from the ravine in the mountain. The *PPO* tore down the old *monomacheion* (the amphitheatre meant for gladiatorial fights) on the acropolis and the aqueduct leading up to the acropolis to obtain building material for the wall.[10]

My own educated guess is that the walls of Antioch were enlarged twice, once under Theodosius I and a second time during the reign of Theodosius II at the request of Eudocia. There is actually circumstantial evidence for the enlargement of the walls also under Theodosius I because Libanius mentions that in 383/4 the population of the city had increased after the previous enlargements of the Plethorion building in 332 and 336 so that a new attempt was made to enlarge it. This project is also noted by Downey (1958, p. 87: Lib. Or. 10.9, 13, 25), but he (Downey 1941) has not connected it with the statement that the walls were enlarged under Theodosius I. In my opinion, Libanius' statement lends credence to Malalas' statement that the walls were enlarged under Theodosius I. The problem with this is that the extant evidence doesn't know any Antiochus Chouzon for the reign of Theodosius I. However, the sources do know several Antiochuses for the same period (PLRE1 Antiochus 5–10) that could fit the description and it is possible that one of them was called Chouzon as well. In particular Antiochus 6 (PLRE2), who was at the Imperial Court in 388–90 and whose influence Libanius courted, would fit the bill. Consequently I would connect the enlargement of the walls at the instigation of Eudocia with her visit of Antioch in 438/9, but not with her later visit in ca. 444 because by then she had lost most of her influence with the emperor (see later). I would also suggest that Eudocia's project was not actually an enlargement of the walls (it is probable that the sources have confused the two projects) but an improvement of the work done under Theodosius I – or if the walls were actually enlarged that it cannot have been as extensive an enlargement as under Theodosius I. What is almost certain however, is that it was under Theodosius II that the walls received the sophisticated prow-towers, the remains of one of which still exists together with other improvements. What is notable about the likely timing of the project is that it also took place when Anatolius was *MVM per Orientem* and it is actually probable that Anatolius had made the suggestion to the empress in person because the HQ of the *MVM per Orientem* was located at Antioch. The improvement of the defences also appears to have been connected with the simultaneous legislation against the corruption of the officers of the *Limitanei* (see below) and can therefore be considered to have been a conscientious project to improve the defences initiated by the *MVM per Orientem* Anatolius.

The improvement of the walls of Antioch was a very important addition to its defences because the city served as the logistical hub of the eastern armies (with the port city of Seleucia) and as the HQ of the *MVM per Orientem*. My own estimate for the size of the population of Antioch is that there were about 200,000 free males in the city so that with the women, children and slaves there were altogether about 600,000 inhabitants.[11]

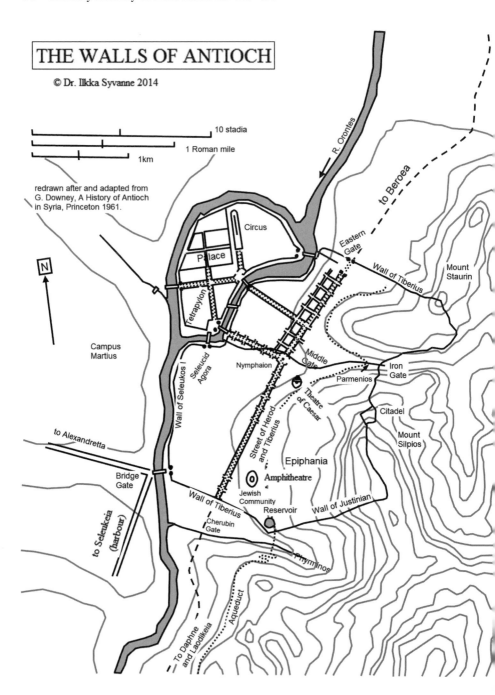

THE WALLS OF ANTIOCH

© Dr. Ilkka Syvänne 2014

10 stadia

1 Roman mile

1km

redrawn after and adapted from
G. Downey, A History of Antioch
in Syria, Princeton 1961.

After Eudocia had completed her visit of Antioch, she continued her journey to Jerusalem where she built many buildings and reconstructed the wall of Jerusalem (Mal. 14.8). Once again it is probable that Anatolius used Eudocia's influence over the Emperor to obtain what he considered necessary for the defence of the city and area. The reconstruction of the walls of Jerusalem secured the area so that the Arab invaders would have to turn their eyes towards other targets, which they appear to have already done in 440 (see below).

It is difficult to know whether the improvement of the defences made any real difference to the defence of the east. We do know that the city of Antioch remained secure until the Persian invasion of 540, but this had probably more to do with the general state of peace prevailing between the empires until 502. Jerusalem remained secure until 614, but once again it is probable that this had more to do with the fact that the Persians would first have to defeat the Roman main army and take the cities of Mesopotamia and Syria before they could march against Jerusalem. However, if the fortifications were meant to secure Jerusalem against the Arabs then the project can be considered to have been a success.

At the same time as Theodosius launched the fortification programme in the East, he also issued a series of *Novellae* that had military significance for the defence of the area. He legislated against Jews and Samaritans (NTh 3 issued on 31 Jan. 438) by forbidding them from holding any honours or dignities, any administrative civil duties, any position in the imperial service, or the position of defender of a municipality. See above. In addition, Jews and Samaritans were forbidden to build new synagogues or to proselytize their religion. The stated reason for these laws was that they were 'heretical monsters'. The likeliest reason for this anti-Semitic legislation is Pulcheria's hatred of the Jews as suggested by Holum (1982, 188–9). This means that Theodosius' administration did not trust that these religious groups would fight loyally for the Empire; they did not even trust that they would defend their own communities. We do not know whether there were good reasons for these suspicions – none of the sources mention any for this period – but it is known that the Jews and Samaritans did cooperate with the Persian invaders during the sixth and seventh centuries. It is certain that the distrust shown by the imperial authorities would have caused plenty of distrust amongst the authorities of these religious groups because it is well known that distrust creates distrust. Unsurprisingly, this legislation resulted in communal strife in Palestine which resulted in the deaths of Jews and Christians alike and required military intervention (Holum 1982, 188).

Theodosius' legislation betrays particular problems related to the defences along the eastern frontier which involved cases of corruption that had diminished the serviceable numbers of *Limitanei* forces and Saracen Federates. On 25 February 438 (NTh 4.1–3) Theodosius exempted all *Limitanei* from the duty of appearing before a civilian court at the request of the *MVM per Orientem* Anatolius. Henceforth the cases involving the *Limitanei* were to be judged by competent military judges. This decision released those apparently numerous *Limitanei* from being sued so that they were able to go back to their duties in their respective areas of responsibility. On 8 June 439 (NTh 5.2) Theodosius ordered that henceforth no person was allowed to transfer to private ownership through petition imperial farms, farms used to support the *Limitanei*, and woodland pastures situated in the orient. This proves that numbers of *Limitanei* had dimished throughout the eastern frontier due to the fact that the lands used to support them had been transferred to other hands. It also proves that similar legislation issued in 423 had proved ineffective (or that it had been followed only for a while after which old bad habits had resurfaced) while subsequent legislation (NTh 5.3, 24) after the war of 441 proves that this *Novella* had failed to address the situation before the war especially in Armenia. See below.

When Eudocia returned from her pilgrimage in early 439, her prestige had risen significantly in the eyes of her husband. She was back in favour and was able to influence her husband's policies. One of the results of this was the rise of the poet Cyrus as *PVC* and *PPO* in 439. This appointment was to have long reaching consequences. Firstly, and most importantly, as *PPO* Cyrus stopped using Latin as the official language in the East and replaced it with Greek.[12] This was to have momentuous consequences. Even though the East Romans continued to call themselves Romans (*Romaioi/Rhomaioi*), the adoption of the Greek language eventually separated them from the West Romans and from the Latin-speaking successor states which started to consider East Romans as Greeks. The adoption of Greek also meant that the East Romans would eventually stop using the military manuals written in Latin as their sources of inspiration. The East Romans are known to have produced a copy of the *Epitoma rei Militaris* of Vegetius at Constantinople in 450 and it was still known alongside other Latin treatises in the sixth century, but thereafter their influence waned in the East while the influence of Vegetius only kept growing in the West.

Cyrus also became well-known for his many construction projects in Constantinople that appear to have resulted from the need to rebuild much of the city together with its walls after an earthquake had damaged them (Marc. a.446/7; PLRE2). One of his most important innovations was the introduction of street lighting in Constantinople. Theodosius ordered Cyrus to fortify the whole seafront of the city with a circuit wall, which means that he rebuilt those sections of the sea wall that had been levelled by the earthquake. The order to cover the seaward side of the city with rebuilt walls immediately was particularly relevant for the year 439 because in that year the Vandals conquered Carthage and became a real naval threat for the entire Mediterranean Sea. The rebuilding of the sea walls for the vulnerable sections was also particularly timely because it effectively secured the city against the invasion of the Huns which came in 441. Cyrus was nominated as *Patricius* and then appointed sole consul for the year 441.

Ominously it was in the same year that the ex-*PSC* and *Patricius* Antiochus fell from favour once again. The reason for his downfall is not know, but it is probable that it came about as a result of the plotting of the eunuch Chrysaphius who held the position of *spatharius* (sword-bearer). Antiochus was forced to enter the clergy and the emperor passed a law which forbade ex-*PSC*s from becoming *patricii*. Chrysaphius appears to have been nominated *PSC* in about 439/40.[13] It is possible that Antiochus's fall together with the fortification project of the years 438/9 was partially responsible for the start of the Persian war next year. We do not know whether Eudocia had any role in the downfall of Antiochus, but since Chrysaphius was able to influence her to take steps against Pulcheria this is quite possible. This was only the first stage in Chrysaphius's plan to become the real power behind the throne.

The Persian War of 440/441[14]

On the basis of John Lydus's account, the casus belli for the Persian War of 440/1 was the Persian demand that the Romans pay their share of the upkeep of the Derbend Walls. The Romans refused and the Persians invaded. Another probable reason is that the Romans had once again received Christian fugitives from Persia. The removal of the ex-*PSC*

Antiochus from office in about 439 may also have contributed to the situation because without his help the administration seems to have lacked adequate understanding of how to handle eastern policies with the result that a situation that could have been solved through diplomacy had to be solved through hostilities. The circumstances in which the Persians issued the demands prove that the Persians were opportunistically exploiting the difficulties the Romans were facing.

The extent of troubles the Romans were facing depends on how the war is dated. Marcellinus Comes and some modern historians date the war to the year 441, but a number of modern historians prefer 440. If the war was fought in 440, the Romans faced the Vandal problem (they had conquered Carthage in 439 and raided Sicily in 440) and the revolts of the Saracens, Tzani and Isaurians, but if it was fought in 441, as claimed by Marcellinus, the Romans still faced simultaneously the Vandal problem, together with the revolts of the Saracens, Tzani, and the Isaurians. The Huns appear to have invaded only after the East Roman military expedition had already sailed to Sicily. If the war was fought early in 440, then the building work at Heliopolis in Phoenicia and the rebuilding of the city walls at Geraza/Gerasa in Arabia (PLRE 2 Anatolius) would probably have been done as a response to the damage caused by the war in 440. In support of this, one can state that the *Novella* from the year 443 sets to correct the corrupt practice of the dukes of stealing the provisions meant for the Saracen Federates, which would suggest that the Federates had revolted and pillaged these places in 440. In my opinion however, the statement of Marcellinus Comes that the war was fought in 441 is to be preferred: he states that the Romans fought simultaneously against the Persians, Saracens, Tzani, Isaurians and Huns (in truth the Persian and Hunnic invasions seem to have followed each other very closely), and that Theodosius sent against them Anatolius (to negotiate with the Persians) and Aspar (to negotiate with the Huns) and they made peace with them for one year (this refers to the Huns) – the last mentioned can be dated to the year 441. This means that Anatolius had simply continued his fortification project in Phoenicia and Arabia in 440 and that these projects should not be connected with the war. It is of course possible that all of the events (including the invasion of the Huns) took place in 440.

According to Lydus, the Persians invaded into the Syrias and Cappadocias 'little by little' as a result of which the elder Theodosius (a mistake for Theodosius II) sent Sporacius the Elder to discuss terms of peace with the Persians. Sporacius managed to pacify the situation without resorting to the payment of tribute, which I take to mean some face-saving measure which allowed the Romans to pay money and/or contribute men to the project.

According to Theodoret's version, the Persians attacked neighbouring towns when they learnt that the Roman armies were preoccupied (a fleet was prepared against the Vandals and some soldiers were evidently defending the Balkans), but then failed to make any progress because the fierce thunderstorm and hailstorm (implying early spring) prevented progress for twenty days as a result of which the Romans were able to march their soldiers to the scene of operations.

Moses Khorenatsi states that Yazdgerd II attacked the Greeks at Nisibis while the army of Azerbaijan invaded Armenia. The invasion of Roman Armenia is confirmed by the NTh 5.3 (dating it to 26 June 441), which states that the district of Armenia around Theodosiopolis (Erzurum) and Satala, which borders Persia, had been recently ravaged by the Persians partly because the feudal agreements concerning the royal farms in the form of taxes (soldiers, wagons, supplies, horses etc.) had been illegally abolished when the ownership of the farms had been transferred. The new owners were now required to make the same contributions. Moses' account implies that the Romans had regained the city of Nisibis in 421.

Elishe (p.61–2) in his turn asserts that Yazdgerd attacked as far as Nisibis (this once again implies that the Romans had recaptured Nisibis in 421), ravaged many districts, torched many churches, collected much plunder and many captives and terrified the Romans so that they sent Anatolius to negotiate. This implies that Yazdgerd did cause some damage, but this cannot have been significant because at another place Elishe (p.64) also claims that Yazdgerd subjected the Greeks without fighting. Elishe indicates that Anatolius brought many treasures with him with which he gained Yazdgerd's attention after which he fulfilled every wish of Yazdgerd to obtain peace, which included the handing over of Christian fugitives who had fled to Constantinople. This implies that one of the causes of the war had been the flight of some important Persian Christians to Constantinople.

If the Armenian sources are correct, then the city of Nisibis had indeed been captured by the Romans in 421 but was now either handed back to the Persians or at least its taxes were granted to the Persians for a specific number of years to assist them in their campaigns against the Huns. One can actually use Isaac of Antioch's version to support this if one assumes that the inhabitants of Nisibis had not been replaced in 421 because he states that when the Persians plundered the Roman frontiers, the people of Nisibis joined them.[15] This statement can be interpreted to mean that even after 421 most of the people of Nisibis consisted of the Persians because they rose against the Romans when the Persian army reached the neighbourhood of Nisibis. The obvious problem with all of these would of course be that it is difficult to see how the Roman historians would have forgotten to mention that Ardaburius had captured the place in 421, but at the same time it has to be remembered that the handing over of the city of Nisibis in 422 would explain the very joyous feeling of victory the Romans felt in 422 and the sense of humiliation in 441 so it is very likely that the Romans did indeed conquer it in 421. See vol.3.

When the above pieces of evidence are taken together with the evidence preserved in the law codes, it seems probable that the Persians made a two-pronged invasion against the Romans, the northern force being directed against Roman Armenia while the main army marched to the neighbourhood of Nisibis. The Romans were simultaneously preoccupied with the revolts of the Tzani, Isaurians and Saracens in the East which may also have been caused by the withdrawal of the forces from the area to fight against the Vandals. There is a clear pattern in the East that the revolts of the Tzani, Isaurians and Saracens coincided with the Persian invasions, which suggests two alternatives: 1) Persian agents may have incited the revolts; 2) the tribesmen may have exploited the opportunity provided by the Persian invasions. The probable sequence of these events is that (1) the Praesental armies and part of the Federate Army had been assembled against the Vandals in the fall of 440 with the result that (2) the Persians invaded in the spring of 441 which was supported by the simultaneous revolts of the Tzani, Isaurians and Saracens, which were then followed up (3) by the Hunnic invasion in the summer of 441 and the transferral of forces from the East to the Balkans, with the result that (4) the Eastern rebels remained unsubdued, which in its turn (5) resulted in the conclusion of a one-year truce with the Huns so that (6) the Eastern Field Army could be marched back to crush the Tzani, Isaurians and Saracens. These troubles in their turn made the Eastern Government (7) ready to conclude peace with the Vandals (see above) so that the Praesental and Federate forces could be recalled.

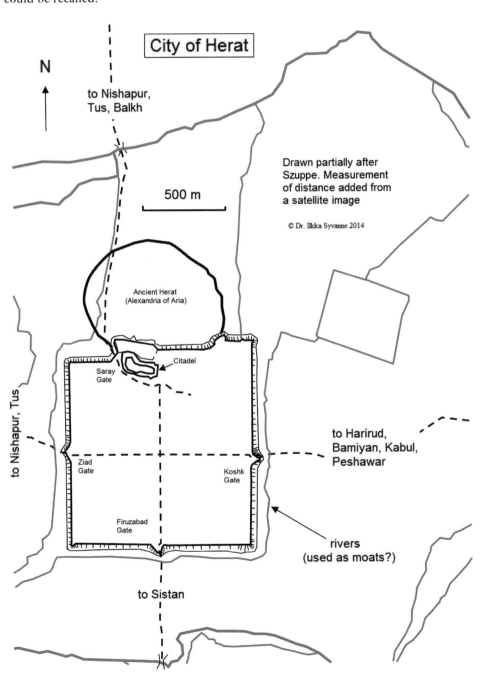

City of Herat

N

to Nishapur,
Tus, Balkh

500 m

Drawn partially after
Szuppe. Measurement
of distance added from
a satellite image

© Dr. Ilkka Syvänne 2014

Ancient Herat
(Alexandria of Aria)

Citadel

Saray
Gate

to Nishapur, Tus

Ziad
Gate

Koshk
Gate

to Harirud,
Bamiyan, Kabul,
Peshawar

Firuzabad
Gate

rivers
(used as moats?)

to Sistan

On the basis of the Armenians sources, the terms of peace with Persia were humiliating but necessary. Anatolius agreed to fulfil all the requirements put forth by the Persians. These included the transfer of Christian Iberia and other similar areas into the Persian sphere of influence (e.g. Elishe pp.64–5). It is possible that the negotiations were conducted on the Persian side by Mihr-Narseh and that he also visited Constantinople to obtain the emperor's signature to the treaty (see vol.3). Despite what John Lydus states, Elishe's account makes it clear that the Romans did make a contribution to the defence of the Derbend Pass and that they also contributed soldiers/engineers for Yazdgerd's campaign against the Hephthalite Huns and probably also for the construction of the Gurgan Walls. Elishe's account (e.g. p.64) also makes it clear that the Romans contributed actual military detachments for the Persian military campaigns. The continued payments to the Persians for the upkeep of the defences of the Derbend Pass until the reign of Peroz (459–484) are confirmed by (Pseudo-) Joshua the Stylite 9. He states that Peroz provoked the Romans to contribute money for his wars against the Chionite Huns (in truth the Hephthalites) by threatening to let the Huns through the Derbend Pass. These payments were stopped later, because Sidonius (letter to Lambridius 8.9 dated to 476) states that the Persian *Shahanshah* paid tribute to the East Romans in return for peace. This must have resulted from the very poor success Peroz was having against the Hephthalites which the Romans must have exploited. However, see also *MHLR* Vol.5.

As regards the immediate aftermath of the 441 war, I would go so far as to suggest that Roman military engineers also built the new city of Herat for the Persians in about 442/3, so that it was not only inspired by the Greek-Roman inheritance as suggested by Maria Szuppe but also designed and partially constructed by Roman engineers/architects. See the map. The Roman square fort incorporated into its northern defences the Hellenistic round Herat called Alexandria Aria so that the Saray Gate was built on the side of the wall structure. The Tzani, Isaurians and Saracens were presumably pacified by 443 because *Novella NTh 24* clearly expects the situation to have normalized in the East.

If the Blemyomachia (see vol.1) is to be dated to the reign of Theodosius II, then Germanus's (*MVM vacans* in 441) exploits against the Blemmyes are to be connected with the Persian war of 441 so that Germanus's march north against the Persians was delayed by the simultaneous invasion by the Blemmyes. After Germanus had inflicted a severe defeat on them, he restarted his journey, but was once again forced to return. On the latter occasion Germanus trashed the enemy so completely that he was able to join the expedition against the Vandals. However, as stated in vol. 1, it is quite possible to connect the poem Blemyomachia with the events that took place during the reign of Constantine the Great.

The Huns and East Rome in 441–446[16]

As noted above, the Huns invaded East Roman territory by making a surprise attack against some unnamed trading town (presumably Constantia opposite Margus) in the summer of 440/1. The excuse for the attack was that the Bishop of Margus had looted royal tombs on the other side of the Danube and that the Romans were protecting some fugitives from the Hunnic realm. It is not known whether the accusations were true or just an excuse, but the former appears more likely. Theodosius dispatched Aspar to negotiate because the Romans lacked adequate resources to face the Huns at a time when their armies were needed against the Vandals, Huns and Persians. Aspar managed to obtain a one year truce. At about the same time as this happened, the Gothic general Arnegisclus murdered the *MVM per Thracias* John the Vandal presumably at the instigation of Chrysaphius and with the acceptance of the court. The probable reason for the murder was that John's Vandal background made him suspect at a time when the East Romans were fighting against the Vandals (PLRE2). The other likely reason is that Chrysaphius appears to have allied himself with the Gothic faction led by Aspar whose rise to a dominant position coincides with the rise of Chrysaphius. After the death of John, the Germanic faction of Aspar was quite soundly in control of the East Roman high commands.

When the Huns realized that the Romans had transferred their forces against the Vandals, they broke the truce and invaded, in 441. The sources name a number of cities that the Huns besieged and sacked, but unfortunately fail to give a detailed discussion of the Hunnic invasion. The Huns sacked Sirmium (Sremska Mitrovica, the HQ of *PPIl.*), Singidunum (Belgrade), Margus (Dubrovica), Viminacium (Kostolac), Naissus (Nish), Serdica (Sofia) and an unknown number of other cities, towns, villages, and forts in Illyricum. It is possible that the invasion progressed south-east from Pannonia II or that the brothers Attila and Bleda invaded with at least two separate armies. The latter option receives support from Priscus's fragment 6.1, which states that the Huns crossed the Danube and pillaged many cities and forts along the river. He also states that the Huns took Viminacium before Margus with the result that the scared Bishop betrayed his city rather than take the risk of being handed over to the Huns by the populace. This suggests the alternative that one Hunnic army marched from Pannonia II while another crossed the Danube close to Viminacium and then marched west towards the other army. The sum total of the first year of campaigning was that the Huns managed to obtain the key cities for further advance into Thrace in 442, which they duly did in that year. We do not possess any details of the ravages committed by the Huns in Thrace beyond the general statement that they pillaged it. The Hunnic invasion was over before August 442. The reason for the end of the war is not known. Speculation ranges from the conclusion of peace to the return of the army from Sicily. On balance, despite the arrival of the army, it seems probable that some sort of peace agreement was reached in 442, which required the Romans to double their payments to the Huns, but which the East Romans proceeded to break immediately either in 443 or 444 at the same time as Aetius fought his successful campaign against the Huns. We do not know what the East Roman armies did during the war, but since no major engagement is recorded one can make the educated guess that the heavily outnumbered Aspar and Arnegisclus chose to conduct a guerrilla campaign with the men they had. As noted above, the Huns were preoccupied with a war against Aetius in 443/4 after which Attila murdered his brother, presumably either in 444 or 445. Then Attila secured his position amongst the tribes by conducting operations in the steppes and forests of Eastern Europe. In 446 he was able to extort concessions from the West Romans which included the handing over of Aetius's son as hostage. As a result of this he obtained operational freedom towards East Rome for the year 447.

Siege of Naissus in 441

The only detailed piece of evidence for the Hunnic invasion of 441/2 concerns siege of Naissus (Priscus fr. 6.2). It is worth discussing this siege in detail, because it sheds light on the sudden and unexpected ability of the Huns to besiege cities successfully. After the capture of Margus and Viminacium, the next in line of attack was the populous city of Naissus. The modern estimation for the size of the city is twenty hectares (Bajenaru), which would imply (if pop. density resembled that of Philippopolis with refugees from the countryside) a population of about 25,000 inhabitants. However, as Naissus has not been subjected to a thorough archaeological research it is possible that it may have been considerably larger. Priscus' text suggests that the Huns knew that the operation would be difficult because Naissus was 'populous' and 'well-fortified'. So they made thorough preparations and assembled a truly awesome array of siege equipment together with masses of men. The siege equipment the Huns brought to the scene consisted of Greco-Roman machines that could have been taken straight out of siege manuals, which proves that the Huns had obtained Roman architects (the siege specialists were called such) and engineers. These could have been obtained through war as prisoners, or their services could have been bought.

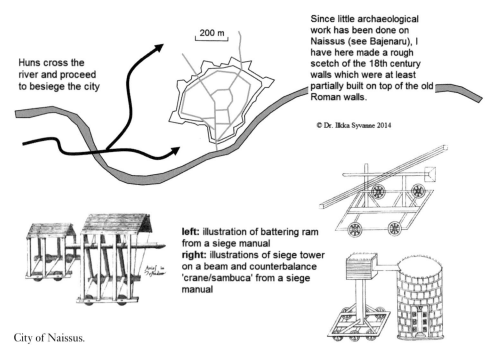

Huns cross the river and proceed to besiege the city

200 m

Since little archaeological work has been done on Naissus (see Bajenaru), I have here made a rough scetch of the 18th century walls which were at least partially built on top of the old Roman walls.

© Dr. Ilkka Syvänne 2014

left: illustration of battering ram from a siege manual
right: illustrations of siege tower on a beam and counterbalance 'crane/sambuca' from a siege manual

City of Naissus.

Priscus points out that since the citizens (which would probably have included members of the local garrison) did not dare to fight in the open, the 'Scythians' (i.e. the Huns with the assistance of their Roman collaborators) were able to bridge the river from the southern side and bring their siege machines against the circuit wall. The Huns had prepared large numbers of wheeled siege engines that had beams on top of which stood archers protected by screens made out of woven willow, rawhide and leather. The screens protected the archers from missiles and fire darts, and the superior height of the beams placed them above the heads of the defenders giving them a clear view over them. Behind the beam (and evidently the protecting screens) were men who pushed the beam towers wherever they were needed 'so that one could shoot successfully through the openings made in the screen'.[17]

Priscus' text allows two different interpretations for the screens. It states that archers on top of the beams were protected by the screens, but in addition to this there may have been another screen that covered the entire length of the siege operation except those sections through which the Huns intended to push through their battering rams. I would suggest that they used both techniques. See the illustrations. The tactic proved a great success. The archers on the beams cleared the walls of defenders which enabled the Huns to bring their battering rams forward. According to Priscus, these battering rams were very large machines in which there was a beam with an iron head suspended by chains from the roof of a shed which was covered by screens of willow, rawhide and leather. The men inside swung the battering ram from inside the shed against the chosen point in the wall. The defenders had prepared wagon-sized boulders against these, and managed to crush a number of rams, but the Huns had brought many replacements.

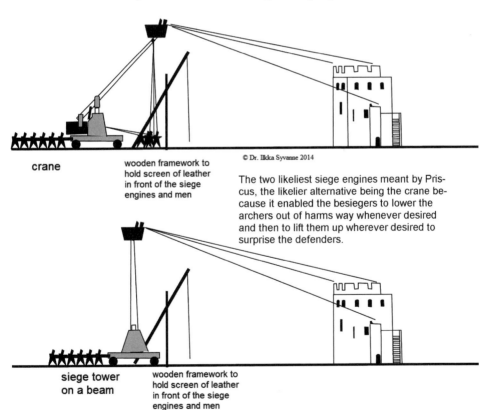

crane

wooden framework to hold screen of leather in front of the siege engines and men

© Dr. Ilkka Syvänne 2014

The two likeliest siege engines meant by Priscus, the likelier alternative being the crane because it enabled the besiegers to lower the archers out of harms way whenever desired and then to lift them up wherever desired to surprise the defenders.

siege tower on a beam

wooden framework to hold screen of leather in front of the siege engines and men

In the end, the Huns brought down part of the wall with their large number of rams. They sent part of their army into the breach and the rest up scaling ladders against other sections of the wall. The defenders were overwhelmed by the sheer mass of attackers and their machines.

The Walls of Thessalonica

The date when the so-called Theodosian Walls of the city of Thessalonica were built is a contested issue, the suggested dates ranging from the years 380–382 (Theodosius I) to 441–443 or 447–450 (Theodosius II). It is probable that some repairs were done during Theodosius I's reign when he resided in the city, but it is still more likely that the major rebuilding work should be dated to the reign of Theodosius II. The first alternative is that the walls were built during 441–443, because it is probable that the fortifications of the city received additional attention at a time when Attila had invaded and the capital of the Prefecture of Illyricum had been transferred to Thessalonica. However, if the major repairs were undertaken only in 447 (there are stamps in the tiles that can be dated to that year), it would have occurred simultaneously with the repairs of the Theodosian Walls of Constantinople which would mean that Thessalonica had suffered damage from the same earthquake as Constantinople. It is unfortunate that we do not know the exact date for the Theodosian Walls of Thessalonica, because that means that we cannot know the exact circumstances in which the project was undertaken. This should be taken into account when reading the section devoted to the Hunnic War of 447. However, what we do know is that the refortification of Thessalonica in the 440s made the city almost as impregnable as the city of Constantinople.[18]

The new walls were built in such a way that they exploited the structures of the previous Hellenistic and Roman walls. The fortifications had been strengthened during the third century by new hastily built walls and strong new square-shaped towers. It is also probable that both Galerius and Theodosius I strengthened the walls when they resided in the city. On the basis of an inscription, it is usually believed that Hormisdas (as *PPII*) was the person who built the new 'Theodosian Walls'. These walls incorporated the latest fashions in fortification, which were based on the concepts put forth by Philon of Byzantium so that the existing walls received new triangular projecting structures called *proboloi* (sing. *probolos*) most of which were redans rather than towers – the old *proboloi* consisted of a variety of rectangular, polygonal, round and semicircular structures. The old walls were refaced to make them stronger and deeper; new sections of wall with improved arcs of fire together with triangular redans and towers were added to the curtain wall in the Lower Town, both east and west; and rectangular towers were added to the Upper Town. There was no uniform shape or size for the towers and the distance between the towers varied between 8 and 60 metres. After the rebuilding was completed, the Land Walls (including the Heptapyrgion but excluding the maritime towers) had about 120 redans and towers.[19]

The walls covered an area of 350 hectares, which means that the city had a minimum of 87,500–175,000 inhabitants (based on the estimate that the Roman marching camp had either 5,000 or 10,000 persons per 20ha) and a maximum of about 437,500 inhabitants (based on the figure that 80-hectare Philippolis had 100,000 inhabitants); my best educated guess is that the city had about 200,000–300,000 inhabitants. Thessalonica was a major city, a true Jewel in the Crown.

The dating of the Sea Walls is even more controversial, and researchers have not found any consensus in this. It is known that the Macedonians and Romans both built sea walls, and that the Romans hastily repaired these during the third century against the Goths. It is also known that Constantine the Great added a new military harbour for the city in 323/4, but we do not know whether he strengthened the walls or built new ones at the same time. The researchers disagree whether the Sea Wall was again strengthened during the fifth century. In addition to this, the statement in Miracula St. Demetrii that there was an unwalled section in the Sea Walls when the Slavs attacked the city in 613 has led some researchers to suggest that Constantine did not build walls to protect his new military harbour. The Sea Walls were not nearly as strong and high as the Land Walls because the Romans expected that they would retain the mastery of the seas, which held true until the seventh century.[20] The reinforcement of the walls was strategically very significant for it secured the city until the early tenth century.

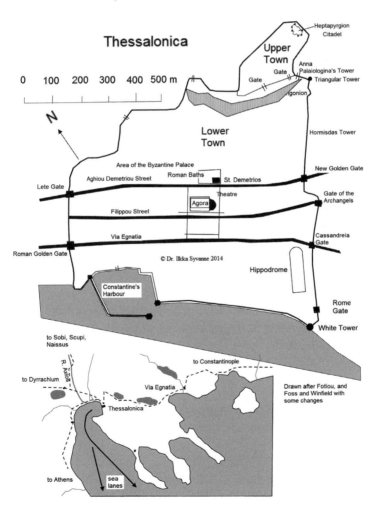

The improvement of the city defences was very important because of the strategic location of the city of Thessalonica. It was on the strategic crossroads connecting North with South and East with West. The sea lanes connected it with the Mediterranean and Black Sea. The navigable Axios (Vardar) River together with the road from Naissus connected it with the Danube frontier. The *Via Egnatia*, running from Dyrrachium to Constantinople, connected it with East and West. It was also a logistical hub for the armies operating in the Balkans. As a well fortified coastal city it was practically impregnable as long as the Romans controlled the sea lanes leading into it, and even then the Sea Walls provided some protection for it. The maps are based on those of Fotiou, and Foss and Winfield. The city layout includes some later features like Anna Palaiologina's Tower, but I have included these because it is probable that such structures were just built on top of earlier ones.

The Legislative Reforms of 443

The wars of 441/2 brought to light the old problems, which the state set out to solve by issuing new *Novella 24* (NTh 24) to *Mag.Off.* Nomus on 12 September 443. *Novella* (NTh 24.1–2) acknowledges that the frontier forces and the dukes commanding them were not up to the task. It states that this was a particular concern on those borders which faced dangerous tribes (i.e. the Huns). The *duces* were to be promoted on the basis of their ability and not as a result of corrupt solicitation, on pain of capital punishment. The *duces* were to restore the units to their ancient numbers under the supervision of the *MVM* and see to it that the soldiers were properly trained. The dukes were also to see to it that there were the required number of boats and river patrol boats. The *duces*, together with the *princeps* (commandant duties unknown) and *praepositi castrorum* (provosts of the camps), were to receive as a compensation for their troubles 1/12th of the *annona* of the *Limitanei* from the *MVM*.

Novella NTh 24.2 acknowledges that the *duces* had confiscated the *annona* of the Saracen *Foederati* and of other tribes (Tzani, Isaurians?) presumably with the result that these had revolted (note above).[21] This was strictly forbidden by the *Novella* on pain of death. *Novella* NTh 24.3 suggests that the *magistri militum* had acted as the principal culprits for the above offences by stating that in the future they and their staff should not extort money from the *Limitanei* and Federate tribes or face a fine of 100 lbs of gold. *Novella* NTh 24.4 states once again that the lands used to support the *Limitanei* were to be free from extortion so that the lands would be used for their orginal purpose.

The most important part of the new legislation (NTh 24.5) was that the control over the *magistri*, *duces* and frontier defences was handed over to the *Magister Officiorum* who now had the duty of inspecting and reporting the number of soldiers, the condition of the camps, the condition and number of river patrol boats in Thrace, Illyricum, Orient, Pontus, Egyptian Thebes and Libya. He was to present this report annually in the Sacred Imperial Consistory in the month of January. Theodosius foresaw that if military affairs were observed as decreed, Rome's enemies would not pose any threat.

Eudocia's Fall from grace in 443[22]

In 441 Chrysaphius manipulated Eudocia to initiate a number of projects against Pulcheria who was outmanoeuvred. Pulcheria chose to step down to avoid open conflict. She handed over her imperial staff to Eudocia and withdrew to the Hebdomon palace. Now the only obstacle left to Chrysaphius was Eudocia, but then Eudocia made a momentuous blunder. On the Epiphany feast of the year 443 Theodosius II went alone to attend the ceremony in the Great Church. A poor man brought an unusually large Phrygian apple as a gift to the Emperor. When Theodosius saw the apple, he dispatched it back to the empress as a token of love, and when the Empress saw it, she 'innocently' gave it as a present to their mutual friend *Mag. Off.* Paulinus. Paulinus in his turn sent the apple as a present to the Emperor. The Emperor recognized the apple and asked his wife what she had done with the apple he had sent. Eudocia foolishly answered that she had eaten it. As a result, Theodosius naturally suspected that Eudocia was having an affair with Paulinus, and Paulinus was executed. Eudocia, who claimed to be innocent and may have been but we do not know this for certain, was horrified and demanded to be dismissed. Theodosius agreed and exiled her to Jerusalem. This story has unnecessarily been suspected by most modern historians. There is nothing inherently improbable in it. Sometimes life imitates art just as art sometimes imitates life. However, it is probable that the incident as such was not enough to bring about the downfall of Paulinus and Eudocia and that it was Chrysaphius who inflamed Theodosius' passions to jealousy and anger with the above-mentioned result. Eudocia's destiny was sealed in 444. It was then that Theodosius received reports of Eudocia's close relationship with the priest Severus and deacon John. Theodosius dispatched *Com. Dom.* Saturninus to Jerusalem to execute both, which he did with the result that the furious Eudocia murdered Saturninus. When a report of this was brought to Theodosius, he removed the royal attendants from Eudocia who then spent the rest of her years in the city of Jerusalem.

Unsurprisingly the downfall of the patroness meant that Cyrus's position was also on shaky grounds. The reason for Cyrus's disgrace was that he became too popular for his own good as a result of his restoration work and reforms. When the circus factions shouted in 443, 'Constantine founded, Cyrus restored', in the Hippodrome in the presence of the Emperor, the Emperor became jealous and decided to get rid of the prefect. Theodosius found a willing collaborator in Chrysaphius who also wanted to get rid off him. The Emperor first stripped Cyrus of his offices and confiscated his property, and then exiled him to Phrygia at the instigation of Chrysaphius. It is quite possible that Chrysaphius had engineered the shouting of the incriminating words by the factions with a suitable bribe. It is not known whether we should connect the rise of Chrysaphius with any change in imperial foreign policy. Theodosius II clearly sought to avoid having to fight multiple conflicts simultaneously, but this was the standard operating procedure for most of Roman history.

The End of Late Roman Balkans: Attila's Invasion in 447–448[23]

In 447, presumably prompted by news that the walls of Constantinople had suffered horrible damage in the earthquake which occurred on 26 January, Attila assembled a truly massive force against the East Romans. It included Gepids under Ardaric and Ostrogoths under Valamir, which suggests that the composition was almost the same as in the Battle of the Catalaunian Fields in 451. This army obviously did not include the Franks, Alamanni and Burgundians, but they must have been replaced by some other eastern tribes so that Attila could put to the field an army of at least 400,000 warriors.

At about the same time (ca. 446–449), the Austurians were also causing serious troubles in Libya. We do not know any details of this action beyond what is stated in Priscus' fragment 14 (Blockley fr. 4.4. p.298 4.16ff.), which states that Armatus/Armatius, son of Plintha/Plinta/Plinthas, had fought against the Austuriani in Libya and had distinguished himself but had then fallen ill and died with the result that his wife was available to be married to Constantius, *notarius* of Attila who had been sent by Aetius, in 450.[24]

Once again the sources provide only sparse details of the war, but some conclusions can be made on the basis of the scattered references. The *PPO* Flavius Constantinus rebuilt the walls of Constantinople in three months by assigning the rebuilding to the factions. The Blues were assigned to the sector from the Blanchernae to the Porta Myriandi and the Greens from there to the Sea of Marmara. The work was finished by the end of March 447. Consequently the Romans were able to rebuild the defences before the Huns were able to reach the vicinity of Constantinople. Theophanes states that the Romans dispatched Aspar, Areobindus and Arnegisclus against Attila who had already devastated Ratiaria, Naissus (in truth probably in 441), Philippopolis, Arcadiopolis, Constantia (in truth probably in 441) and many other towns. The Roman generals then suffered a series of defeats in battles with the result that Attila reached both the Pontus and Propontis, and took the cities of Calliopolis and Sestus in the Chersonese. He took every town and fortress including the fortress of Athyras in the area except Adrianople (Hadrianopolis) and Heraclea (Perinthus). After this Theodosius sought peace and sent ambassadors. The *Chronicon Paschale* adds to the list of conquered cities Marcianopolis, and Marcellinus states that Attila advanced as far south as Thermopylae.

On the basis of the fact that the *MVM per Thraciam* Arnegisclus advanced from Marcianopolis to the River Utus where he fought against Attila bravely to the death after his horse had collapsed under him, it is possible to conclude that the Romans and Huns both employed separate armies. According to Marcellinus (a. 446–7), by the time Arnegisclus died most enemy forces had been destroyed. Even if this is probably an exaggeration, it is still clear that the Huns had suffered terrible losses in this battle. Since the site was close to the city of Asamus (Asemus, Asimos, Anasamos), it is clear that the Huns had indeed suffered terrible losses in this battle and that it was commanded by Scythian generals rather than by Attila. The fact that Arnegisclus was able to destroy 'most' of the enemy force proves beyond doubt that the Huns had divided their army into at least two separate armies. In fact, the locations mentioned by the sources suggest strongly that the Huns invaded as three separate armies which the Romans opposed with three separate armies. Arnegisclus would have marched from Marcianopolis against the Hunnic army which advanced along the Danube from Ratiaria towards Marcianopolis and Odessus, while *MVM* Aspar engaged Attila's main army in Thrace and *MVM* Areobindus engaged the Hunnic army advancing towards Greece. Attila's intention was clearly to distract parts of the Roman army for the protection of the Danube line and Greece so that he would be able to direct his main strike straight at the weakened heart of the enemy territory in Thrace and Constantinople. See the map. It was thanks to this that the Huns were able to engage each of the three Roman armies with numerically superior forces which ensured victory for them. In contrast, it would have been in the Roman interest to unite their forces and engage each of the invading armies separately by exploiting the inner lines of communication. It is no wonder that Theodosius now lost all confidence in the military abilities of Aspar and Areobindus. Attila had outgeneralled both of them!

Some of the remnants of Arnegisclus's army appear to have fled to the nearby fortress of Asemus. When the Huns followed, the garrison of Asemus was deployed outside the walls despite being heavily outnumbered. The defence was so successful that when the numbers of casualties started to mount up the Huns withdrew slowly from the fortress. When the spies/scouts reported this to the garrison, they set out in hot pursuit and managed to surprise the retreating Huns, and thereby the Asemuntians achieved a complete victory over the overwhelmingly superior numbers. They killed many Huns, freed Roman prisoners, retook booty taken from them, and captured large numbers of Huns. Arnegisclus and the garrison of Asemus had effectively annihilated one of the Hunnic armies. Theodolus was appointed as Arnegisclus's successor.

The other diversionary force which advanced towards Greece proved relatively successful because we know that Areobindus was also defeated, but at the same time we also know that this army failed to achieve anything remarkable because its progress was stopped at Thermopylae, which means that its principal usefulness for the Huns was that it too tied up Roman resources that could have been more fruitfully used against the main army advancing straight into Thrace.

Meanwhile Attila had led the main army along the road leading from Serdica to Constantinople via Philippopolis and Adrianople and Arcadiopolis to Constantinople. It is probable that Attila had about 200,000–250,000 warriors with him. His march appears to have been opposed by some elements of the Praesental Armies and the Goths of Thrace under Aspar. The Romans may therefore have had about 80,000 men because they would have needed to leave a considerable number of soldiers behind to defend Constantinople. At the same time as this happened, the Emperor appears to have ordered Zeno (Zenon) to bring his Isaurians to defend the capital. It seems probable that the Romans assembled their forces when Attila was preoccupied with the siege of Philoppopolis and then advanced against him. Theophanes's account makes it clear that the Romans suffered a series of defeats and Jordanes' account of the battle of the Catalaunian Fields proves that the East Romans had fielded large numbers of infantry because Attila's speech in Jordanes' *Getica* refers to it in the past tense. Taken together it is probable that the Romans used a combination of hollow infantry squares and cavalry which were defeated somewhere near Adrianople and Arcadiopolis with the result that the Huns were able to take the latter. It seems probable that the Romans regrouped during that siege, but were again defeated and then forced to retreat towards Constantinople. It is possible that the Roman army or parts of it had taken refuge in Adrianople because the Huns failed to capture it, or that Aspar had reinforced it some other way. Aspar's line of retreat to Constantinople, however, appears to have been cut off by the more mobile Huns before Heraclea because the Huns captured it and the fort of Athyras while we find the Roman main army in Chersonesus. It is probable that Aspar attempted to form a line of defence along the wall of Chersonesus, but with equally poor results. Attila defeated the Romans and captured the cities of Calliopolis and Sestus. The Roman generals presumably fled in ships. It was after the defeat in Chersonesus that Theodosius decided to seek peace.

Nestorius's account of this war in the *Bazaar of Heracleides* sheds additional light on the events. According to him, when the towers of the wall of Constantinople had collapsed and the barbarians invaded, Theodosius sent one wooden cross with the field army against the enemy (presumably Aspar's force), placed another in the Palace, and another in the forum to encourage the army and populace. In other words, Theodosius used the same form of religious encouragement as previously to unite his people against the heathen enemy. According to Nestorius, the Huns then withdrew even though no-one was pursuing (i.e. the Huns turned towards Chersonese after having taken Athyras), but then returned and subjected the Romans into slavery.

Kallipolis (Gallipoli) drawn after *Librum insularum archipelagi*. It is very probable that the fortress is built on top of the late Roman fortress as this was one of the standard shapes for forts built on the shore. The fort clearly included a landing beach for warships that would have enabled the evacuation of at least some of the troops and commanders. The windmills date from a later era, but the smaller forts inland may have existed in antiquity as well. The same is true of the civilian buildings surrounding the fort.

It is notable that the Huns did not attempt to besiege or even threaten the East Roman capital in earnest after they had inflicted a crushing defeat on Aspar's army in Chersonesus. There are several probable reasons for this. Attila was undoubtedly aware that the defences had been repaired, but at the same time he must have been aware that newly built towers and walls were still vulnerable to battering rams, so this was not the real reason for Attila's readiness to withdraw. He certainly knew that he would have to take the city through direct assault, because it was impossible to blockade it when the Romans possessed naval supremacy. He also knew that it would be very costly to attempt to storm the city because it was well garrisoned (imperial bodyguards, marines and Isaurians) and had vast numbers of civilian paramilitary forces, but this appears not to have been the true reason for the abandonment of the attack. Isaac of Antioch's account states that the Huns were overcome by sickness of the bowels, in other words by diarrhoea. I would suggest that the Romans had used one of the forms of biological warfare mentioned in their collections of stratagems: the poisoning of water sources (rivers, aqueducts etc) with hellebore or human feces/corpses or something similar. When this happened the Huns withdrew from Constantinople and marched north. The need to take revenge against the Asemutians and others in the north provided Attila with a suitable excuse. He marched his army to Marcianopolis, and then besieged and conquered it.

EAST ROME IN 447-450

Hunnic apocalypse in the Balkans in 447

Vandals raided Italian and East Roman coastal areas in 448-451. The targets of Vandal raiding included at least Rhodes as a result of which even the Alexandrians feared the prospect of having to face the Vandals.

Isaurians revolt under Zeno in 450. Maximinus sent to Asia Minor and a fleet prepared for a war against him. The death of Theodosius I in 450 prevents a full scale hostilities.

300miles

© Dr. Ilkka Syvänne 2014

Raids by Austuriani and Mazices in ca. 447-453

Raids by Nobatae and Blemmyes in ca. 447-453

Persian preparations for war in ca. 448-450

Saracen raids in 448-453

Persarmenian revolt in 449-451

Meanwhile Theodosius sacked Aspar and Areobindus from office, appointed Anatolius as the new *MVM Praes* and Zeno as the new *MVM per Orientem*. After this he dispatched Senator (former consul and Theodosius's advisor) and Anatolius to negotiate terms of peace with Attila. They feared to take the land route so they sailed to Odessus where they met the new *MVM Thracias* Theodulus. Theodulus clearly did not trust the defences of Marcianopolis. These three men acted as negotiators even if the leader of the mission was Anatolius. The Roman negotiators felt that they had to agree to every term demanded of them. Attila's terms were as follows: 1) all fugitives were to be handed over; 2) the Romans were to pay 6,000 lbs of gold they owed as tribute and from then on 2,100 lbs of gold per year; 3) all Roman prisoners who had escaped were to be returned unless 12 solidi were paid for each; 4) Romans were not to give a place of refuge to any barbarians; 5) a no man's land was to be created for the distance of five days' journey from Pannonia to the south-east so that the border between the Huns and Romans ran from Novae to Naissus.

The Romans pretended to agree to these voluntarily and apparently nominated Attila as *MVM* for this purpose. According to Priscus, the Emperor initially faced some difficulties finding enough gold because he had squandered the imperial treasury on spectacles, pleasures, banquets and generosity, so he forced all taxpayers to contribute. Priscus exaggerates the hardship caused to the senatorial class, but he is undoubtedly correct in saying that some of them were forced to sell their wives' jewellery and furniture to pay the tax. This problem would have been acute for the poorer senators because the taxes fell more heavily on them than on the rich. In truth, as we have seen, the richest senators could have paid the entire tribute from their own yearly income. The acceptance of these heavy terms was unavoidable, but it led to further troubles as it became necessary for the Romans to start paying tribute to the other neighbours in return for peace, and as we shall see new troubles surfaced soon enough.

After having obtained these terms, Attila decided to extort additional concessions from the Romans. He stated that he would not ratify this treaty unless the Romans who had fled to Asemus were returned or had been ransomed and the Hunnic prisoners taken by the Asemutians were returned. Anatolius and Theodulus felt compelled to agree and sent these demands to the Asemuntians. The Asemuntians claimed that all Roman fugitives had departed, and that they had killed all Huns except for two that they had kept as hostages. The Asemuntians claimed that the Huns had ambushed and captured twelve children during the siege and that they intended to exchange the two Huns for these. The Huns did a search and claimed that they did not have the children, with the result that the two Huns were released and the terms of peace were ratified.

The Troubled Years 447–450

The peace treaty of 447 was effectively forced on the East Romans by a combination of facts. Firstly, it is clear that Aspar and Areobindus had failed miserably as commanders as a result of which the Huns were before the gates of Constantinople. Secondly, Vandal pirates were roaming the Mediterranean. Thirdly, the East Romans were facing a series of troubles in the east: the Persarmenian and Kidarite situations were boiling over and the Persians were making military preparations apparently on both fronts that were troubling to the East Romans who did not know what the Persians planned to do; the Isaurians and Saracens were causing troubles with their pillaging; the Blemmyes and Nobatae were troubling Egypt. It is possible that it was because of these troubles that the Thebaid was divided into two provinces and the border region of Upper Thebais was placed under a *dux limitis* with extra powers which united both civilian and military spheres under a single man.

The peace was considered humiliating and several important persons opposed it, the most vocal of whom appears to have been *MVM per Orientem* Zeno because he considered the appeasement of the Huns and the tribute paid to them to have been exacted under duress. Blockley has suggested that it was because of this that the East Romans may have attempted to bribe tribes to revolt against Attila, the best evidence of which is the sending of envoys to a Hunnic tribe called the Akatiri/Akatziri. It is in fact clear that the Romans engaged in subversive tactics because the Huns caught and then executed one Roman spy after which the Huns also exposed the assassination attempt against Attila at the behest of *praepositus sacri cubiculi* Chrysaphius and *magister officiorum* Martialis in 449, the information about which is most famously preserved in Priscus' account of the Roman embassy to the court of Attila. Attila exploited the exposure of this plot by demanding more money from the East Romans and by forcing the East Romans to promise to hand over a high-born woman to his secretary Constantius (he had been dispatched by Aetius) and by forcing them to send another embassy to him with gifts. By this time Theodosius was adamant that the policy of appeasement should continue, because he planned to support the revolt of the Christian Persarmenians against the oppression of the Zoroastrian Sasanians. Zeno, however, had other thoughts. Firstly, he made certain that the intended wife of Constantius was married to another man, and secondly he prepared to revolt against Theodosius if Theodosius intended to carry through his intentions regardless of his opposition. Theodosius in his turn prepared to dispatch a naval expedition to get rid off Zeno. It was then that Theodosius II died as a result of a riding accident. The timing of the death was very fortunate because it saved the Roman Empire and Europe from the horrors of the savage Huns.

Theodosius II (408–450): The Orthodox Christian Ruler

Despite the problems with Attila in the 440s the reign of Theodosius II can be seen to have been a great success, which ensured the survival of East Rome. In great contrast to West Rome, Theodosius' realm was not a hostage of any barbarian or Roman generalissimos. Despite being under the influence of his sister Pucheria or his wife Eudocia or his favourites, Theodosius II always had the last say and could and did remove from positions of power anyone (e.g. Aspar) who had lost his favour.

drawing by Beger 1696

Theodosius' greatest achievements were the reinstatement of his family back to power in the West (see vol.3), the keeping of power in his own hands, the building and strengthening of the so-called Theodosian Wall of Constantinople, the fortification programme along the eastern frontier, and the legal reforms, the most important of which was the compiling of the *Codex Theodosianus* together with the laws that curbed the worst expressions of corruption among the military.

He was ill served by his military commanders after ca. 427. The disastrously poor performance of Aspar and Areobindus against Attila in 447 brought ruin and misery to the people of the Balkans and financial troubles or even ruin to many upper class people. It is therefore not surprising that he sacked both.

The strict Christian upbringing that Theodosius had received at the behest of his sister Pulcheria had a direct influence on all his policy decisions, even if towards the end of his rule he adopted a different view of Christianity than his sister had. The best example of this Christian influence is that Theodosius was ready to support the Persarmenian revolt in 449/50 despite the fact that the Huns were far more threatening to the Roman Empire than the Persians were at this stage. In this case it was his Christianity that affected his policy decisions. He wanted to protect his co-religionists against Zoroastrian persecution. It was lucky for the Romans and Europeans that Theodosius II died before he could implement this policy.

Chapter Eight

The War of the Nations in 451–454[1]

The Road to War

In the course of 449–450 the situation inexorably moved towards another confrontation between Attila and Rome while Attila attempted to extort further concessions and payments through various excuses. According to Jordanes, the wily Gaiseric attempted to incite Attila with bribes to attack the Visigoths. This is not surprising after the mutilation of Theoderic's daughter by Gaiseric. From Gaiseric's point of view it was quite OK if such a move also resulted in a war between West Rome and Attila, because the latter needed to pass through Roman territory to attack the Visigoths.

In 449 Iusta Grata Honoria, the sister of Valentinian III, was caught having a love affair with her manager of estates Eugenius. She became visibly pregnant. Eugenius was duly killed and Honoria sent to Constantinople to give birth to the illegitimate child. We do not know what happened to the child, but we do know that Honoria was then sent back, where she was kept in custody and bethrothed to trustworthy senator Herculanus. Honoria was naturally quite upset. She had lost her lover and child and was now forced to marry Herculanus who was 'no Hercules'. She managed to dispatch her trusted eunuch Hyacinthus to the court of Attila to seek his help. According to the official Roman version, she asked Attila to help her and as a token of her good faith she gave her ring to Attila. In my opinion however, Attila's version, which is that Honoria promised to marry Attila, is to be trusted in this case. It is not at all impossible that Honoria would have sought to marry Attila in the same manner as her mother had married Athaulf. Valentinian's first reaction was to order the execution of Honoria for treason, but Galla Placidia prevented this. When Attila then duly demanded Honoria's hand in marriage in 450, Theodosius II recommended that Valentianian should agree. Valentinian did agree and decided to send Honoria to Attila, but once again Galla Placidia intervened. Valentinian relented and forced Honoria to marry Herculanus. This marriage then enabled Valentinian to state that Honoria was already married and could not marry Attila.

The year 450 saw the deaths of three rulers, all of which shaped the future.

In the East Theodosius II died as a result of a riding accident. Before his death, Theodosius had concluded a humiliating peace with Attila so that he would be able to support the Persarmenian revolt by launching a war against the Persians. This policy decision brought him into conflict with the Isaurian *MVM per Orientem* Zeno, and it was to be expected that Theodosius would have to eliminate him first. The death of Theodosius obviously altered the picture. It meant that Valentinian III was now the sole ruler of the Roman Empire. But the East Romans were having other ideas and chose Marcian as the new Emperor. He was Aspar's former *domesticus* and it is quite clear that Aspar contributed to his unexpected rise to dominance. Marcian's appointment was also supported by *MVM per Orientem* Zeno, who promoted a more aggressive stance against Attila, and by the *Augusta* Pulcheria. Marcian's rise to the throne was secured with a marriage to Pulcheria. It seems probable that Marcian had managed to gain Pulcheria's full backing with promises regarding religious policies, the most important of which would be the assembly of a Church Council at Nicaea, which was then transferred to Chalcedon. Obviously one cannot preclude the possibility that Pulcheria would also have had other urges, because despite the official version that Marcian did not sleep with Pulcheria, the loose-tongued claimed otherwise.

The reign of Marcian signified a break with the policies of his predecessor. Marcian was a native of the Balkans and the neglect shown towards this region was to stop. Instead of letting the Huns roam free in the Balkans or be paid to stay away while the Roman armies fought either in the East, or in Italy, or against the Vandals, the Balkans now became a top priority while the other fronts were neglected.

The second of the momentuous deaths was the death of the *Augusta* Galla Placidia on 27 November 450. This meant that Valentinian no longer possessed a trusted advisor who could hold his worst character straits in check. This was to have dire consequences when the emperor started to listen more closely to the enemies of Aetius.

The third important death was that of some unnamed Frankish king (Priscus Blockley ed. fr. 20.3). Aetius backed the younger son for the throne with the result that the elder sought support from Attila. Aetius and Valentinian both adopted the younger son and sent him back home as a friend and ally. It is unfortunate that we do not know the name of the ruler and which Frankish tribe was involved, but in my opinion Blockley's (1982, p.390, n.107) educated guess that the dead king was Merovech and that the younger son was Childeric is quite plausible, the other possible identification being that the younger son was Merovech. The invasion route of Attila suggests that the Franks in question were the Salians.

After this, Attila once again sent envoys to both courts. His demands to the Western Court were that Honoria was to marry him and that Valentinian was to give her half of his Empire. Valentinian's response was that in Rome only men ruled and that Honoria was already married. From the East Attila demanded the paying of the agreed tribute. Marcian's response was that he would not pay any tribute, but if Attila would agree to keep the peace he would be ready to give him gifts. If this did not satisfy Attila, Marcian was prepared to assemble men and arms equal to the number possessed by Attila.[2] There are two ways to interpret this. It is possible to think that Marcian's government acted foolishly if he was prepared to pay the same sum of money as gifts but not as tribute in return for peace. Or it is possible to think that Marcian calculated that the response would result in war [previous agreement broken plus the threat of military response] and that the referral to the paying of gifts was just meant to make it seem as if the East Romans had acted moderately [i.e. the war would be just]. In my opinion the latter alternative is more likely. Of note is the referral to the use of the same number of men by the Romans now with the implication that the Huns had outnumbered the East Romans in 447.

We do not know when Attila decided to attack West Rome and Gaul in particular, but it must have happened at the latest when he received the above-mentioned answers. The case for Gaul was considerably better than the other alternatives. Attila knew that if he attacked either Italy or Thrace he could be put between two Roman armies now that he no longer had Aetius's son as hostage. This left Gaul as his best chance. If he could keep part of the Western Army in Italy, he would face a divided enemy in Gaul. After all, he had the support of the elder of the Frankish princes and the former leader of the Bacaudae, which he could use to create dissensions among the enemy ranks. In addition to this, he could also hope that the Visigoths and Romans would be unable to cooperate. By attacking the Visigoths, Attila could gain the goodwill of the Vandals and if things went well he could also hope to gain Honoria's hand in marriage together with part of the Roman Empire.

When Attila received the two answers, he decided to employ a further round of diplomacy and military movements to keep his enemies guessing where he intended to attack. He sent a message to Theoderic in which he asked his assistance against the Romans by claiming that his quarrel was with the Romans and not with him. At the same time Attila sent another message to Valentinian in which he claimed to act as Valentinian's *MVM* when he attacked the Visigoths. Essentially Attila claimed to perform a service to the Romans similar to that of the crushing of the Burgundians. The only purpose of this diplomacy was to create dissension and uncertainty among the enemy.

At the same time as Attila used these diplomatic ploys to confuse his enemies, he assembled two armies: 1) a diversionary army posted in Pannonia which threatened simultaneously Italy and East Rome; 2) the main invasion force which marched to Gaul. This latter army was assembled and marched through Attila's own tributary territories to keep its existence unknown to the enemy as long as possible. After preparations had been completed, Attila began his campaign earlier than was usual because he was in Gaul by April. At the same time as Attila started his march towards Gaul, as a final diplomatic ploy he dispatched still another set of envoys to both Roman courts. He ordered Valentinian to prepare a palace for him in Rome while he ordered Marcian to prepare a palace for him in Constantinople. The presence of another army in Pannonia together with the messages caused both emperors to suspect that Attila intended to attack either Italy or Thrace, whereas in truth Attila led his main army to Gaul.

The Armies

Sidonius Apollinaris and Jordanes give us a list of nations that Attila had assembled for the invasion. Naturally the core of the army consisted of the Huns. It is difficult to estimate the size of Attila's army on the basis of the extant evidence. Jordanes' (Get. 182) claim that Attila had about 500,000 men is usually considered suspect, but as stated in the introduction there are actually reasons to believe that it may be close to reality. The other figures given by the sources also support the use of a huge army: both sides lost 165,000 men in the battle in addition to the 15,000 dead of the previous night (Jord. Get. 217); Paulus Diaconus (Rom. 13.6) 180,000 killed; 300,000 fell in this battle (Hydatius, Olymp. 308); Attila's army had myriads of men (Chro. Pasch. Olympiad.450). It is possible to verify the figures by comparing the different nations in the lists provided by Sidonius and Jordanes making up the army.[3] The following conservative estimates are based on the assumption that all the nations in question would have left a significant proportion of their fighting strength behind to protect their homes, but in such manner that those nations that fought closer to their homes used a greater proportion of their manpower for the war with the exception of the Gepids and Ostrogoths. In sum, my conservative estimate for Attila's army is that he fielded about 410,000 or even the claimed 500,000 warriors and about 100,000 non-combatants against Gaul in order to achieve a significant numerical advantage. In addition to this, he used another field army of 100,000–150,000 men (Huns, Germans, Dacians, nomads) in Pannonia and Illyricum to create a diversion.

HUNS (my conservative estimate)

Sidonius (my estimate based on:

Huns	110,000 horsemen
(Ostrogoths added)	40,000 inf. and 60,000 cav.
Bellonoti	8,000 cav.
Rugi	7,000 inf. and 3,000 cav.
Gepids	50,000 horsemen
Gelonians	10,000 horsemen
Burgundians	17,000 inf. and 3,000 cav.
Sciri	7,000 inf. and 3,000 cav.
Neurians	25,000 inf. and 5,000 cav.
Bastarnae	8,000 inf. and 2,000 cav.
Thuringians	17,000 inf. 3,000 cav.
Bructeri	17,000 inf. and 3,000 cav.

(subjects of the Salian Franks and supporters of the elder brother against Childeric)

Franks of Neckar (Ripuarians)	17,000 inf. and 3,000 cav.
	145,000 inf. and 265,000 cav.

to which one should add the non-combatants possibly about 100,000 men for a total of 500,000 men?

Jordanes:

Huns	100,000 horse
Ostrogoths	100,000 inf. and cav.
Gepids	50,000 cav.
Various nations	?

Paris 500 AD

Drawn after M. Rouche, p. 317.

Necropolis
Urban area   500m

ROMANS (my conservative estimate)

GAUL:

Sidonius (my estimate based on:
Aetius's *bucellarii*   15,000 cav.
[Aetius leading a small elite force of auxiliaries (*bucellarii*) but no *militia* (legions) across the Alps in the expectation that he would obtain support from the Visigoths. Avitus managed to convince the Visigoths to join Aetius. Even though Sidonius fails to mention this, it is probable that when Aetius reached the neighbourhoods of Arles, Valence and Lyon that his army was reinforced by the Field Army of Gaul and Alans.]

Jordanes and Paul the Deacon (Rom. 13.4):
Auxiliaries of Aetius:

Franks	45,000 inf. 5,000 cav.
Sarmatians	15,000 cav.
Armoricans	18,000 inf. 2,000 cav.
Liticians (Laeti?)	18,000 inf. 2,000 cav.
Burgundians	22,000 inf. 3,000 cav.
Saxons	5,000 inf.
Ripari/Ripari[oli]/Riparians	18,000 inf. 2,000 cav.

(Ripuarian Franks or less probably *Ripenses*)
[Oli]briones/Briones 5,000 inf.?
 (once Roman soldiers, now *auxilia*, Lebedynsky 2011.43 suggests Bri[tt]ones, i.e. Britons which seems the best guess)

Other Celtic or German tribes	8,000 inf. 2,000 cav.
Romans (implied in the speech)	ND
Alans	60,000 cav.
Visigoths	40,000 inf. 60,000 cav.

ND - Gaul *Comitatenses*   6,000 cav. 76,000 inf.
- An unknown number of remnants from the *Limitanei* and an unknown number of Federates and *bucellarii*.
- The Field Army of Gaul enlarged with new recruits in 443-444: 10,000 inf.?

ITALY AND ILLYRICUM

ND - *Comitatenses* 3,500 cav. 48,000 inf.
   Intra Italiam
   - **15 Sarmatian *praefecti***   15,000 cav.?
   - ***Comes Illyrici*** 27,000 inf.
- An unknown number of remnants from the *Limitanei* and an unknown number of Federates and *bucellarii*.
- The Italian Field Army enlarged with new recruits in 443-444: 3,000 cav. (?) and 30,000 inf. (?)

Aetius and the Roman High Command were clearly fooled into believing that Attila intended to attack Italy in 451 (note that Aetius and his small retinue marched to Gaul only after Attila had devastated the north of Gaul) so that they in all probability transferred regulars (possibly about 3,000 cavalry and 40,000 infantry) from Gaul to Italy. My educated guess is that in the spring of 451 Aetius had at his disposal in Italy and Illyricum an army of about 118,000 infantry and 36,500 cavalry (Italian army, Illyrian army, Aetius's *bucellarii*, and reinforcements from Gaul). This is a very conservative estimate, because I have not included in these figures any *Limitanei* or the retinues of the officers. In this case it is probable that the units were close to their paper strengths because the West Roman government was well aware of the threat and could prepare accordingly against enemy invasion. It should be remembered however that Aetius would not have been able to put this whole force to the field. He would have needed to leave some behind to protect the Emperor and some of the more important places. On the basis of this my educated guess is that Aetius's Field Army of Italy in the spring of 451 probably consisted of about 100,000 infantry and 36,500 cavalry. In addition to these, there would also have been the citizen levies/paramilitary forces to protect the cities; the *bucellarii* of the senators, officers and nobility; the bodyguard units of the Emperor; and the remnants of the navy and other Federate forces. In my opinion it is improbable that these forces could have been used to bolster Aetius's Field Army because they were needed for the security of important persons and cities.

This means that Gaul was protected by the remaining forces of the Field Army of Gaul (ca. 3,000 cavalry and 46,000 infantry) posted in and around Arles, and by the auxiliaries (ca. 139,000 infantry and 91,000 cavalry). The Visigoths (a field army of ca. 40,000 infantry and 60,000 cavalry, but which could be enlarged even further by a complete mobilization of the tribal levy) formed an independent force and the Romans could not trust in their loyalty even if they expected that the Visigoths as Federates would provide soldiers for the campaign.

It should also be noted that the above-mentioned figures agree with the usually suggested locale for the battle of the Catalaunian Fields near the city of Troyes. I have used this terrain to verify my estimates even at the risk of being accused of circular argumentation. As we shall see, the terrain, my conservative estimates for the different tribal contingents, and the figures provided by the ancient sources correspond with each other.

The Invasion of Gaul in late March or early April 451

In the spring of 451 Attila the Hun launched his well-planned campaign in Gaul. According to Sidonius, the invaders felled the Hercynian forest to build boats for the crossing, which presumably means that the boats were used to make several pontoon bridges over the Rhine. The earliest definite date that we have of Attila's whereabouts is that he sacked the city of Metz (Divodorum) on Easter Eve which fell on 7 April 451. The various medieval hagiograpies of saints and chronicles name a number of other cities that were sacked by the Huns: Strasbourg, Worms, Mainz, Cologne, Cambrai, Arras, Tongres, Tournai, Therouanne, Cologne, Rheims, Amiens, Beauvais, Nymaie (Nijmegen?), Nerbonne (Nervii?),[4] Langres, and Paris. Paris is controversial because one of the hagiographic sources, the *Life of Saint Geneviève*, claims that when the men were about to evacuate the city, Geneviève and the other women managed to force the men to stay, after which the city was saved thanks to their prayers.[5] The likeliest explanation is that that the Huns did indeed sack the city on both sides of the Seine, but not Paris proper, the 'Isle of France', because their goal was just to continue their march towards Orleans. See the map.

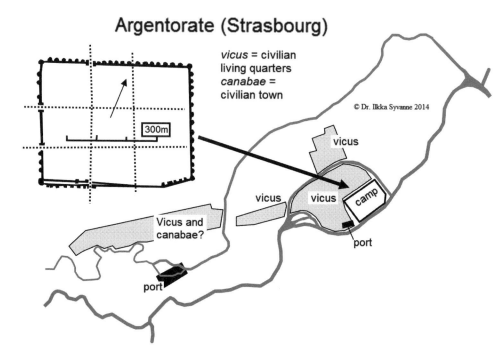

The list of cities included four bordering the Rhine – Nijmegen, Cologne, Mainz, and Strasbourg – which makes it possible that Attila's army could have crossed the river at four different points, but this is unlikely for several reasons, the most important of which is that Attila needed to possess numerical superiority at all points of his chosen invasion route. Operational security also rules out Strasbourg, because the route of march would have taken Attila through the territories close to the Romans, and because Attila's army did not include Suevi/Alamanni which would otherwise have been added to its strength. It is also improbable that Attila would have chosen to invade Gaul at one point (e.g. at Mainz) from which he would then have spread out his army, because his massive force needed to be fed and it was easier to supply if he used at least two marching columns; this approach would also have enabled the collecting of different tribes for the army along the route. In my opinion, the use of two massive corps is the likeliest alternative because it gave both marching columns a significant numerical superiority regardless of what enemy they faced in the north of Gaul. However, one still cannot rule out the use of other numbers of columns.

The southern division under Attila would have consisted at least of the Huns and the Gepids, and they would have approached the Rhine through the lands occupied by the Ripuarian Franks and Burgundians. They crossed the Rhine near the city of Mainz where Attila divided his force into two divisions, one advancing south to Strasbourg (the army HQ) and another division advancing against Trier, so that both divisions were united close to Metz. Attila's corps then conquered Metz and Reims and advanced west to unite with the other corps.

The northern corps approached the Rhine through the lands occupied by the Thuringians and Bructeri, crossed the Rhine near Cologne, and then divided itself into two divisions, one of which advanced to Nijmegen and the other to Tongres where both divisions met and advanced into Belgia. The mission of the northern corps was to secure the area held by the Salian Franks. Both corps met somewhere near Beuavais and then advanced through Paris to the city of Orleans with the purpose of then crossing the Loire to attack the Visigoths of Aquitania.

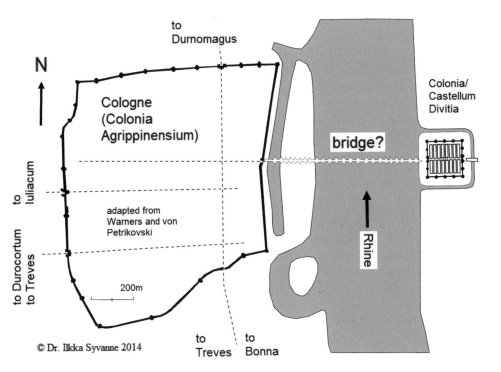

© Dr. Ilkka Syvänne 2014

When the Huns marched through Gaul it is probable that they followed the typical nomad tactic of always posting one main marching camp on some chosen position under the leader (e.g. to besiege a city) from which they sent roving bands/units of horsemen to reconnoitre, pillage, forage and terrorize the enemy. The enemy would be terrorized far and wide, weakening his ability to form a united defensive plan, enabling the Huns to live off the land and gather intelligence of enemy activities.

Some time during the Hunnic invasion Attila's forces had come very close to achieving their objective of securing the Salian throne for their candidate because, as Fredegar (FRMG 612) claims, the Huns managed to capture both Childeric and his mother. Fredegar goes on to state cryptically that the Frank Wiomad was more loyal to Childeric than others because he freed Childeric and his mother. I take this to mean that the warriors of the elder brother, which included Wiomad, had captured Childeric, and that Wiomad then betrayed the elder brother, freed the captives and fled. The likeliest date for this occurrence would be the beginning of the war when the northern corps was securing the Salian lands for the elder brother.

Siege of Orleans

The sources make it clear that Orleans was defended by its citizen militia and by the Alans under their king Sangiban, but it is also possible that some regular troops had been posted there to operate the siege equipment. The city had a population of about 30,000, which may have been bolstered by refugees from the surrounding areas. When Attila reached the city he decided to besiege it, presumably because it was held by the King of the Alans. Attila would have been eager to re-establish Hunnic superiority over their former 'slaves'. The fact that the defender of the city of Orleans was Sangiban suggests that Goar had either died or had withdrawn from public duties in shame. The Alans frowned upon all those males who had not died in battle but had become old and frail.[6]

The city walls were 10 metres high with round towers placed at distances of 54.5 metres. The towers had a diameter of 8 metres and protruded out of the walls for two metres.[7] It is also possible that it had earthworks outside the walls built by the Alans. The defences were by no means impressive in comparison with the fortifications that the Huns had already conquered in the Balkans, but in spite of this and despite the massive superiority of the Hun military machine, the city managed to hold on long enough for the local bishop, Anianus, to seek help from Aetius who had reached the city of Arles where Anianus met him. This proves that Aetius had finally reached the conclusion that the Gallic invasion was the main invasion in May and had then, accompanied by only his own retinue, hurried at the double to Gaul to organize its defence. Anianus's message appears to have been that unless Aetius relieved the city by a certain date Sangiban would surrender it to Attila because of the agreement made by them. This is the likeliest reason for Jordanes's claim that Sangiban intended to betray the city to Attila. Sangiban knew that his position was untenable unless he received help from Aetius, but one cannot rule out the possibility that Sangiban would have played out a ruse against Attila by agreeing to surrender if Aetius did not arrive by the time specified. This would have bought time for the Romans because it is probable that Attila would have halted the assault under these circumstances.

Aetius, however, had one serious problem. He had apparently managed to order the remnants of the Salian Franks, Saxons and Armoricans to join him somewhere south of the Loire, and had managed to order the assembly of the regular forces, Alans, Sarmatians, Burgundians, and other auxiliaries in the neighbourhood of Lyons for the forthcoming campaign, but he still needed to gain the support of the Visigoths. Consequently, he had apparently already dispatched an embassy to Theoderic which carried a conciliatory personal message from Valentinian to Theoderic stating that they must unite against their common treacherous foe and which reminded Theoderic that the Visigoths were part of the Roman Empire. Aetius appears to have trusted that this message would do the trick and joined his army near Lyons from which they then marched to Clermont. It was close to Clermont that Aetius then learnt that the Visigoths had indeed assembled their army and had advanced northwards from Toulouse but that the Visigoths did not intend to join forces with the Romans. The Visigoths intended to fight against the Huns independently in their own territory. So Aetius had no alternative but to recall Avitus from his retirement (he lived on his estates near Clermont) back to service to convince Theoderic to change his mind. Avitus did as asked and managed to convince his old friend Theoderic that unless they united their forces, the war would be lost. Theoderic agreed and the Gothic nobility shouted their eagerness to fight against the Huns. After this, Theoderic sent four of his sons back home (Frideric, Euric, Retemer, Himnerith), keeping with him his two older sons (Thorismund and Theodoric). The fact that Theoderic had marched north with all his sons suggests that he had initially assembled his entire force for the war, but when he then decided to join forces with the Romans he decided that he would not need his entire army and dispatched part of it back with his four sons. This proved to be a costly mistake.[8] It is probable that the armies were united somewhere near the city of Argentomagus from which the united force advanced directly north to relieve Orleans.

In the meantime Attila seems to have become aware of the imminent approach of the relief army, because he had launched a massive assault against the city walls with his siege engines. Anianus appears to have dispatched one last desperate call for help to Aetius while the battering rams were already pounding against the walls and *tormenta* shooting

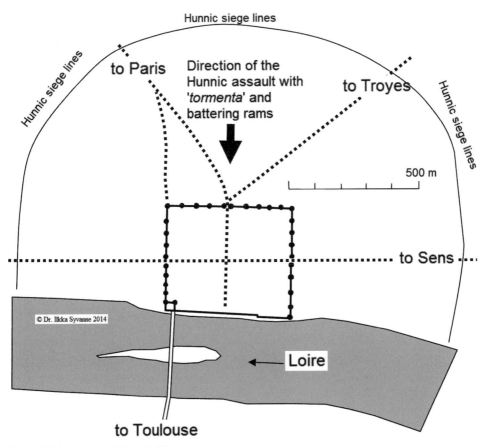

Siege of Orleans by the Huns in 451.

fire bombs. His last message to Aetius was to hurry because the city would fall on the same day. Aetius used forced marches to reach the city and arrived in the nick of time. The battering rams had already breached the wall and the Huns were pouring into the city. The Bishop had kept up the morale of the defenders by ordering the people on the wall to watch the horizon because Aetius would arrive on that day. The people did this twice and saw nothing, but the third time they looked they saw a cloud of dust in the distance. The arrival of reinforcements tilted the balance, the defenders fought back with renewed vigour, and the demoralized Huns retreated back to their camp. Aetius's army marched into the city via the bridge and then advanced out of the gates to build the great earthworks outside the city mentioned by Jordanes. He claims that the earthworks were built in front of the city before the arrival of the Huns. This is possible if the Alans had initially been deployed outside, and if this was the case then the Romans merely rebuilt those. The city was relieved on 14 June 451.

The Battle of the Nations: The Catalaunian Fields on 19–20 June 451[9]

Attila realized that his position near Orleans was untenable because of the arrival of Aetius and Theoderic and because his huge army had consumed all the supplies in the vicinity. Consequently he decided to retreat north-east towards the Rhine. Historians have suggested two other reasons for the retreat: 1) feigned retreat to lure Aetius to a suitable battlefield; 2) retreat all the way back to the Rhine because with the arrival of Aetius it would be impossible to inflict a serious defeat on the enemy. The former is inherently more likely, because as a warlord of the barbarian nations Attila would have needed to prove his manhood and not just flee. Aetius and his allies pursued the Huns to ensure that they would have to evacuate Gaul. It is also probable that Aetius was actively seeking a favourable occasion to force the Huns to fight in a place that would be favourable for his mostly infantry-based army. The standard tactic against the nomads was to force them against a river, so they would have to fight a frontal pitched battle with no chance of conducting a feigned flight, and this is what appears to have happened.

The location of the resulting confrontation between the nations is a heavily contested issue because the sources provide imprecise and conflicting information, but I am inclined to accept the reasoning presented by Lebedynsky for the case that the famous Battle of Mauriacus or Catalaunian Fields/Plains took place about 7.5 km west of the city of Troyes. The battle became inevitable when Attila approached the city and the River Seine and realized that it would be impossible to cross the river securely when Aetius and his allies were hot on their heels. The fact that Aetius sent the Franks to the assault to occupy the hills west of Troyes made the situation clear. Attila had made the Bishop of Troyes his hostage and guide in return for not pillaging Troyes, but Aetius, who knew Gaul inside out, had managed to force his enemy to a position which was quite unfavourable for the invader.[10]

According to Jordanes (*Getica* 217), the Gepids and Franks, who fought against each other during the night before the general engagement, lost 15,000 men in this combat. The Franks fought for the Romans and the Gepids for the Huns. The encounter between the Franks and Gepids is likely to have been a preliminary encounter between the Roman vanguard and Hun rearguard which would have been the first stage in the fighting for possession of the ridge. Since the Franks consisted predominantly of infantry, it is not surprising that they were able to force the Gepids to abandon their positions on the ridge. This action would have been followed up by the advance of the Roman forces along the ridge close to the actual battle site. Roman combat doctrine stated that when the infantry was led out from the marching camp to the battle, the distance there was not to exceed 2–3 miles (3–4.5 km; See Syvänne 2004). When one remembers this, it is obvious that Aetius would have marched his army during the night close to the battle site.

Jordanes (196ff.) claims that the arrival of Visigoths and Aetius and the loss of the ridge to the Franks unnerved Attila so that he lost confidence in his own troops. It was then as a result of this that Attila meditated the possibility of flight. In my opinion, Attila thought that this was very difficult now that the Romans had arrived and had effectively pinned him against a river. Jordanes then continues his account by stating that Attila decided to inquire into the future through soothsayers, which I interpret to mean that Attila wanted to encourage his men in a situation which appeared very unfavourable to the Huns. Jordanes however claims that the soothsayers foretold disaster to the Huns, but prophesied that the chief commander of the enemy would die in this battle. In my opinion this story smacks of legend to explain the death of Theoderic, because it is improbable that Attila's soothsayers would have foretold disaster publicly. I am sure that Attila was good enough as a commander to make certain that the soothsayers prophesied victory so that this message would encourage the men to fight with greater fervour in a desperate situation. Jordanes, however, claims that Attila chose to fight only because he considered the death of Aetius a thing to be desired, because Aetius was the man who stood in the way of his plans. This implies that Jordanes or his source thought that it was largely thanks to Aetius that Attila had suffered defeats or had been stalemated and that Attila realized this. According to Jordanes, it was then because of this that Attila began the battle. However, he then goes on to state that Attila was not confident in his success because he started it in the ninth hour of the day (i.e. at about 3 pm) so that the impending darkness would come to his aid if the outcome of the battle was disastrous. This was standard operating procedure in all armies when one doubted the outcome and it is probable that this was the case now.

The different stages of the battle have also been misunderstood by previous researchers as a result of which it is necessary to quote Jordanes's description (Get. 197ff.) in greater detail. The translation is by Mierow into which I have added comments and explanations inside parentheses.

The armies met …in the Catalaunian Plains. The battlefield was a plain rising by a sharp slope to a ridge, which both armies sought to gain [*Hughes 2012 is correct that this implies that the hill was between the armies, but subsequent details prove that the hill was located on the Roman left wing*]; … The Huns with their forces seized the right side [*this means the Gepids et al.*], the Romans, the Visigoths and their allies the left [*this means the Roman left flank*], and then began a struggle for the yet untaken crest [*this would refer to the end of the ridge near Troyes*]. … [*Theoderic*] with the Visigoths held the right wing and Aetius with the Romans the left. They placed in the centre Sangiban … On the other side, … Attila and his bravest followers were stationed in the centre. …The innumerable peoples …formed the wings. Amid them …the

Ostrogoths under the leadership of the brothers Valamir, Thiudimer and Vidimer,...
The renowned king of the Gepidae, Ardaric, was there also with a countless host,
and because of his great loyalty to Attila, he shared his plans. For Attila, comparing
them in his wisdom, prized him and Valamir, king of the Ostrogoths, above all the
other chieftains. ... Attila might well feel sure that they would fight against the
Visigoths, their kinsmen. Now the rest of the crowd of kings ... and the leaders of
various nations hung upon Attila's nod like slaves, ... Attila alone was king of all
kings...

... the struggle began for the advantage of position we have mentioned. Attila sent
his men to take the summit of the mountain, but was outstripped by Thorismund
and Aetius [*Thorismund with his followers clearly served as a sort of hostage under
Aetius*], who ...through this advantage of position easily routed the Huns [*in truth
the Gepids et al. because it would have been next to impossible to transfer the wings
in the middle of the battle. The fact that Thorismund and Aetius reached the top first
suggests that the top of the hill could be reached by cavalry. The account leaves open
whether Thorismund and Aetius then dismounted their troops or still fought mounted, but
whatever they did they were able to buy enough time for the infantry to reach the scene
before the enemy could occupy it. The ability to deploy the Roman and allied infantry in
a timely fashion to the edge of the ridge proves that Aetius had marched them close to the
site during the night and had then rested them in a marching camp for the battle which
commenced at about 3 pm*].

... when Attila saw his army thrown into confusion by this event, he thought
it best to encourage them by an extemporaneous address [*the speech is obviously
invented but does accurately reflect the situation facing the Huns*] ...: ... 'Let us then
attack the foe eagerly; for they are ever the bolder who make the attack [*Julius Caesar
would have approved of this*]. Despise this union of discordant races! [*partly true
because the different tribes had not trained to fight together, but the fact that all followed
similar military systems which were based either on the use of infantry phalanxes or on
similar cavalry tactics still enabled all the different sections to cooperate.*] To defend
oneself by alliance is proof of cowardice. [*Aetius was forced to form such an alliance
because he would have otherwise lacked adequate numbers to engage the masses facing
him; his opposition however was a similar conglomeration of various tribal forces*] ...
They seek the heights ...and ...clamour for protection against battle in the open
fields. [*Aetius had wisely occupied the higher ground which gave his force of mostly
infantry a clear advantage over the enemy cavalry.*] You know how slight a matter the
Roman attack is [*this implies the presence of Roman regulars too*]. While they are still
gathering in order and forming in one line with locked shields [*in ordine coneunt
et acies testudineque conectunt*], they are checked, I will not say by the first wound,
but even by the dust of battle [*this implies that on their previous fights against the
Romans, the Huns had faced infantry-based Roman armies and the encouragement in
the speech came from the successes achieved against the East Romans!*]. ... Despise their
battle line [*despicientesque eorum aciem*], attack the Alani [*Alanos invadite*], smite the
Visigoths [*in Visigothas incumbite*]! [*Since the attack against the Romans had failed,
Attila directed the main attack against the Alans and Visigoths! This was a sound tactical
decision. The defeated Gepids and others were now used as a holding force against the*

Roman auxiliaries] … Who, moreover, made armed men yield to you, when you were as yet unarmed? [*This implies that the Huns were now more fully armoured than they had previously been.*] Even a mass of federated nations could not endure the sight of the Huns. … I shall hurl the first spear at the foe. If any can stand at rest while Attila fights, he is a dead man.'…

… Hand-to-hand they clashed in battle [*the Huns charged into contact*], and the fight grew fierce, …a fight who like no ancient time has ever recorded [*the numbers involved were such that this is actually likely to be true*]. … a brook flowing between low banks through the plain was greatly increased by blood …of the slain. [*this suggests that the Visigoths had deployed behind a small brook for protection*] …Those whose wounds drove them to slake their parching thirst drank water mingled with gore [*this proves that the battle lasted for hours and probably involved advances and retreats by cavalry units and then pauses in fighting during which the participants rested and drank and filled their quivers with arrows*]…

…[*Theoderic*] while riding by to encourage his army, was thrown from his horse and trampled under foot by his own men… ['*hic Theodoridus rex dum adhortans discurrit exercitum, equo depulsus pedibusque suorum conculcatus vitam maturae senectutis conclusit.*' *This means that the Ostrogoths crushed the Visigothic battle line with the result that the panicked Visigoths trampled their king underfoot. It also means that the Visigoths had probably deployed their force in two lines with cavalry front and infantry reserve or the other way around, both of which were crushed. It is possible that the Ostrogoths had outflanked their cousins especially if they outnumbered them as I have assumed here. The terrain is heavily forested today and one may make the educated guess that it was also so in antiquity; it is possible that lack of visibility may have contributed to the defeat. Aetius's plan appears to have been to use infantry to secure both flanks so that the Huns could be induced to charge against the Alans and then crushed between the two wings.*] But others say that he was slain by the spear of Andag of the host of the Ostrogoths, who were then under the sway of Attila. … Then the Visigoths, separating from the Alani [*tunc Visigothae dividentes se ab Alanis invadunt Hunnorum caterva et pene Attilam trucidarent*], fell upon the horde of the Huns and nearly slew Attila [*This is inaccurate because the previous chapter proves that the Ostrogoths had crushed the Visigoths. The Visigoths who attacked Attila were Thorismund's cavalry as his subsequent presence close to their camp proves. The text however leaves several alternative ways to interpret it. It is possible that Aetius had placed Thorismund on the left flank of the Alan line and that Thorismund charged out of the array straight at Attila when he realized that his father's line had collapsed. It is unlikely that such a tactic could have worked without a simultaneous charge by the Alans and one can practically rule out such an Alan charge when their right flank was threatened by the Ostrogoths. It is more likely that the Alans retreated so that their right wing could not be outflanked. The second alternative is that the Alan line retreated when its right was exposed and that Thorismund then wheeled back against the Huns, but once again it is unlikely that such a tactic could have worked without support. If this is what happened, then it is probable that Aetius supported it with a flank attack against the pursuing Huns. In support of this one can state that Aetius was among those forces that pursued the Huns back to their camp, but it is possible that he may have pursued the fleeing Gepids there.*

The third alternative is that Thorismund and Aetius had both stayed on the left and then attacked the Huns in the flank when the Huns followed the retreating Alans. This alternative is supported by the fact that Thorismund and Aetius were both on the left, but it leaves open the statement how the Visigoths separated from the Alans; it is possible that this could refer to the separation of the two lines resulting from the retreat of the Alans and Visigoths. The fourth and likeliest alternative is that the Roman left wing, which included Aetius and Thorismund, defeated the enemy opposite them so that Thorismund spearheaded the pursuit and was followed by Aetius and the rest of the forces. Thorismund would then have outflanked the enemy and charged towards the reserve under Attila. This would explain why Thorismund supposedly separated from the Alans and also why the Romans were unable to block Ardaric's retreat back into the Hunnic camp. He would have retreated there immediately. This alternative is supported by the fact that Jordanes fails to mention any retreat by the Alans, which he certainly would have done had it happened. The probable reason for the confusion of the account is that Jordanes's source was an Ostrogoth who did not know what had happened on the other flank, and as stated, the circumstances actually suggest that the Romans had defeated their opposition. Notably, Gregory of Tours 2.7 precisely states that it was Aetius who won the battle with the help of Thorismund.]. ... [Attila] took flight and straightaway shut himself and his companions within the barriers of the camp, which he had fortified with wagons *[This presumably means that the Hunnic wings also retreated. Since Jordanes mentions only one camp, one may presume that the Huns and their subjects were housed in one massive camp with a circumference of more than 5 km. The use of one single camp may have contributed to the Hunnic defeat because this would have forced their units to travel greater distances to reach their positions in the battle line than was the case on the opposite side. The sixth century Strategikon refers to this Roman combat doctrine by stating that the allies were to be housed in a separate marching camp. See Syvänne, 2004.]. ...* But Thorismund, ...who with Aetius had seized the hill and repulsed the enemy from the higher ground, came unwittingly to the wagons of the enemy in the darkness of night, thinking he had reached his own lines. *[Note that this statement once again implies that Aetius and Thorismund were fighting on the left flank and note that it was Thorismund and not the Visigoths of the right flank who reached the enemy camp!]* As he was fighting bravely, someone wounded him in the head and dragged him from his horse. Then he was rescued by the watchful care of his followers and withdrew ... *[obviously to the Visigothic camp]*. Aetius also became separated from his men in the confusion of night and wandered about in the midst of the enemy. *[The fact that Aetius was in the midst of his enemies suggests that he had also pursued the enemy close to their camp.]* Fearing disaster had happened, he went about in search of the Goths *[Aetius feared that the Visigoths had been completely crushed and went in search of his allies]*. ... *[Aetius]* reached the camp of his allies and passed the remainder of the night in the protection of their shields *[This could mean the auxiliaries, but the fact that Aetius was seeking the Goths means that the Visigoths are meant. This also means that the defeated Visigoths had been able to regroup inside their wagon laager when the enemy had retreated back into their own camp]*.

At dawn on the following day, when the Romans saw the fields were piled high with bodies and that the Huns did not venture forth, they thought the victory was theirs… Even so this warlike king [*Attila*] …terrified his conquerors. …the Goths and Romans assembled [*and the Alans too!*] and considered what to do with the vanquished Attila. They determined to wear him out by a siege, because he had no supply of provisions and was hindered from approaching by a shower of arrows from the bowmen placed within the confines of the Roman camp [*Note the effectiveness of the Roman archers against the Huns, the supposed masters of this art! This also suggests that the Romans had defeated Ardaric and had blocked the route to the city of Troyes with a new marching camp. It also proves that Aetius and the PPG Ferreolus had organized the provisioning of their massive forces with great care, even if it appears probable that the subsequent departure of the Visigoths and Salian Franks back to their homes was at least partly meant to ease the supplying of the army*].

Now …the Visigoths sought their king and the king's sons their father, … When, after a long search, they found him where the dead lay thickest [*Theoderic had encouraged his footmen from behind the line and had died in their midst when the battle line collapsed*], …, they honoured him.

On the basis of the above analysis of the quote, I would suggest that Aetius's battle plan was to force the Huns to fight a pitched battle in which the Romans possessed the advantageous terrain and the Huns lacked the ability to flee because they were fighting with their backs against the river. Aetius's battle array was a variation of the so-called mixed formation in which the centre consisted of the Alan cavalry while the wings were secured by infantry. The massive size of the allied army (at least ca. 219,000 infantry and 169,000 cavalry = ca. 388,000) enabled Aetius to post the Visigothic right flank on higher terrain so that the Alan cavalry forces occupied the entire space between the securely anchored wings.

The Roman left flank formed the most powerful corps and consisted of the regulars, auxiliaries, Aetius's *bucellarii* and of Thorismund's division. Thorismund's presence on the left had two purposes: Firstly he served as a hostage, ensuring Theoderic's loyalty; Secondly, Aetius needed to bolster the number of horsemen on the left. I have also made the assumption that Aetius would have left about 6,000 footmen behind to protect Arles. Therefore the left flank consisted of about 179,000 infantry (regular and auxiliary) and 44,000 cavalry (Aetius's c.15,000 *bucellarii*; Thorismund's c.10,000; the auxiliaries and regulars without the Sarmatians). It seems probable that the Alans in the centre included their tribal brothers, the Sarmatians, so that Sangiban commanded about 75,000 horsemen altogether. The Visigothic right flank must have consisted of slightly more men because they needed to deploy their forces in two lines, one of cavalry and one of infantry.

One can calculate the approximate length of the infantry line by calculating the width of each file in the *testudo* formation with the file width being 60 to 70 cm, onto which is then added the intervals between the units and divisions. If the infantry phalanx was deployed 24 ranks deep (16 heavy and 8 light) so that it was possible for each unit to form a double front or double phalanx if it was outflanked, then the length of the line without any intervals would have been about 7,458 metres. The figure of 179,000 footmen would equal about 36 divisions (called either *legiones* or *mere*) each of which was separated from the others by intervals of 30–60 metres which would add up to an additional length of 1,050–2,100 metres for the phalanx for a total width of 8,508–9,558 metres. If the legions were deployed as 24-deep phalanxes, there would also have been small intervals between the smaller units of about 300 men (I have estimated the intervals at 2 metres per 'cohortal' interval for a total of 1,192 metres) so that the total length of the phalanx battleline with all intervals and units would have been 9,700–10,750 metres. If these legions were deployed as hollow oblongs (2,000 men front and rear, 500-man flanks), then the length of the line would have been (I have given each of the files the width of one metre to take into account the intervals in the line) 8,112 metres (units 6,012 metres, intervals between the squares 2,100 metres). It is possible that a mix of phalanxes and squares/oblongs were used depending upon the nationality of the unit, but it should still be recognized that even the Germanic auxiliaries could use both tactical variants.[11] If there was a need to lengthen the line, the infantry could assume a shallower array of eight heavy and four light infantry, which still allowed the forming of double front. The terrain suggests that the Romans would have deployed their infantry to cover a distance of ten kilometres. The cavalry units could also be used to lengthen the line, but the huge size of the infantry contingent would have made this unnecessary. I have estimated the depth of all 'barbarian' cavalry units to be seven ranks on the basis of the depth of Federate units in the *Strategikon* (six ranks of regulars and one rank of squires). It is probable that the infantry units formed the front so that the cavalry was either stationed behind them and/or on the flanks.

The about 75,000 Alans and Sarmatians would have been deployed as 2,000–3,000-man rank-and-file units (seven ranks with file widths of about 1–1.5 m) with intervals of 60–120m according to their standard tactical doctrine. I have made the educated guess that Sangiban would have varied the depth of his units and the intervals between so that it would have equalled the width of the Hunnic line opposite him so that the array occupied the entire open field of 15 km between the hills just like their enemy line.

The Visigothic line formed the right anchor of the array, but it was fatally weakened by the detachment of Thorismund's forces because this appears to be the likeliest reason for its collapse in the face of Ostrogothic attack. If Thorismund took about 10,000 horsemen with him as I have guessed this would have left about 40,000 foot and 50,000 horse to the main formation so that the front of the array would have been formed of cavalry which would have retreated behind the infantry whenever threatened and then charged back after regrouping. The Ostrogoths on the opposite side would have followed a similar tactic. Depending on the tightness of the array (cavalry file 1–1.5 m in witdh) and slight variations in intervals, the cavalry would have occupied about 8,000–11,600 metres (both figures rounded up) in length. The infantry in its turn would have occupied only about 2,351 metres if deployed 24 deep and about 4,702 if deployed 12 deep. Considering the fact that the Ostrogoths were able to charge through the infantry phalanx, it is quite probable that the Visigoths would have used only six-deep formation (four heavies and one light) to widen the width to about 7,351 metres, which would have made their infantry array roughly equal in width to their cavalry line.

The Hun battle plan for their now ca. 400,000 warriors was a simple desperate attempt to defeat the pursuers first by trying to push the Romans away from the hills and after this had failed to defeat the Alans and Visigoths. The following numbers and widths of the lines are only conjectural, because we should remember that the Huns and their allies had suffered significant numbers of casualties in the course of their invasion.

The Hun combat doctrine suggests that their 110,000 men were divided into 10,000-man divisions each of which consisted of small units of about 40–50 men. The Huns deployed as one continuous battleline which consisted of units of irregular size behind which they deployed a reserve line. There were two standard ways to use this array. The first was to charge straight into contact and the second was to spread the array into multiple small units in irregular formation to wear out the enemy with volleys of arrows; they might also feign flight or use the reserve for ambush. In this case the Huns were forced to charge into close combat as rank-and-file units as stated by Jordanes.

The 110,000 Huns would have consisted of the 10,000-man divisions ('tümets') with 60 metre intervals, each of which would have consisted of small units of about 50 men. This would mean that the intervals between the 11 divisions would have encompassed about (10 x 60 = 600 metres) and the intervals between the 2,200 small units (2,199 x 2 m = 4,398 rounded up to 4,400 m) which gives a total of 5,000 m for the intervals. The 110,000 men (1–1.5 metres per file) with a depth of seven ranks would have occupied a width of about 15,714–23,571 metres without any intervals. With intervals the length of the array it would therefore have been about 20,714–28,571 metres wide. If the Huns posted about 80,000 men in the frontline then the length of their battle line was about 15,000 (rounded down from 15,059) to 20,000 metres (rounded down from 20,775).

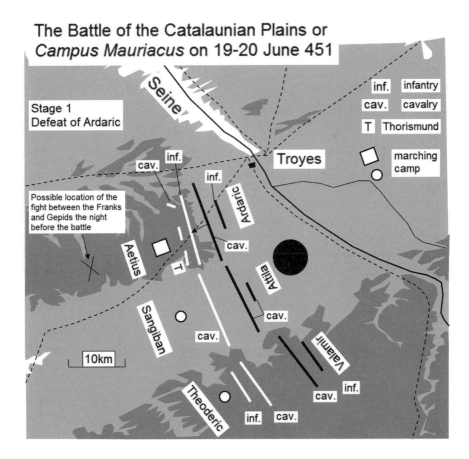

The Battle of the Catalaunian Plains or Campus Mauriacus on 19-20 June 451

Since the open terrain between the hills was only 15 km wide, I suspect that the Huns would have made the intervals between their 'tümets' smaller to shorten the line and/or placed an even greater proportion of their men in reserve. The corresponding width of the cavalry line of 87,500 horsemen (95,000 minus 7,500 lost during the night) under Ardaric would have probably been close to 15 kilometres as well (if one takes into account the casualties taken during the campaign) while the 115,000-strong infantry array behind it would probably have been about 6,876 metres in width (depth 24 ranks equals the width of 4,792 metres plus the intervals of about 2,084 metres) or 9,583 metres with the depth of 12 ranks. The Ostrogothic cavalry line was probably slightly longer or deeper than the Visigothic line because it was eventually able to overrun the opposing lines. Their infantry line was probably equal to that of the Visigothic line.

On the basis of the above analysis of Jordanes' narrative, the principal stages of the battle are as follows. The Battle started with the night encounter between the Franks and Gepids, which enabled the Romans to occupy the advantageous position overlooking the city of Troyes. It was this that forced Attila to attempt to retake the heights the next day. Attila launched his attack late in the afternoon because he feared defeat. The attack led by the Gepids against the Roman and allied cavalry and infantry formations ended in complete defeat. Attila regrouped his army and attempted to encourage it. After this,

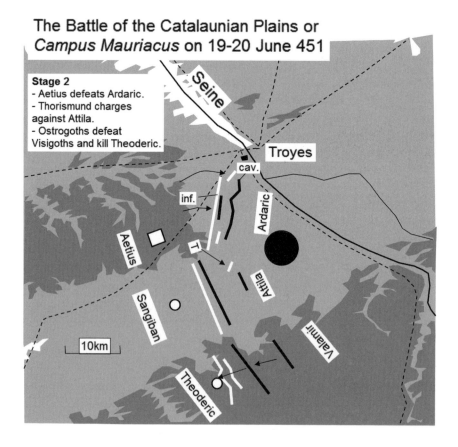

The Battle of the Catalaunian Plains or *Campus Mauriacus* on 19-20 June 451

Stage 2
- Aetius defeats Ardaric.
- Thorismund charges against Attila.
- Ostrogoths defeat Visigoths and kill Theoderic.

Seine

Troyes

cav.

inf.

Ardaric

Aetius

Attila

Sangiban

Valamir

10km

Theoderic

Attila launched an attack against the Alans and Visigoths. This resulted in a bloody stalemate lasting for hours until close to nightfall the Ostrogoths managed to defeat the Visigoths and the Romans the mixed forces opposite them. When the Roman left wing forced the Hunnic right wing back, Thorismund launched an attack against Attila and his reserve which forced the latter to flee back to his camp. Even though Jordanes fails to mention this, it is probable that when the Huns started to retreat, the Alans launched a pursuit which completed the Hunnic rout. Both Aetius and Thorismund appear to have reached the Hunnic camp before the Hunnic centre started its flight back to the camp with the result that Aetius and Thorismund both became embroiled in a chaotic fight in the midst of the retreating enemy during the night. When Thorismund was wounded, his retainers took him back to their own encampment. In the meantime, Aetius had galloped further south in search of his Visigothic allies until he finally found them in their camp where he spent the following night.

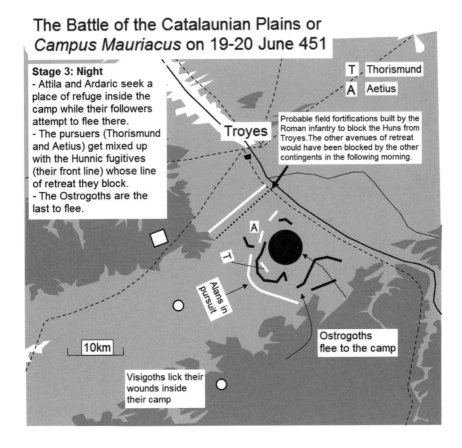

The Battle of the Catalaunian Plains or Campus Mauriacus on 19-20 June 451

Stage 3: Night
- Attila and Ardaric seek a place of refuge inside the camp while their followers attempt to flee there.
- The pursuers (Thorismund and Aetius) get mixed up with the Hunnic fugitives (their front line) whose line of retreat they block.
- The Ostrogoths are the last to flee.

T — Thorismund
A — Aetius

Probable field fortifications built by the Roman infantry to block the Huns from Troyes. The other avenues of retreat would have been blocked by the other contingents in the following morning.

Troyes

Alans in pursuit

10km

Ostrogoths flee to the camp

Visigoths lick their wounds inside their camp

Aftermath
Owing to the confusion resulting from the great length of the battleline and the night fighting, Aetius and the Romans were uncertain who had won the battle. However, when at dawn Aetius saw that the Huns remained inside their camp, he realized that he had won. After this the commanders held a council and decided to starve the enemy out

rather than attempt to attack them in the camp. The Romans appear to have built some sort of field fortifications to accomplish this. According to Jordanes (*Getica* 217), 165,000 men of the bravest tribes on both sides were killed in this battle, not including the 15,000 men who had died in the encounter between the Franks and Gepids. It is impossible to know how accurate the figures are, but at least they show the unprecedented magnitude of the fight.

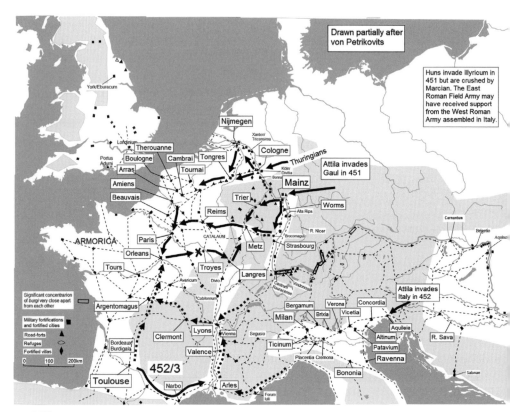

Military campaigns in Gaul and Italy in 451–453.

At some point in time after the Visigoths had found their fallen king and had buried him, Aetius decided that it was in his interest to convince Thorismund to return to Toulouse to secure his throne against his brothers. According to the sources, this was a ruse to lure Thorismund away so that the Huns would not be destroyed, but in my opinion there are other rational reasons for such advice and policy. There was a very real danger that the Visigothic realm could become embroiled in a civil war which Attila could exploit, and if Aetius thought that Thorismund was the preferred candidate it is quite obvious why he wanted to send Thorismund back to secure his position. The second reason is that it was easier for Aetius to provision the army if the Visigoths returned. According to Gregory of Tours, Aetius also convinced the king of the Franks (presumably Childeric) to return home so that he would be able to collect the booty lying on the ground.[12] Once again there were very logical reasons for Aetius's policy. When Attila was besieged inside his camp, it was possible for the king of the Franks to secure his realm both for himself and for Rome.

Once again the absence of the Franks eased the provisioning of the army. This is not to say that Aetius would not have wanted to keep the Hunnic realm in existence. It is quite possible that he intended to use the Huns as a possible source of help against the other tribes, but if this was his aim, he was mistaken, as the events of the following year prove: when the Visigoths and Franks marched back to their homes, the Romans opened up a route of retreat for the Huns presumably through the city of Troyes.

At first the Huns did not dare use the route of retreat opened up for them because they feared that the retreat of the Visigoths and Franks was a ruse, but when they finally realized that they were allowed to retreat they used the opportunity given. The likeliest reason for the readiness of the Huns to retreat instead of attempting to fight against the remaining forces is that they had suffered many casualties. According to Jordanes, a total of 180,000 men died on both sides (15,000 + 165,000), a figure which can also be found in Paulus Diaconus (*Romana* 13.6). Hydatius claimed that 300,000 fell in this battle, but one may make the educated guess that he may have misunderstood the meaning, doubled the figure and rounded it down. One may perhaps make the educated guess that 2/3rds (right wing and centre defeated) of the casualties were suffered by the Huns and 1/3rd (Visigothic right wing defeated) by the Romans. This would mean that the Huns had about 290,000 men (410,000 minus 120,000) left and the Romans about 328,000 (388,000 minus 60,000), which would have given the allies a slight numerical advantage over the Huns. On top of that it is probable that the Huns had suffered terribly because their route of retreat had been partially blocked by the Roman cavalry. One may make the educated guess that the bulk of the casualties would have consisted of the footmen of the Hunnic right wing (perhaps about 80,000 dead). On the Roman side the vast majority of the casualties would have been borne by the Visigoths: they may have lost as many as 40,000 men.[13] Consequently, when Aetius sent the Visigoths and Salian Franks (10,000 killed?) away he still had about 228,000 men – enough to face the Huns if needed.

According to Gregory of Tours, when the Visigoths and Franks had left, Aetius collected booty lying on the ground and then retreated, after which the Huns withdrew. This is contradicted by Fredegar's claim that Aetius and the Franks pursued the retreating Huns up to Thuringia (FRMG 598) with the apparent purpose of securing the area for Childeric and the Salian Franks. These accounts can be reconciled if one takes Gregory to be referring to the immediate aftermath of the battle, so that Aetius did indeed loot the dead after which he withdrew his forces so that the Huns were able to retreat through Troyes after which Aetius shadowed the Huns out of Roman territory all the way up to Thuringia. The shadowing of the Huns up to Thuringia means that Aetius managed to secure both banks of the Rhine for his Federate allies.

Operations in Illyricum in 451

Things went equally badly for the Huns in Illyricum. The letters of the Emperor Marcian to the attendees of the Council of Chalcedon (originally Nicaea) before the opening of the council prove that the Huns had invaded East Roman Illyricum and had been thoroughly trashed. But the situation had still demanded the personal attention of the Emperor and he had taken charge of the operations in person. Priscus' text (fr. 20, Blockley fr.19) proves that Ardabur/Ardaburius, son of Aspar, made so great a contribution to the success of the war in 451–53 that he rewarded him with the position of the *Mag.Mil. per Orientem* in 453. The PLRE2 speculates that Ardabur probably held the position of *MVM vacans* or *comes rei militaris* during this Balkan campaign. The defence had been such a success that the East Romans were already poised to cross the Danube in early September 451, but the operation was postponed to the next year because Marcian wanted to participate in the council, which he transferred to Chalcedon as he did not want to travel as far as Nicaea. Marcian needed to reconcile the rift between the Eastern and Western Churches resulting from the Council of Ephesus. This was doubly important when the two halves of the Empire needed to cooperate and when Marcian also needed to keep his wife happy. The end result of the council did satisfy these two needs, but at the same time it created an even worse situation that dawned upon the participants only slowly. The Syrian, Egyptian and Armenian churches could not accept the result and came to be considered as Monophysites.[14] This was to have dire consequences for the defence of the Empire at a later date.

It is unfortunate that we do not know what the West Roman field army in Italy did at the time the East Romans crushed the Huns in Illyricum. My own educated guess is that they would have participated in the operation and that the two halves coordinated their actions, because we find them doing precisely the same thing next year when the East Romans dispatched reinforcements to Italy to help Aetius defend it against the Huns.

Invasion of Italy in 452

The double defeat of the year 451 did not deter Attila from making another attempt the next year. His own position was dependent upon his ability to provide loot for his followers and the invasion of Gaul had not been the success he had hoped for. This time Attila aimed to strike at the heart of the Roman Empire by invading Italy. Attila's actual campaign plan consisted of two elements: 1) of the diversionary invasion of Gaul against the Alans of the Loire to tie up both the Alans and Visigoths in that area (Jordanes); 2) of the main invasion into Italy under Attila himself.

The Alans appear to have defeated the diversionary invasion of the Huns before the Visigoths were able to reach the scene because Jordanes (Get. 228) states that the Alans had repulsed the Huns without any loss to the Visigoths. In this context it is important to note the statements of Gregory of Tours (2.7) and Prosper (a.453). Gregory states that Thorismund defeated the Alans in battle, which must refer to the situation in which Thorismund had supposedly come to help the Alans against the Huns. In other words, Thorismund had attacked the Alans with the excuse that Sangiban had betrayed them to the Huns. After this Thorismund threw away all pretenses and invaded the south of Gaul in 452/3 and besieged Arles. He evidently exploited the absence of part of the Field Army of Gaul in Italy to fight the Huns. *PPG* Ferreolus managed to convince Thorismund to abandon the siege through diplomacy, which can be considered to be among the greatest successes of Roman diplomacy for this period. In fact Ferreolus was among the very few skilled administrators of the era. In the midst of all the troubles he had managed to provision Aetius's massive forces in 451, then convince Thorismund to abandon his invasion, and at the same time manage the public tax system in such a manner that he was able to reduce the tax burden on the provincials with the result that he was publicly thanked by them. It is unfortunate that we do not know why Ferreolus was forced to give up his position as *PPG*, considering that in the same year he had managed to turn Thorismund back. Perhaps, the likeliest reason is that he was just too good at his job. Aetius and other powerful men could see him as a potential threat to their own power.

It is in light of the above that we should see Prosper's statement that Thorismund's brothers killed him in 453 because he attempted to act against the Romans and thereby cause harm to the Visigoths. Thorismund had effectively destroyed the loyal Alans of the Loire and presumably intended to continue his campaign against the Romans in 453 and it was because of this that his brothers, who were loyal to the Romans, decided to garrotte him, undoubtedly with the backing of at least some of the Roman authorities. Thorismund's successor Theoderic was a personal friend of Avitus and one may make the guess that he had urged Theoderic to get rid off Thorismund.

Attila's diversionary invasion of Gaul proved a great success because it tied up all the auxiliaries of the previous year together with the Visigoths and a part of the Field Army of Gaul with the result that Aetius had far too few men available for the defence of Italy. The

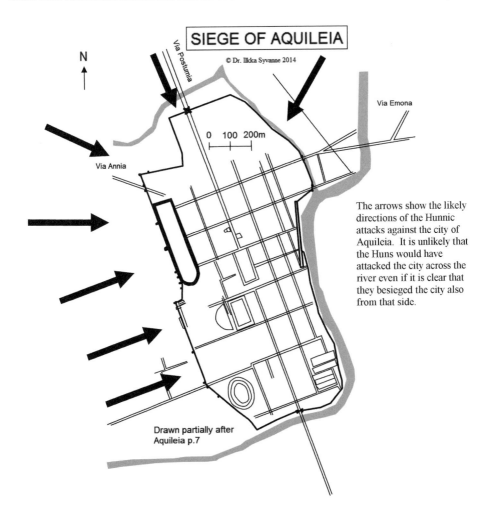

SIEGE OF AQUILEIA

© Dr. Ilkka Syvänne 2014

Via Postumia

Via Annia

Via Emona

N

0   100   200m

The arrows show the likely directions of the Hunnic attacks against the city of Aquileia. It is unlikely that the Huns would have attacked the city across the river even if it is clear that they besieged the city also from that side.

Drawn partially after Aquileia p.7

lack of adequate numbers of cavalry to face the Huns was a particularly acute problem for Aetius. He could not conduct truly effective guerrilla war if the enemy possessed vastly superior numbers of more mobile cavalry forces. But this was not the only decisive factor because this time the two halves of the Empire coordinated their efforts against the Huns. Aetius was not completely surprised by the Huns as claimed by Prosper. He was just following the standard late-Roman strategy against the major invasion of the north of Italy (Radagaisus in 395, Alaric in 401 and 408, Aspar in 425, Attila in 452, Theoderic in 489), which was to attempt to delay the enemy with fortifications and then to defeat the invader through guerrilla war, famine and disease. There is no reason to reiterate the reasons for this conclusion because Maenchen-Helfen (132–143) has already provided a detailed discussion of these. The following discussion is based on his analysis, except where I state otherwise.

The Huns invaded through the Julian Alps either in May or early June 452 and then halted to besiege Aquileia for three months. The city was very populous and had a sizable garrison, which meant that the Huns could not bypass it safely. The length of the siege is proven by Valentinian's *Novella* 36 (29 June 452) which states that in the midst of all his warlike troubles, Aetius had found enough time to secure Rome's meat supply, and by Priscus's referral to the end of the siege after the storks had left Aquileia, which always happened after 23 August. This means that the siege of Aquileia started either in May or June and ended either in late August or September. This means that I do not agree with Maenchen-Helfen regarding the reliability of the story of the storks leaving Aquileia. The information provided by the *Novella* means that Aetius took precautions against the possibility of the Huns advancing against the city of Rome by providing it with adequate supplies for the siege.

When, after a very long period, the Huns had made no progress against the defenders of Aquileia because these consisted of elite soldiers, the Huns started to voice their dissatisfaction openly. The Huns were already leaving their siege lines when Attila noted that the storks were carrying their young ones away from the city. With a keen mind he exploited this to renew the fighting spirit of his superstitious army. He claimed that this predicted the fall of the city and ordered machines and artillery (*tormenta*) to be built for immediate assault. I would suggest that the building of the siege engines actually means that the soldiers were ordered to rebuild the machines that had already been taken apart for transportation or had been destroyed. This time the attack was a success. The siege engines brought down the same section of the wall from which the storks had flown. I would suggest that when Attila had observed the flight of the storks he had also recognized that the wall of that section had decayed and could be crumbled with siege engines. The Huns, together with their allies, burst inside and devastated the city. See the map.

Attila celebrated his victory by marching his army along the main road to Concordia, which was then pillaged. It is not known whether Attila divided his army at this point so that one branch conquered Vicetia and the other Altinum, or whether the entire army advanced to Altinum and then turned towards Vicetia ravaging Patavium en route. The advance along the coastal road to Altinum was meant to threaten the city of Ravenna. We do not know why Attila chose not to complete his march, but the likeliest reasons are: that by then the defenders of Ravenna would have been reinforced by the East Roman field army (which must have been shipped to Ravenna because the road via Pannonia was blocked) which in combination with the lateness of the season and the strong fortifications spelled potential disaster for the Huns if they had chosen to besiege the city.

The Huns continued their march from Vicetia to Verona, Brixia and Bergamum, and from there to Mediolanum (Milan), and Ticinum (Pavia). The route suggests that Attila had kept his army united, which in turn suggests that Aetius was conducting an effective guerrilla campaign which forced the Huns to remain united with the result that they consumed their foodstuffs faster than they could replenish their stocks. The other reason for keeping the army united would obviously have been the need to take the strongly fortified cities, but as far as the evidence permits us to make educated guesses Aetius actually appears to have abandoned the cities so that he could unite their garrisons into his army. The sources clearly imply that the cities were not effectively defended and that most of the populace had fled. This if anything proves how large an army the Huns had and how depleted the resources of West Rome were. Aetius needed to horde all his forces into one major field army and he also urgently needed help from the east to bolster his depleted numbers – and he needed help because this time the Visigoths and Alans were not coming to his help.

After the conquest of Ticinum, the Huns crossed the Po and advanced into Aemilia, but it was apparently then that the Huns were hit by an 'illness sent from heaven'. I would suggest that this illness was caused by human intervention. It is very probable that the Romans had poisoned the aqueducts of Milan (or one of the rivers) with bacteria/viruses and/or hellebore (or some other poison) as instructed by their military manuals (instructions for this can be found for example in Polyaenus and Julius Africanus) just as had happened when the Huns approached Constantinople in 447. It is also possible that the Romans could have poisoned some food sources and even the fields as instructed by the military manuals. The third possible way to 'poison' the enemy was to release 'bottled' illnesses to be carried by the wind into the enemy camp. For further information regarding these methods, see Syvänne (2004, 2006) together with Mayor. It is very likely that one of the reasons for the abandoning of the cities to the Huns was to cause them to advance into these cities so that the spreading of the poisons and diseases would become easier. The use of diseases had the added benefit of weakening the attackers even after the invasion was over because they would bring the diseases back to their homes; this was recognized by the Romans (Syvänne, 2006).

The two key texts for the end of the war are provided by Hydatius and Prosper (see the relevant year). According to Hydatius, the Huns were struck by heaven-sent disasters, hunger and disease, and were being killed by the auxiliaries sent by the Emperor Marcian and commanded by Aetius, and at the same time they were also being destroyed in their homelands by the heaven-sent disasters and by the army of Marcian. Since the Huns were being defeated on every front, they concluded peace with the Romans and returned to their home territories. I agree with Maenchen-Helfen that there is no need to postulate any second Aetius (the *Com. Dom.* of East Rome was another Aetius) in this case. Hydatius's Latin is quite clear. There were two separate armies, one in the west consisting of easterners and westerners under the western *MVM* Aetius, and another army in the Balkans, which was Marcian's eastern field army and which also included the Emperor himself and Ardabur/Ardaburius.

Prosper refers to the instance in which the Romans sent an embassy to Attila consisting of Pope Leo, ex-consul Avienus and ex-prefect Trygetius. According to Prosper, Attila received the envoys and was so flattered by the presence of the Pope that he ordered his men to stop the hostilities and promised peace, after which he returned to the Danube. The key piece of information is actually the promise of peace, which means that no peace was actually concluded then. The Huns just bought a respite from the fighting so that they could retreat unmolested. Maenchen-Helfen (141) has noted that the only thing that the envoys really achieved was the return of captives in exchange for ransom. Those who had no-one to pay their ransoms were forced to follow the Huns. The meeting of the envoys and Attila took place in the Ambuleian district of the Veneti at the ford of the River Mincius. This means that the summit occurred when the Huns were already retreating. When one combines this with the map of the region it means that the Huns had probably crossed the Po near Ticinum, marched along *Via Iulia Augusta* (east of Placentia) past Placentia, then *Via Postumia* (between Placentia and Cremona) past Cremona and then eastwards up to the Mincius River where they met the ambassadors asking for the release of the prisoners. This means that Aetius had somehow managed to force the Huns to abandon their campaign in Aemilia along the *Via Aemilia* with the purpose either of advancing against Ravenna and/or over the Apennines. The likeliest reason for the retreat of the Huns would of course be that if the already weakened Huns advanced any further they would have been forced to fight against the main field army under Aetius which was still intact and waiting for the Huns. The Huns faced the prospect of having to fight another Battle of the Catalaunian Fields in a location of Aetius's choosing, which Aetius also chose not to fight for the risks it would have entailed. It was always risky to fight a pitched battle that could end either way, on top of which it would have been very unwise to fight against a foe suffering from a disease that the victors could also have contracted – and, if the disease had been spread by the Romans themselves it would have been doubly foolish to prevent the enemy from retreating.

In short, Attila's Italian campaign had ended in a dismal failure despite the many cities and people captured. The Hun army had suffered terribly as a result of fighting, hunger and disease, and their homelands had been ravaged by the East Roman field army. The time was almost ripe for the revolt of the Hunnish subjects. Only Attila's death in 453 spared him from the humiliation of having to witness the desctruction of his Hunnic Empire, which would have followed soon enough now that the two halves of the Roman Empire cooperated.

The defeat of the Huns in 452, the death of Attila in early 453, and the resulting civil war among the sons of Attila and then with the subject peoples of the Huns (see the discussion later), enabled Aetius to modify his military priorities. Malalas (14.10) claims that Aetius had managed to assassinate Attila by bribing Attila's *spatharius* to stab him and that it was because of this that Aetius was able to return victorius to Rome. This would imply that Aetius had followed Attila to the Danube and stayed there until his assassin had accomplished his mission, but this is not the only version, for there exist several alternative ones. Regardless, it was thanks to the death of Attila that in 453/4 (Hydatius) Aetius was able to dispatch Theoderic II's brother Frederic to subdue the Bacaudae of Tarraconensis, which he did with great slaughter. In other words, the West Romans did not possess enough regulars for these tasks and were entirely reliant on their

Federates. This also means that Aetius probably kept most of his forces concentrated in Italy during the civil war that ravaged the Hun Empire. This would have been wise as it was undoubtedly impossible to know how the multiple wars wrecking the Hun Empire would end, on top of which it is clear that the decisive battle of Nedao River in 453/4, which was fought in Pannonia, was also fought dangerously close to Italy.

The Murder of Aetius on 21/22 September 454[15]

Just when Aetius had managed to bring some sense of stability to the West Roman Empire, things started to unravel once again. According to Procopius (3.16ff.), this resulted from the sexual urges of Valentinian III. According to him, Valentinian lusted after the beautiful wife of *Patricius* Maximus and developed a plot to bed her. He summoned Maximus to the palace to play a game of draughts which, unsurprisingly, the Emperor won, and since Maximus did not have enough money, he left his ring as a pledge for the amount owed. Valentinian then sent a messenger with the ring to summon Maximus' wife in Maximus's name to the Palace to meet the Empress Eudoxia. When she arrived, Valentinian raped her. After this, she returned home and accused her husband Maximus of complicity in the rape. The enraged Maximus decided to kill Valentinian, but since he knew it would be impossible to do that while Aetius was alive, he decided to kill him first.

Maximus convinced *PSC* Heraclius the Eunuch to persuade Valentinian into the false belief that Aetius aimed to kill him and then appoint his son Gaudentius as the new Emperor. This mission was easily accomplished in a situation in which Aetius and his wife Pelagia had managed to force Valentinian III to agree to the marriage of Gaudentius and Placidia, and the West Romans no longer needed to fear that the Huns would take revenge on Aetius's behalf. Valentinian swallowed the bait. On 21 or 22 September, when Aetius came to the Palace to discuss matters of revenue (note that Aetius controlled these too without any official position), Valentinian and Heraclius drew their bladed weapons and hit Aetius on the head – so died a brave man at the hands of two cowards. When Valentinian then asked a man in his entourage whether his deed was a good one, he bravely answered that he did not know whether it was good or bad, but that he knew that the emperor had cut off his right hand with his left. After the death of Aetius, Valentinian admitted *honorati* inside the palace one by one, all of whom were murdered by Valentinian's *spatharius* (Hyd. 454). The most important of these was Aetius's friend the *PPI* Boethius. The lifeless bodies of Aetius and Boethius were laid out in the forum for all to see so that their friends would desist from attempting to rise against Valentinian.

According to Hydatius (a.454), Valentinian's first order of importance was to send envoys to the barbarian tribes to secure their continued loyalty, but this was apparently ineffective; Sidonius's text makes it clear that the barbarians broke their treaties almost immediately. In short, the murder of Aetius had several immediate consequences: Aetius's friend Marcellinus revolted in Dalmatia; the Ripuarian Franks revolted; the Alamanni revolted; the Saxons exploited the situation and invaded; the Visigoths revolted; and Gaiseric once again renounced his alliance with West Rome and resumed his piratical raids. In addition to this, Valentinan and Eudoxia now recalled their favourite Majorian from early retirement and appointed him *Com. Dom.* They clearly intended to make him heir apparent by marrying him with Placidia, but this was not to be.

The exact position of Marcellinus in Dalmatia is not known. He may have been a *dux*, *comes* or *MVM Dalmatiae*, but he was to play an important role in the events that unfolded. His military campaigns prove that he possessed significant numbers of land forces and a fleet. This is not surprising because Dalmatia needed sizable forces against the Huns and other barbarians. We do not know whether Marcellinus's land forces included regulars, but his army was disciplined and well-equipped and included large numbers of 'Scythians' (presumably mainly Huns, but may also have included other tribesmen like Goths) in 461. It is not known whether the 'Scythians' were federates or *bucellarii* or both, but it is clear that Marcellinus must have possessed very significant numbers of *bucellarii* for him to be able to take the whole of Dalmatia as his own personal domain/ fiefdom. The composition of his fleet has caused much speculation among historians, some claiming that he had true war galleys, others claiming that his fleet consisted merely of levied or hired ships, the numbers of which were occasionally bolstered by the eastern fleet. My own view is that Marcellinus had at his disposal a small number of real war galleys that had been detached to the city of Salona in the past (i.e. after 425) in addition to which he would have possessed some war galleys manned by civilian paramilitary forces against pirates, some war galleys that had been laid up in the docks, and levies of civilian galleys and sailing ships. We should not forget that the Dalmatians/Illyrians had long naval traditions![16]

Notably, Marcellinus was known to be a devout pagan and skilled soothsayer. In my opinion it is unlikely to be a coincidence that the two principal West Roman commanders of the Huns, Litorius and Marcellinus, were both pagans who practised soothsaying. This must have been a conscious decision taken by Aetius who would have known Hunnic culture intimately. The Huns clearly needed the encouragement provided by soothsayers before they would be prepared to engage the enemy. For the Romans however, the use of soothsaying appears to have been nothing but a cynical ploy to encourage the Hunnic mercenaries. The best evidence for this is that the cynic philosopher Sallustius of Emesa, who ridiculed the gods, was a close companion of Marcellinus. As a form of ridicule, Sallustius acted as if he were able to foretell a person's manner of death just by looking into his eyes. The use of soothsaying and the supernatural to control the morale of an army was nothing new. Military manuals from Frontinus onwards recommended that generals make use of superstitions and religion (e.g. ceremonies, standards, weather patterns, eagles, crosses, icons etc.) before and during battle. It is possible that Marcellinus may have used Sallustius as his personal undercover operative because it is known that Sallustius travelled widely barefoot and these travels would have enabled him to make observations and to carry messages inconspicuously. Note also the pairing of Illus with Pamprepius and King Arthur with Merlin. For the former see *MHLR* Vol.5 and for latter see my *Britain in the Age of Arthur*.

If Procopius's reasons for the death of Aetius are correct, then this stands as yet another example of the depraved sex life of the Emperor adversely affecting the destiny of the Empire. However, there is another possibility, which is that Maximus had pimped his wife when he became aware of Valentinian's desires, with the intention of taking Aetius's place as supreme leader. This version receives support from the fragment 201.4 of John of Antioch which states that after the murder of Aetius, Maximus at first sought to gain Aetius's position, and only when the Emperor failed to fulfil his wishes did Maximus move to kill the Emperor. This Maximus did by summoning Aetius's comrades-in-arms Optila (possibly Aetius's son-in-law) and Thraustila (both either Huns or Goths). He then accused the Emperor of the murder and promised to reward them if they killed Valentinian.

Maximus had chosen his accomplices well. Valentinian had made the foolish mistake of retaining these men as his bodyguards. A few days later when Valentinian, together with his bodyguards and followers of Optila and Thraustila, rode to the Campus Martius to train in archery, the conspirators struck. When Valentinian dismounted to shoot, Optila slew him with a sword while Thraustila killed Heraclius the same way. The killers took Valentinian's diadem and horse and presented them to Maximus. Valentinian had died on 16 March 455 at the age of 36 or 37 and Maximus became emperor on 17 March. There had been a short period during which there were three candidates for the throne. The military was divided in its support between two men, Maximus and Maximian (Maximinianus). The latter was the son of an Egyptian merchant called Dominus. The third contender for the throne was *Comes Domesticorum* Majorian who was favoured by the Empress and naturally by the imperial bodyguards. Maximus secured the throne for himself by bribing the palace guards and staff.

Aetius, the Last Roman

Aetius can justifiably be called the last Roman (Procopius' title for both Aetius and Boniface/Bonifatius) on the grounds that he was the last native Roman in the West who was able to hold the tottering whole together. He did so by playing the various different sides against each other in a great balancing act during the time he controlled the affairs of West Rome from 433 until his death in 454, despite the massive problems he inherited as a result of Honorius' policies, which had been worsened by the shipping of the Vandals to North Africa by Bonifatius' supporters.

Aetius in the so-called Diptych of Aetius (drawing by © Dr. Ilkka Syvänne 2014). I agree with Ian Hughes (Plate 1) that the individual in the Diptych appears older than Aetius, but I have included this drawing because one cannot entirely rule out the possibility that he is indeed Aetius.

Aetius lacked the financial means to build up a native Roman armed force to stem the tide in a situation in which the entire state apparatus, including its armed forces, was wracked by massive corruption and in which the rich senatorial class refused to contribute its fair share for the defence of the Empire. Aetius' principal problem was that he needed to court senatorial opinion, at least to the extent that the senators did not actively seek a way to overthrow him, so as to enable him to secure his own position vis-à-vis the Emperor. This left him the only option of relying on federate and private forces for most of the fighting while the regular native forces were massed together into a single field army for the protection of Italy and/or Gaul. It is possible that this suited his personal ambitions, because these forces were loyal to him and in most cases only to him. However, it is clear that Aetius still did his best to increase the size of the regular field armies in the 440s, because the Edicts issued then prove that the Roman government recruited new men into the army and also sought to find revenue for their upkeep. This means that once Aetius was securely in power he was prepared to take such measures as were necessary even when this was not liked by the senators.

One of Aetius's greatest achievements was the creation of a loyal and capable class of native officers, the best examples of which are Avitus, Majorian and Marcellinus, all of whom were superb and brave military commanders. Marcellinus may in fact have been the most gifted commander of his age. In addition to this, Aetius schooled the future generalissimo Ricimer in the art of war, but in this case his legacy was not a good one, because in the years following the death of Aetius, Ricimer's actions contributed more than anything else to the downfall of the West. Ricimer was a barbarian whose only goal in life was to promote his career at the expense of all else. It was thanks to Ricimer's devious plotting against Avitus, Majorian and Marcellinus that these excellent native commanders failed to stem the barbarian onslaught against the Roman Empire. The barbarian that they should have dealt with first was their comrade-in-arms Ricimer.

Aetius' greatest achievement was undoubtedly his successful defence of Gaul. The defeat of Attila at the battle of the Catalaunian Fields in 451 was another great triumph for Aetius. Probably the greatest battle of antiquity, a true battle of nations, this was the beginning of the end for Attila. At least equal to this in importance was the successful defence of Italy with East Roman help against Attila in 452, even if Aetius has not been given his due for this, largely thanks to the mix-up of the two Aetiuses by some modern authors. These two military campaigns, the defence of Gaul and Italy against the savage barbarian Huns, saved the western civilization from destruction. The defeats inflicted on the Huns by Aetius also ensured that the Eastern Empire would survive even if it is possible that the walls of Constantinople and its very effective naval forces might have been enough to ensure its survival anyway, but we cannot know that for certain because had the Huns conquered the West, they could have obtained a fleet to challenge the East Romans.

We in the Western World can therefore be particularly thankful to Aetius and Emperor Marcian, because it was ultimately their political and military decisions that saved the Greco-Roman civilization which by the nineteenth century had risen to a position of global dominance. Much has been lost recently as a result of two world wars and a cold war which have destroyed nations and empires much as the Roman civil wars destroyed them. Other civilizations have wisely copied from us what they have thought useful (e.g. scientific thinking) and are now turning our own former weapons against us.

Chapter Nine

Maximus 17 March–31 May 455 and the Sack of Rome by the Vandals[1]

Maximus's first order of importance was to secure his position. With this in mind, he married the widow Eudoxia, and married his son Palladius to Eudocia, the daughter of Eudoxia and Valentinian III, and made him Caesar. We do not know what happened to Maximus's first wife. This marriage made political sense because it tied Maximus with the ruling house. Eudoxia had wanted her favourite Majorian to take the throne, but Maximus managed to secure his position within the Palace with plentiful bribes after which he forced Eudoxia to marry him. John of Antioch claims that Maximus attempted to gain Eudoxia's acceptance by stating that he had killed Valentinian because he loved Eudoxia. If this was the real reason, the sexual desires of Maximus had really far reaching consequences because Eudoxia was not at all pleased that her husband had been killed. Since East Rome was now ruled by Marcian, Eudoxia decided to seek help from the Vandals and wrote to Gaiseric. She urged him to come to Rome to save her and her children from the usurper. Gaiseric was happy to oblige and sailed his fleet presumably to Portus and Ostia where he disembarked the troops. When the Vandals reached Azestus, a place near Rome, Maximus panicked and attempted to flee on horseback. Those who saw this started to insult him, calling him a coward with the result that the imperial bodyguards and the freemen deserted Maximus. It is quite possible the the future emperor Majorian, who was *Comes Domesticorum*, had a role in the death of Maximus. When Maximus was about to ride out of the gates someone threw a stone which hit him on the temple. Maximus fell to the ground dead and the mob tore his body into pieces and carried his limbs on poles while singing and shouting.

According to Sidonius's cryptic statement (Pan. Avit. 441ff.), when the Vandals were about to attack Rome, the traitorous Burgundian leadership caused Maximus to panic, and that led to his death. There are three possible explanations for this. Firstly, it is possible that the Burgundians made up part of the garrison of the city of Rome (e.g. as imperial bodyguards) and then abandoned the city. Secondly, it is possible that the Burgundian kings Gundiocus and Chilperic I (note that they were allied with the Visigoths in 455) had revolted at the same time as the Visigoths with the result that Maximus had felt it necessary to march north to protect the north of Italy. Thirdly, both of the previous explanations could be correct.

Gaiseric entered Rome three days later on 2 June 455 and subjected the city to fourteen days of such pillage that it had never seen before. It would have been easy for the Romans to protect their city by posting the populace and the imperial bodyguards on the walls against the Vandals, but since this was not done it is clear that Eudoxia prevented effective defence through her own personal interference. The Vandals carried to their ships all the wealth that they could carry, and Gaiseric took Eudoxia, Eudocia, Placidia

(Eudoxia's other daughter and wife of Olybrius) and Gaudentius son of Aetius, with him to Carthage, which provided a place of safe haven for them and their hostages. Gaiseric soon married Eudocia with his son Huneric and thereby connected his House with the Imperial House. He also claimed the right to the personal possessions of Eudoxia and Gaudentius.

Before his death however, Maximus had initiated other projects to secure his position. The most important of these was his appointment of Avitus as *MVM* (of Gaul or Praesental) to secure the support of the Gallic nobility. In addition to this, Avitus had to deal with the Saxon attacks against the Armorican coast (they used stitched boats made out of hides, i.e. Irish-style curraghs), the Frankish (Chatti) attacks against Germania I (capital Mainz) and Belgica II (capital Rheims), Alamannic attacks along the Rhine, and the mustering of the Visigothic army for an invasion of Roman territory. The Suevi had also renounced their treaties and were pillaging the areas of Carthagensis in 455 that they had previously surrendered back to the Romans in 452/3 (Hyd. 452–55). It is just possible that all these invasions and revolts could have resulted from the murder of Valentinian if messengers travelled really fast, but it is inherently more likely in light of the time it would have taken to organize the raids and invasions that all of these had resulted from the murder of Aetius in the fall and that the invasions just took place after the death of Valentinian because the traditional fighting season began in late March. It was clearly the name of Aetius that had kept the barbarians in check. According to Sidonius, when the Alamanni, Saxons and Franks learnt that Avitus, who had had a brilliant military career, had been appointed *MVM*, they all renewed the peace with Rome, but as we have seen this probably did not include the Burgundians who appear to have revolted just before the Vandal attack against Rome and were still in revolt after his death.

This left only the Visigoths to deal with, but since Avitus was a known friend of the Visigoths and had taught Latin to Theoderic II, he was in an excellent position to negotiate. Consequently, Avitus travelled to Bordeaux (where the Garonne met the tides of the ocean) to renew the peace treaty with Theoderic II. When Avitus was there, the news of the sack of Rome and death of Maximus arrived. Theoderic discussed the matter with his *duces* and the senate (the Visigothic elders) after which he urged Avitus to take the purple and promised his support. Avitus agreed and signed the treaty with the Visigoths when they all reached Toulouse. After this, Avitus convened the Gallic nobility in the hall of Viernum (Ugernum, mod. Beaucaire) near Arles who duly proclaimed him *Augustus* on 9 July 455. After this, Avitus assembled the army, which also duly declared its support. This was made possible by the lack of any desicive action in Italy in the aftermath of the sack of Rome. *Comes Domesticorum* Majorian, as the designated successor of Valentinian III, would have been the obvious choice, but he or his supporters failed to act in a timely manner. The threat posed by the combined forces of the Gallic army and the Visigoths may also have paralyzed all opposition at this stage.

Chapter Ten

Avitus 9 July 455–17 October 456[1]

Augustus Eparchius Avitus (455-456). Source: Hodgkin

Italy was ripe for the taking, but Avitus, the Visigoths, and the Gallic Field Army did not march straight into Rome, because, according to Sidonius (*Pan.Av.* 589–90), Avitus recovered the two Pannonias for the Empire at the very beginning of his rule. This means that Avitus advanced first against the territories held by the Ostrogoths on behalf of East Rome (see the reign of Marcian). Avitus was basically reacting to the settlement of *foederati* by the East Romans that had taken place in the previous year, 454, in which Marcian had effectively taken control of West Roman territory by settling the Ostrogoths in Pannonia. It is very unlikely that there would have been any fighting involved between the armies when Avitus reached Pannonia. Avitus had been chosen as Emperor by the Visigoths and Gauls and was accompanied by a Visigothic army and Visigothic bodyguards. This would have made him the ideal ruler also for the Ostrogoths. Therefore it is clear that the Ostrogoths were glad to become Avitus's *foederati* and to recognize him as their Emperor, but we should not forget that they did this while still receiving payments from Marcian in return for being his *foederati*. This was to become one of the causes of quarrel between the Ostrogoths and the Eastern Empire. See the reigns of Marcian and Leo.

There was another question that needed to be taken care before advancing into Italy, which was referred to by Sidonius in the context of Maximus' last days. The Burgundians needed to be pacified. It is probably in this context that we should see the referral in the so-called *Auctar.Prosp.Haun* (*MGH AA Chron. Min.* 1, p.304, a.455), which states that the Gepids attacked the Burgundians in 455. Katalin Escher (71–72) has suggested that the Gepids did this as allies of Rome, and this is indeed the likeliest reason. Avitus would have used the Gepids so that he could himself march with his Gallic army strengthened by the Visigoths first to Pannonia and from there to Italy. It is possible or even probable that Avitus stayed in Gaul until the Gepid attack had convinced the Burgundians to make a peace with him, but one cannot entirely rule out the possibility that he used the Gepid campaign as a diversion which allowed him to lead his forces to Pannonia while the attack against the Burgundians was still ongoing.

Even though there is no certainty regarding the dating of the appointment of Aegidius as *MVM per Gallias* I would suggest that Avitus kept Agrippinus as *MVM per Gallias* and that Aegidius was appointed as his successor by Majorian. See later. Avitus's *Mag. Ped.* was Remistus who was probably a Visigoth and his *Mag.Eq.* was Ricimer. It was the latter who was destined to become Aetius's successor as the power behind the throne. However, unlike Aetius, Ricimer was a pure-bred barbarian who was closely linked to three Germanic royal families. His father belonged to the royal family of the Suevi, his mother a Visigoth (daughter of Vallia) and his sister had married the Burgundian king Gundioc. In addition to this, he had had a long and distinguished military career under Aetius in the course of which he had befriended Majorian.

After having been confirmed as Emperor by the Roman people (i.e. the Senate), Avitus sent ambassadors to Constantinople to seek their acceptance. It is not known whether this was successful, but most historians think that the Eastern government did not recognize Avitus; but the fact that both halves of the Empire appear to have coordinated their actions towards the Vandals seems to contradict this. Similarly, it is possible to see Sidonius's statement (*Pan.* 589–90) that Avitus recovered the two Pannonias merely with a march either as a sign of cooperation between the empires to subject the Ostrogoths under Roman rule, or as Avitus's way to put pressure on the eastern empire by subjecting the Ostrogoths under his rule. The latter is actually more likely because we find the East Romans denying payments to the Ostrogoths after this. So there is no certainty about this, but in light of the presence of Marcian's fleet close to Corsica (see below) I would suggest that it is more likely that the Eastern Empire did indeed lend its support, even if it was more modest than before. Avitus's position was also precarious because the Italian nobility was very apprehensive of being ruled by a Gaul who brought with him his own supporters from Gaul, a Visigothic army and Visigothic bodyguards. In addition to this, Avitus had to prove himself a successful defender of Italy against the Vandals who had just sacked Rome. It was the Eastern Emperor who dispatched the first ambassador to Gaiseric with the demand that he was to stop his raids against Italy (this implies some cooperation between the courts) and to hand over the Empress and her daughters. This produced no results. It was then that Avitus dispatched his own envoys which reminded Gaiseric of his agreements; Avitus threatened to use his own army and allies if Gaiseric failed to abide by the treaty. Gaiseric's response was to send his fleet to ravage Sicily and the areas (presumably Bruttium) close to it (*Priscus*).[2]

Avitus dispatched Ricimer to Sicily with an army where Ricimer inflicted a crushing defeat on the Vandals on the plain of Agrigentum (Agrigento). The sources do not provide any details, but it seems probable that Ricimer cleared Bruttium of the Vandals before shipping his army across to Sicily at the Straits of Messina. Even though Sidonius refers only to the victorious land battle on the plains of Agrigentum, it is still probable that

Ricimer would have used his fleet to transport supplies and simultaneously to attack the anchored Vandal fleet from the sea. The Roman war effort would have been aided by the fact that Agrigentum was one of the metropolises of the ancient world and on top of that well-fortified. According to modern estimates it had a population of 200,000–600,000, while Laertius claimed that it had a population of 800,000. Its urban area covered 456 hectares and the walls were 12.9 km long with nine gates. The city also had natural defences in the form of hills, gorges and hollows. In short, it is clear that the Vandals would have needed a huge army to besiege the place and even then they would have faced serious troubles.[3]

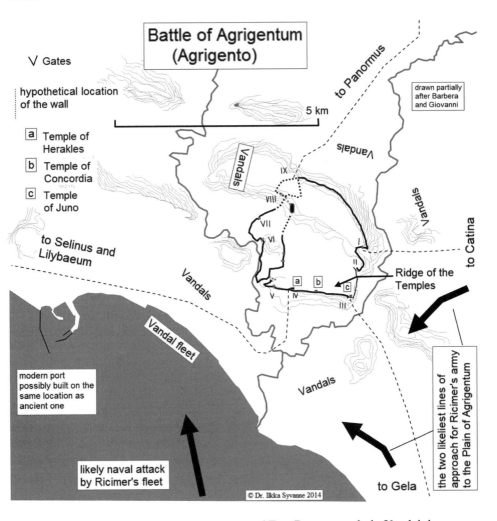

It is no wonder that at this time both West and East Romans took the Vandal threat very seriously. They had not only sacked Rome, but Sidonius's list of tribes (Pan.Maj. 335ff.) subjected by Gaiseric proves that the Vandals had conquered Mauretania Tingitana (Autololi), Mauretania Caesariensis, Numidia (Numidians, Gaetuli) and Tripolitania (Garamantes, Arzuges, Psylli, Nasamones, Marmaridae) by about 456/8. The last two

(Nasamones and Marmaridae) suggest the possibility that the Vandals may have also invaded East Roman territory just south of Cyrenican Pentapolis. It is no wonder that even the Alexandrians felt threatened!

According to Hydatius (a.456), Avitus sent a message to Theoderic in Spain that Ricimer had destroyed through stratagem/encirclement/ambush a Vandal naval detachment consisting of sixty ships in Italy which had been advancing towards Gaul. The next sentence suggests that it was actually destroyed off Corsica because it states that a multitude of Vandals had died in Corsica at a time when Avitus had moved from Italy to Arles in Gaul. It is possible, however, that the Vandals had actually been destroyed by the East Roman fleet (or marines?) serving under Ricimer, because it was the Easterners who arrived in ships at Hispalis and reported a bloody victory by Marcian's army.[4] Still another possibility is that these are two separate incidents, so that in the former case Ricimer had destroyed sixty Vandal ships in Italy (possibly at Agrigento in Sicily), while in the latter case the East Romans had killed a multitude of Vandals at a time when Avitus had fled to Arles. This would have been the first example of Marcian's changing attitude to the Vandals towards the end of his rule. I would suggest that the latter is true and that we are here dealing with two separate defeats suffered by the Vandals. MacGeorge notes that the vocabulary used by Hydatius doesn't necessarily mean that the encounter was a naval battle. In her opinion, the Vandals could have been ambushed after they had embarked their forces. Considering that the news included the number of ships and the word meaning encirclement/ambush this is a distinct possibility, but I would suggest that it is still very probable that the action included also the use of a Roman fleet, so that Roman ships were either able to surprise the Vandal ships at anchor or were able to encircle them from the sea side so that the Vandals had land behind them. These victories naturally strengthened Ricimer's standing among the military.

In the meantime, the Suevi under their king Rechiarius had continued their ravaging of the Roman territory with the result that Avitus sent the *comes* Fronto and Mansuetus as his envoy to demand the immediate evacuation of the territories invaded at the same time as Theoderic II dispatched his own envoys to the Suevi for the same purpose (Hyd a.456.; Jord *Get.* 230ff.). The Suevi responded by invading Tarraconensis. Their attack met with success and they were able to take large numbers of captives and booty back to their own territory in Gallaecia. Avitus dispatched the angered Theoderic II to Spain.

Theoderic's forces consisted of his own men and of the Burgundians under their kings Gundioc and Hilperic. The Burgundians had been promised Lyon and other territories in Gaul in return for their assistance.[5] Rechiarius's army opposed the allies at the River Urbicus/Ulbius twelve miles from the city of Asturica (Astorga) on Friday, 5 October 456. The deployment of the forces in defensive position behind a river was typical for those who feared the Gothic cavalry charge. The Burgundians were deployed on the left and the Visigoths on the right. The Visigoths crushed their opposition and annihilated almost the entire enemy force. Rechiarius was wounded by a javelin but still managed to flee via Bracara to Portus Cale (Oporto). The Visigoths were admitted into Bracara without opposition, but the Visigoths paid this kindness back by sacking it on Sunday, 28 October 456. Since Avitus had been overthrown on 17 October (see below), it is just possible that the sack of the city resulted from this if the news of this had been brought by relays of fast moving horsemen to Theoderic. However, since Hydatius (a.457) states that Theoderic was in or close to Emerita (Merita) when he received the news of the death, it seems likelier that Theoderic just rewarded his men by allowing them to pillage. The Visigoths took many Roman captives from Bracara including nuns and children. The churches were turned into stables.

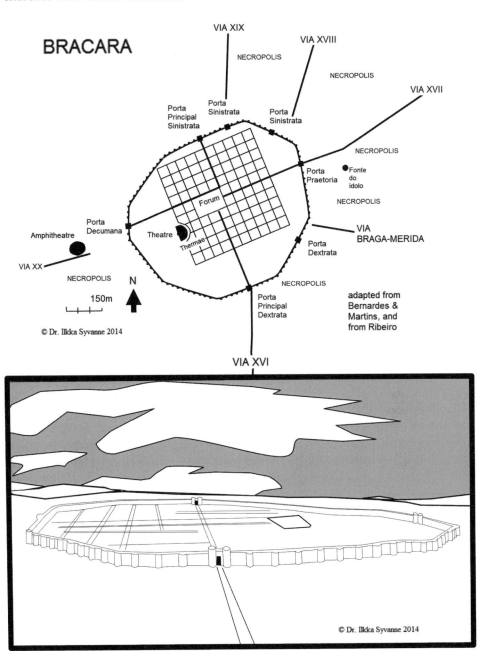

After this, the Visigoths continued their pursuit of the defeated foe and caught him at Portus Cale. Rechiarius had attempted to flee in a ship before the arrival of the Visigoths, but then unluckily for him the adverse wind forced his ship back into the harbour. Theoderic executed Rechiarius in December 456 and then continued his march to Lusitania with the result that Aiolfus deserted the Visigoths intending to become king of the Suevi in Gallaecia. But the Suevi of Gallaecia chose Maldras (or Masdra) as their new king. This resulted in a chaos which was exploited by some bandits who pillaged part of the assizes (*conventus*) of Bracara.

Ricimer knew that his opportunity to overthrow Avitus had come when Avitus's supporters, the Visigoths, were preoccupied with the Suevic war. Avitus's position in Italy was very weak because he had not been able to gather enough support for his cause among the Italian upper classes and among the field army posted there. In fact Avitus had managed to do the exact opposite, so he became even more hated. Avitus had appointed his Gallic supporters to high positions; the populace blamed him for the hunger they were facing thanks to the Vandalic war; he had been forced to strip the metal (mainly bronze) from public buildings to reward his Visigothic supporters and Visigothic bodyguards, which angered the senators in particular. The Italian senators demanded that Avitus send these Visigoths back to Gaul and when he did this after he had cashiered them with money, he sealed his own fate.

According to Gregory of Tours 2.11 and Fredegar 3.7, Avitus was overthrown by the senators because he was a libidinous debaucher of women. According to the latter, Avitus had raped senator Lucius's wife with the result that Lucius betrayed his native city of Trier to the Franks. Fredegar's account is not among the most reliable sources for this period, but if the account of the sack of Cologne and Trier by the Franks in the *LHF 8* is dated to 456/7 then it is possible that Trier could have been betrayed by this Lucius as claimed by Fredegar. However, it is likelier that this actually occurred in 465 because the *LHF* connects this account with events of that year (see later) or even as early as 411 as suggested by Hodgkin (3.393–5) so that Fredegar would have mistaken Iovinus for Avitus. Nevertheless, it is by no means impossible that Gregory and Fredegar are right.

When Avitus could no longer hope to obtain help from the Visigoths, Ricimer decided to act. Two explanations have been put forth for the revolt of Ricimer. Firstly, it is possible that the principal reason for Ricimer's revolts was his lust for power and that he intended from the start to make his friend Majorian emperor, because as a barbarian he could not become one. Since Majorian belonged to the Italian nobility and was supported by the former soldiers of Aetius this was a wise choice. The second of the reasons put forth by Ian Hughes (2015, 63–64) is that Ricimer and Majorian both acted because the hostility of the Roman senators of Italian origin was just too great towards Avitus and that both men just acted in the interest of the Italian nobility. I agree with Ian Hughes's view that the two men were indeed acting on behalf of the Roman Senate in this case. Furthermore, the fact that Avitus was not in the East Roman 'good books' after his Pannonian campaign, which is proven by the refusal of Marcian to recognize the West Roman consul, meant that both men could also expect to be rewarded by the East Roman emperor Marcian for their great services to the Roman Republic.

When the two men declared their revolt, Ricimer marched to Ravenna where he murdered Remistus and anyone else who supported Avitus. There are several different versions of what happened next. John of Antioch (fr. 202) states that the rebels attacked Avitus near Placentia when he was attempting to reach Gaul, but according to the more credible account of Hydatius (a.456), Avitus managed to flee to Arles from which he dispatched tribune Hesychius with gifts to ask Theoderic's help. This same embassy brought the news of the naval victory off the coast of Corsica. The Visigoths were apparently unable to provide any assistance even if it appears likely that they sought to end their war with the Suevi immediately with the result that Avitus was forced to rely on the forces available to him near the city of Arles. These must have consisted primarily of the regular units posted in the cities and of the Alans settled nearby. Avitus appointed Messianus as *MVM Praes.* and marched his forces into Italy. The armies fought a decisive battle near Placentia on 17 October 456, which Ricimer and Majorian won. Messianus was killed while Avitus fled inside Placentia. Avitus was allowed to retire as Bishop of Placentia, but was then killed by Majorian's men. According to Gregory of Tours's version (2.11), when Avitus learnt that the 'Senate' still wanted to kill him, he decided to flee to the church of St.Julian in Clermont, but died en route. As noted by Ian Hughes, the truth of the matter must be that Avitus was attempting to flee to Clermont to raise a revolt against the usurpers and that Majorian's forces caught up with him and then killed him.

The defeat of Avitus at Placentia brought with it a series of new troubles, not least of which was the fact that large numbers of regulars and Alans that had previously protected south-east Gaul had now been killed. The loss of these forces was very costly for the West Roman Empire when the Burgundians and Visigoths started to advance into this area, and the overthrow of Avitus naturally caused them to revolt.

Chapter Eleven

The East: The Reign of Marcian
(Marcianus, 25 August 450–27 January 457)

The Rise

On 26 July 450 Theodosius II died as a result of a riding accident. Before his death he had agreed to renew the humiliating peace with Attila with even more humiliating terms than before. Theodosius' aim was to buy peace from the Huns so that he could support the Persarmenian revolt against the Persians. This policy decision had brought him into direct conflict with the Isaurian *MVM per Orientem* Zeno/ Zenon, and it was to be expected that Theodosius would have to eliminate him first. The death of Theodosius obviously altered the picture.

The Western Emperor Valentinian III was now the sole ruler of the Roman Empire, but the East Romans would not agree to be ruled by him. The Easterners chose Marcian as their new Emperor. Marcian owed his nomination to the support of the *Augusta* Pulcheria, the grey eminence behind the throne, and to the barbarian military faction of the Alan Aspar. It is quite clear that Aspar must have contributed to Marcian's

Augustus Marcianus = emperor Marcian (450-457)
Source: Hodgkin

drawing by Beger 1696

unexpected rise to dominance because Marcian had been Aspar's *domesticus*. Marcian's appointment was also supported by the Isaurian *MVM per Orientem* Zenon/Zeno, who promoted a more aggressive stance against Attila. This meant that the military faction that had lost its power in the course of the years 447–50 had now regained its position thanks to the support of Pulcheria which gave it legitimacy. Marcian's rise to the throne was secured with a marriage to Pulcheria. It seems probable that Marcian had managed to gain Pulcheria's backing by making promises regarding religious policies, the most important of which would be the assembly of a Church Council at Nicaea, which was then transferred to Chalchedon. Obviously one cannot preclude the possibility that Pulcheria would also have had sexual urges, because despite the official version that Marcian did not sleep with Pulcheria, the loose-tongued claimed otherwise. Initially the government of Valentinian III refused to recognize the nomination of Marcian as he did not belong to the imperial family, but military realities, namely the threat posed by the Huns, soon forced him to give his official recognition.

Once it was agreed among the powerbrokers that Marcian would be the Emperor, Marcian and his supporters moved to secure their position. Marcian obtained the support of both the Senate and the army, and was enthroned on 25 August 450 by Pulcheria who handed him the imperial diadem. It is probable that Marcian did this by promising to change the policy of payments to the Huns and by promising financial concessions to the senators. Therefore it is not surprising that among Marcian's first measures was the beheading of the eunuch Chrysaphius (Malalas 14.32–4) who had to have been the brains behind the appeasement of the Huns and who was also the personal enemy of Pulcheria. We should also see Marcian's support of the Blue Faction in every city in this same light. It was a change of policy from the one previously adopted by Chrysaphius who was a supporter of the Greens. Naturally this did not prevent the most ardent fans from continuing their support of the Greens, as can be evidenced from the riot they caused presumably at Constantinople just five months before the death of Marcian from gangrene which caused Marcian to announce a sacred decree according to which the Greens were forbidden to hold any public offices for three years.

Indeed, the reign of Marcian signified an abrupt break with the policies of his predecessor. Marcian was a native of the Balkans and the neglect shown towards this region was to stop. Instead of letting the Huns roam free in the Balkans or be paid to stay away while the Roman armies would fight in the East, or in Italy, or against the Vandals, the Balkans now became a top priority while other fronts were neglected – and there were troubles in the East and in the south. Marcian and his backers had decided to stop payments to the Huns and they had also decided to maintain peace with Persia. Consequently, when the Persian embassy in 450 came to Constantinople to ask what the Romans intended to do with the Armenians, the answer was that the Persians had a free hand to do as they pleased.[1] In contrast, when Attila's envoys came to Constantinople, they were told that the Romans would no longer pay any tribute to them. In addition to this, Marcian abandoned Theodosius' aggressive policies towards the Vandals so that he could concentrate his forces against his enemies in the Balkans.

Religious Policy

As noted above, one of the reasons for Pulcheria's support for Marcian had been his readiness to back up Pulcheria's religious views. It was primarily because of this that Marcian called together the Fourth Ecumenical Council at Chalcedon in late 451, but the urging of Pope Leo I had a role in it too. The idea was to abandon the decisions adopted at the so-called Robber Council (*Latrocinium*) held at Ephesus in 449 that had supported the views of Eutyches, and which had also led to a quarrel between Pope Leo I and Constantinople. The fact that Marcian pardoned Nestorius and allowed him to return to explain his views at the Council suggests that Marcian thought, at least initially, that it would be possible to reincorporate the Nestorians back into the fold of the Orthodox Church. However, this was not to be because Nestorius died en route so that the assembled clerics eventually condemned the Nestorians, Eutychians and the Monophysites as heretics, and declared that Christ had one nature consisting of both the human and the divine. This was actually a wise policy in a situation in which Marcian intended to cooperate with the Westerners against the Huns. However, the council made one decision that proved highly unpopular for Leo I and his successors, namely giving the Archbishop of Constantinople control over all of the eastern churches. At this time, however, it was not significant enough to hinder cooperation. As noted by Nathan, Marcian was also quite prepared to support the policies adopted at the Council with military force so that when the Palestinian monks revolted against the Chalcedon, Marcian sent an army to crush it, and similarly he used military force in support of Proterius, the Archbishop of Alexandria. The idea had undoubtedly been to provide one universally acceptable formula for all Christians, but in practice the so-called Monophysites in the East were never willing to accept the decisions taken at Chalcedon and have not done so even today. According to Haarer, the key point of disagreement for the Monophysites was that by acknowledging that Christ was 'in two natures' rather than 'of two natures', the Council of Chalcedon had gone too far.[2]

Zachariah of Mitylene (Book 3), also known as Zachariah the Rhetor, and Evagrius (2.1–8) provide us with a picture of what happened as a result of the decisions of the Council of Chalcedon. Firstly, the banishment of the Bishop of Alexandria, Dioscorus, to Gangra in Paphlagonia led to trouble when the new bishop Proterius reached Alexandria, presumably in 452. The people rioted presumably because the local monks incited them to do so. When the soldiers (presumably the military retinues protecting the bishop) attempted to intervene, the people routed them with volleys of stones and forced them to seek shelter inside the former temple of Serapis (Serapeum), which the populace duly torched so that all of the soldiers were killed. When the news of this was brought to Marcian he dispatched 2,000 new recruits, which reached Alexandria on the sixth day thanks to the favourable winds, probably in 452. The drunken soldiers abused the local women with impunity and to make matters even worse Florus, the *Comes Aegypti* and *Praefectus Augustalis*, deprived the Alexandrians of the grain allowance, shows and the use of baths. It is probable that Florus had been appointed to hold both the civilian and military positions precisely because of the civil troubles in Alexandria. In the end the populace gathered in the hippodrome where they begged Florus to restore the grain allowance, shows and baths, and stop the abuse by the soldiers. Florus agreed to do this at the instigation of Priscus, probably also in 452 but possibly in 453/4. However, the Alexandrians and other Egyptians were not only subjected to abuse by the military but also to abuse by Proterius, who used the military forces serving under the governors and expelled all those who opposed him after which he confiscated/stole their property but was still wise enough to give part of the loot to the soldiers to keep them happy. Eventually this abuse led to further trouble towards the very end of Marcian's reign, which is discussed later.[3]

The second of the major consequences took place in the Holy Land/Three Palestines, when the monk Theodosius brought back home the news to the local monks and clerics that the Bishop of Jerusalem Juvenalis/Juvenal had backed away from his promise and had signed the Chalcedon Creed. When the local monks raised trouble, Juvenal was forced to flee to Constantinople after which the locals chose Theodosius as their new bishop. Theodosius in his turn appointed new bishops, one of whom was Peter the Iberian, who had been given as a hostage by his father the king of Iberia during the reign of Theodosius II. Bishop Theodosius appointed him Bishop of Maiuma/Gaza. When the news of this was brought to the Emperor, he dispatched *comes* Dorotheus with an army to install Juvenal back on his throne presumably in about 452. The orders were to imprison Theodosius and to depose the bishops nominated by him with the exception of Peter the Iberian who was protected by Pulcheria. When the army reached Neapolis, they came across a large number of monks. Juvenal tried to reason with them, but when this failed, the soldiers and Samaritans who were accompanying him were ordered to kill the lot. The presence of the Samaritans among the armed retinue of the bishop is interesting because it proves that the Samaritans could provide armed forces for the imperial authorities when required to do so. It seems probable that these would have consisted of the members of the local paramilitary citizen militia/police forces. Zachariah claims that some of the Roman soldiers felt pity towards the monks, but that the Samaritans were absolutely ruthless. It is impossible to know whether this was the case, but what is certain is that the Samaritans would not have had any religious compunction that might have hindered them in the performance of their duty. The surviving 'believers' were captured and then exiled; even Peter the Iberian chose to follow them into exile after a short pondering. This, however, was not the end of the story, for the Samaritans, who had assisted in the crushing of the Monophysites, revolted in 453 at the same time as the Arabs were invading.

The Romans cooperate against the Huns: The operations in Illyricum and Italy in 451–452

As noted above, the East Roman military operations against Attila the Hun met with great success in the years 451–2. This is particularly true of the joint defence of Italy against the Huns in 452 in which the role of the Eastern armies was decisive. The expeditionary Eastern army and fleet sent to Ravenna not only saved Italy from immediate collapse, but the main army of the East in the Balkans created a diversion/distraction to the Huns. One can with good reason state that one of the most important decisions of the fifth century was that of Marcian to fight against the Huns in support of the West; it probably saved most of Europe from the savage Huns. This decision has not received its due merit mainly thanks to misrepresenation of the evidence. The price Marcian had to pay was Armenia, which in retrospect was a small price to pay for the East Romans – the Armenians naturally had a different opinion – but for the Romans (and others in Europe) the threat of the Huns of Attila was far more important at the time. If West Rome had fallen under the Hun yoke, East Rome would have been in very serious trouble. In short, from the point of view of Roman and European history, Marcian's decision to fight against the Huns was among the wisest decisions ever made. Thanks to the military defeats inflicted by the two halves of the Roman Empire, the prestige of the Hun military machine was so badly weakened that when Attila died in 453 his subjects were prepared to revolt against their barbarian overlords – the Hun military had been proven vulnerable when its enemy was well-led, motivated, and possessed enough men.

It is also quite possible or even probable that it was thanks to the decision to stop payments to the Huns that Marcian was able to abolish the progressive land tax called *follis* that had been instituted by Constantine the Great. The tax had been very unpopular among the senators and had created very little income for the state. Therefore Marcian's decision was at the same time very popular among the class whose support he needed, and caused no significant loss in revenues especially when there was no longer a need to pay protection money to the Huns. The abolishment of this tax also ensured the support of the moneyed elite towards Marcian in a situation in which his only source of legitimacy was his marriage to Pulcheria. Because of this he no longer required the praetors and consuls to hold games at their own expense and consuls to distribute wealth to the populace of Constantinople. Furthermore, he restricted the holding of these two offices only to the highest ranking senators, the *illustres*. The remission of all old taxes to the state was also particularly beneficial to the richest of the rich. It is possible that even the attempt to put a stop to the sale of offices had similar intent, even if it is clear that this policy was beneficial both for the taxpayers and also for the efficiency of the administration. However, even if it is probable that this campaign did achieve some success, it is still clear that it did not end the corrupt practice altogether because future emperors were required to pay attention to this same problem. We do not know why Marcian abolished Constantine's law which forbade senators from marrying poor women (*humilis*), but at least those senators who loved such women would certainly have found this policy enlighted.[4]

Marcian strengthened his position further by marrying his daughter Aelia Marcia Euphemia into one of the great houses of the East. His choice fell on Anthemius, son of the *MVM* Procopius and grandson of the *PPO* Anthemius. He intended to groom Anthemius as his successor. The choice was a good one. Anthemius belonged to the Houses of Constantine and Anthemius and so was ideally suited to be emperor. On top of that, he proved to be a brilliant military commander.

The Death of Attila in 453: East or West Roman Special Operation?

The cause of the very timely death of Attila has been a mystery ever since it took place and there exist many different versions as to the cause. What is known with certainty is that at the beginning of the year 453 Attila took a new wife whose name was Ildico, then spent the night in feasting and drinking, and after he and his wife entered the bedroom, the king was not seen alive again. When Attila did not appear in the morning the bodyguards broke the doors and encountered a most unwelcome sight: Ildico was weeping hysterically over the dead body of Attila and there was blood on the floor. When no wound was found, it was concluded that the cause of death had been haemorrhage through the nose. Some of the men present and some of the sources suspected Ildico of murder while others thought that Attila had died of natural causes.

According to Jordanes (Get. 254) and Theophanes (AM 5946), drunken Attila suffocated in his sleep in his own blood. Marcellinus Comes (a.453–4) and *Chronicon Paschale* (a.450) included two versions: Attila was stabbed to death or killed in some other way by his wife; Attila was drowned in his own blood. Malalas 14.10 includes three versions: The first is once again the accidental haemorrhage through the nose during the night when he was sleeping with his Hunnish concubine and the second version according to which Ildico was suspected of the murder (both versions credited to Priscus); the third version, from other sources, claimed that Aetius the Patrician had bribed Attila's *spatharius* to stab him. I would add fourth and fifth versions to the above. According to Jordanes (Get. 255 after Priscus), on the same night that Attila died Marcian had a dream in which the bow of Attila was broken, with the implication that the power of the Huns would be broken. On the basis of this, I would suggest the possibility that this was Priscus's way to tell his audience that Attila had been murdered in a special operation set in motion by Marcian. When the message was conveyed in this way, Priscus could claim that the Easterners had not been guilty of the murder while still implying this. The fifth version would be that Ildico acted on behalf of her relatives who wanted to murder Attila to gain freedom from his rule.

It is impossible to know which of these versions is correct, but it would not have been beyond the means or character of either Aetius or Marcian to hire an assassin to do the job for them and for this to be hidden from the official record by Priscus. The Huns would certainly not have wanted to advertise that the death of their beloved leader had been brought about by an assassin hired by the Romans.

The Collapse of the Hun Empire in 453/4

Jordanes describes the collapse of the Hun Empire in his *Getica* (259ff.) and this is basically all that we know of it. According to him, when Attila died, his successors, his sons, started a civil war against each other which led to the collapse of the Hunnic Empire. The tribes and tribal confederations with their kings resented the fact that Attila's sons treated them like a family estate that coud be divided. When the king of the Gepidae, Ardaric, learned of the fighting, he became enraged because he thought that he, who had been highly appreciated by Attila, was now being treated like the basest of slaves. Consequently he was the first to rise against the sons of Attila. According to Jordanes, he was attended by good fortune so that he was able to throw away the disgrace of servitude. His revolt did not only free his own tribe, but all the other tribes who had been equally oppressed. These tribes then took up arms against their common enemy the Huns, and joined battle against them in Pannonia near a river called Nedao. The location is unknown, but it was clearly in that part of Pannonia which had previously been in Gothic and then in Hunnic hands and which after this battle was given back to the Goths. For an analysis of the location, see Maenchen-Helfen, (147ff.). According to Jordanes, there were various nations on both sides who then tore themselves to pieces. He claimed that the sight was a spectacle in which the eyewitnesses could see the Goths fighting with pikes, the Gepids fighting with swords, the Rugi breaking off the spears in their own wounds, the Suevi fighting on foot, the Huns with bows, the Alani arraying a battle-line of heavy-armed and the Heruli of light-armed warriors. This description gives a very generalized image of the battle so that each nation is presented in stereotypical terms with their typical arms and tactics. Regardless, the description is likely to be accurate because it is clear that the Germanic peoples would have sought contact with the enemy and it is in this context that one should see the use of swords by the Gepids. Their king had ordered them to charge into contact with the enemy immediately. The use of swords would also have signalled to the enemy that this was a fight to the death and it seems to have had the desired psychological impact because the Huns lost the battle. One of the tactics used in antiquity was to order the men to fight only with the sword so that they would be forced to advance straight at the enemy. In short, the use of this desperate tactic signalled to the enemy that their foes meant business with all of its psychological implications.

According to Jordanes, the fighting involved many bitter fights after which victory fell unexpectedly to the Gepidae. This may mean that the battle lasted for a long time despite the desperate tactic of using swords. Jordanes claims that Ardaric destroyed almost thirty thousand men, Huns as well as those of the other nations who had brought them aid. This implies that the Gepids bore the brunt of the fighting and that most of the other tribes sided with the Huns. The list of nations that were subsequently handed lands south of the Danube by the Romans suggests that the allies of the Huns consisted of the Sarmatians, Cemandri, Sciri, Sadagarii, and Alani/Alans, and it is also likely that they included Ostrogoths. It is likely that the Heruls and Suevi sided with the Gepids. Similarly, it is possible that the Rugi sided with them too, because they sought land far away from the other *foederati*, but it is more likely that their nation was divided.

The casualties included Ellac, the elder son of Attila, who fell after he had killed several enemies. Jordanes suggests that his death was so glorious and brave that if his father had lived, he would have rejoiced. When Ellac was slain, Jordanes claims that his remaining brothers were put to flight near the shore of the Sea of Pontus, where the Goths had settled earlier. This implies that there was a second battle somewhere north of the Danube on the shore of the Black Sea. If the location can be used as a clue, it is possible that the Gepids would have pushed the Huns against the sea so that the second battle would have been even more disastrous to the Huns than the battle of Nedao. The victory of Ardaric, king of the Gepids, broke the chains that had kept the Hun Empire together, so that their subjects were free to seek their own fortunes. According to Jordanes, many sent ambassadors to Roman territory, and were most graciously received by Marcian. In my opinion this implies that the defeated side, those tribes that had supported the Huns, were the ones who now sought safety in Roman territory.

To sum up, the humiliation of being treated as a slave caused Ardaric and his Gepids to rise against the Huns. This was opportune after the death of Attila in a situation in which his sons were divided and when the defeats of the previous years had proved the Huns to be human after all. In spite of this, most of the subject nations still appear to have sided with the Huns, but thanks to the apparently superb generalship of Ardaric the enemies were decisively crushed in two battles that ended the Hun threat forever. Jordanes' referral to the use of swords by the Gepids and to the light equipment of the Heruls should be seen as an indication of their desperate resolve. In my opinion this should be taken as a hint that both nations charged straight at the enemy to limit the time they had to spend under fire. It also suggests that the greater resolve implied by their equipment carried the day because they appear to have been able to defeat even the Goths and Alans in close quarters fighting.

The Settlement of the Federates in the Balkans in 454–457

Marcian started to promote Anthemius's career immediately after the marriage with his daughter had been consummated. Anthemius was appointed *comes rei militaris* and dispatched to reorganize the Danube frontier in the immediate aftermath of the collapse of the Hunnic Empire in about 453/4. He examined, arranged and equipped forces as needed and was apparently the person responsible for the resettlement of the various tribes that had made up the Hunnic Realm along the Danube frontier as federates. From the East Roman point of view this seemed like a wise policy move because the frontier was entirely in ruins and needed new settlers and defenders. The other benefit of this was that it turned hostile barbarians into allies. Anthemius was duly rewarded for his services with the position of *MVM* which he held from 454 until 467. He was also rewarded with the consulship and with the title of *patricius*, both in 455. His services for the empire were clearly great and well-appreciated.[5]

Jordanes *Getica* (264ff.) describes the settlement of the barbarian federates in Roman territory in the following terms. He states that when the Goths saw that the Gepids had conquered the territory of the Huns (presumably roughly the area of modern Hungary-Romania) and defended it ably, and that the Huns had retreated into the ancient abodes of the Goths in modern Ukraine-Russia, the Goths (Ostrogoths) asked for lands from the Roman Empire in preference to attempting to obtain the lands currently held by the Gepids or Huns. On the basis of this information it is uncertain whether this group of Ostrogoths had sided with the Huns or with the Gepids. The reason for thinking that the Ostrogoths would have sided with the Gepids is that the Ostrogoths were settled in a separate territory rather than together with the Hunnic groups like the other settlers and because the Huns then attacked them almost immediately. On balance, however, it would still seem more likely that the Ostrogoths had at least initially sided with the losing side, because the other groups which were settled on Roman territory were seeking a place of refuge and it would be odd that the Ostrogoths would have been a special case. What is certain, however, is that the Ostrogoths abandoned their alliance after the Huns had been defeated by the Gepids. Whatever the case, the fact that these Ostrogoths felt themselves too weak to challenge the Gepids and Huns on their own suggests that they had suffered badly in the wars fought in Gaul, Italy and then during the war of liberation. According to Jordanes, Marcian granted them Pannonia, which occupied a long plain bordered in the east by Upper Moesia, in the south by Dalmatia, in the west by Noricum and in the north by the Danube. There were several cities in the area, the easternmost being Sirmium and the north-westernmost Vindobona. By doing this Marcian basically took control of areas which officially belonged to West Rome. The Sarmatians, the Cemandri and certain of the Huns were granted territory in Castra Martis. It is probable that these consisted of such Sarmatians and Cemandri that had stayed loyal to the Huns, because their numbers included them. Jordanes noted that Blivila, the Duke of Pentapolis, and his brother Froila, and also Bessas, a Patrician in Jordanes' time, originated from these tribesmen. The Sciri, the Sadagarii (an unknown tribe, a part of which remained loyal to Dengizich in the interior of Pannonia; suggestions include tribes of Hunnic, Turkish, Iranian/Ossetian origin, see Maenchen-Helfen p.441; my own suggestion is that they may have received their name from their overlord Sadagis with the implication that they were Huns; see later) and certain of the Alani under their leader Candac received Scythia Minor and Lower Moesia. It is probable that these had fought on the Hunnic side because they are in the same area as the Huns. Paria, who was the father of Jordanes' father Alanoviamuth (i.e. grandfather), was secretary of this Candac as long as he lived. According to Jordanes, he (Jordanes) was in his turn a secretary of Paria's sister's son Gunthigis, also known as Baza, the *magister militum*, who was the son of Andag the son of Andela, who was also descended from the House of the Amali. In other words, Jordanes was in a position to know the facts and should be trusted in this case. The Rugi and some other races asked and were granted lands in Bizye and Arcadiopolis both of which were located in Thrace very close to Constantinople. These locations are very far away from the other *foederati*, which may suggest that the Rugi would have sided with the Gepids against the Huns.

Hernac/Ernak, the younger son of Attila, with his followers, were granted lands in the most distant part of Lesser Scythia. Emnetzur and Ultzindur, kinsmen of Ernak, were given Oescus, Utus and Almus in Dacia on the bank of the Danube. Other Huns, then swarming everywhere, were also granted territory in 'Romania' (in Rome; the Romans at this time called their country Romania/Rhomania). These Huns later became known

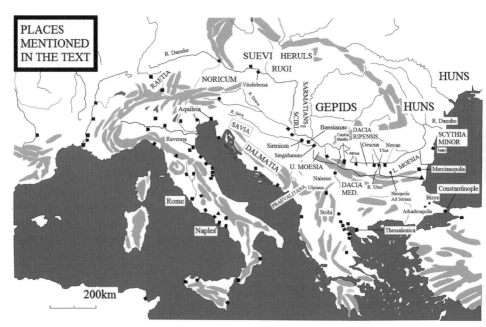

Romans, Barbarians and Settlement of the Federates in 454–457.

as the *Sacromontisi* and the *Fossatii* of Jordanes' own day. Maenchen-Helfen (p.151) speculated that the Hunnic *Fossatii* were probably those of the camp in Moesia while the *Sacromontisi* were probably those who inhabited 'the holy mountain' in Thrace. Maenchen-Helfen also notes that Procopius named four *fossata*: one in Moesia, the one of Longinus in Tzania, the *fossatum* of Germanus in Armenia, and *Gesila-fossatum* in Haemimontus. The last-mentioned consisted of Goths because Gesila meant the Gothic Gaisila. The important point here is that these were clearly permanent garrisons of *foederati* which had been fully incorporated into the Roman army by the sixth century. The so-called Lesser-Goths, whose priest and primate had been Vulfila who had taught them how to read and write, retained their lands in Moesia, where they inhabited the Nicopolitan region as far as the base of Mount Haemus. According to Jordanes they were a numerous people, but poor and unwarlike. See the *MHLR* Vol.1 for the settlement. The Goths always connected the ability to read and write with military weakness – the Greeks and Romans obviously did not share this silly idea. For other earlier and later examples of such Gothic views, see my *Gallienus* and *MHLR* Vol. 6.

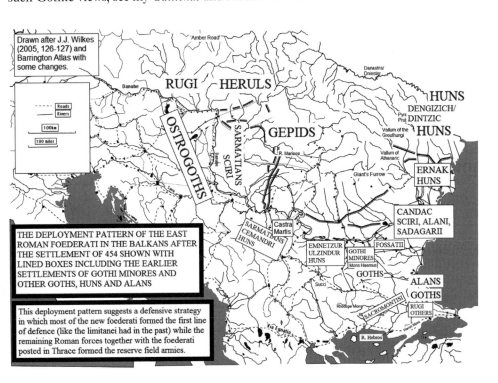

THE DEPLOYMENT PATTERN OF THE EAST ROMAN FOEDERATI IN THE BALKANS AFTER THE SETTLEMENT OF 454 SHOWN WITH LINED BOXES INCLUDING THE EARLIER SETTLEMENTS OF GOTHI MINORES AND OTHER GOTHS, HUNS AND ALANS

This deployment pattern suggests a defensive strategy in which most of the new foederati formed the first line of defence (like the limitanei had in the past) while the remaining Roman forces together with the foederati posted in Thrace formed the reserve field armies.

As noted in the maps (see the accompanying two maps), the above suggests that the initial defensive strategy adopted by the East Romans consisted of the use of the *foederati* along the Danube as the first line of defence (like the *limitanei/ripenses*) while the native Roman forces together with the *foederati* posted in Thrace formed the reserve field army. The locale, Pannonia, given to the Ostrogoths, means that Marcian had effectively taken control of territories which belonged officially to West Rome. The second stage of Roman strategy was the rebuilding of the military forces and civilian settlements in the area, which they achieved relatively quickly, which is proven by Maenchen-Helfen's (p.159, 162) analysis of the sources. According to the ecclesiastical sources analysed by him, cities such as Marcianopolis, Nicopolis, Odessus, Novae, Abrittus, Appiaria, and Durostorum were able to communicate with Constantinople in 457. The only areas where the Emperor Leo did not send letters in 457 were Dacia Ripensis, Dacia Mediterranea, Moesia Superior, and Praevalitana, which proves that those areas were in the midst of a conflict, but by next year, 458, communications worked again. This proves that there was still some fighting in those areas in 457 (see later), but it also shows that life got back to normal relatively quickly after the Huns had been expelled – after all, Jordanes specifically mentions that the area which was handed over to the Ostrogoths was full of cities. This is a sign that the cities at least in Pannonia regained their vitality fast. The only problem with the solution adopted by the East Romans was that the *foederati* started to fight against each other, and some also failed to abide by their agreements.

On the basis of Jordanes' account the initial settlement pattern of the *foederati* could be interpreted to have been a miserable failure, because according to Jordanes (Get. 268ff.), the sons of Attila considered the Goths as deserters from their rule and attacked them. However, as we shall see, there were other reasons for this. The domains of the Ostrogoths were divided between three brothers, Valamir, Thiudimer and Vidimer, all of whom belonged to the House of Amali. Valamir dwelled between the rivers Scarniunga and Aqua Nigra, Thiudimer near Lake Pelso, and Vidimer between them. The locations are unknown, but I would suggest that Valamir lived somewhere close to Sirmium possibly between the rivers Sava and Drava, Thiudimer somewhere close to Vindobona, and Vidimer somewhere between. See the accompanying map. The Huns then attacked Valamir alone, obviously because his territory was closest to the Huns, but Valamir inflicted a complete defeat on the Huns so that the remnants of this force sought safety in those parts of Scythia which border the Danaper (Dnieper), which in their language was called Var.[6] This event is usually dated to the year 454, but I would suggest that it is quite probable that the Huns actually attacked the Ostrogoths on behalf of the Eastern Empire in about 455/6 if Avitus (Sid. *Pan. Av.*, 589–90) had indeed subjected the two Pannonias under his rule in 455 but, as already noted, this is uncertain because the Easterners still appear to have helped Avitus against the Vandals. However, I would still suggest that the East Romans did precisely that. The subsequent negotiations regarding the subsidies paid to the Goths by the East Romans suggest that the Goths had played it both ways and had claimed to be subjects of both halves of the Roman Empire and that the Easterners would have none of that. The use of the Huns by the East Romans in this case should be considered to have been a proxy war in which the East Romans left the dirty work to the Huns so that they could maintain deniability. In other words, the East Romans could deny any responsibility for the attack against the *foederati* of West Rome. Had the Huns been successful, the Ostrogoths would have recognized the Huns as their masters which in turn would have extended the Hunnic alliance with the East Romans to cover also the Ostrogoths. In other words, the use of the Huns gave the East Romans the chance to avoid a civil war with the West.

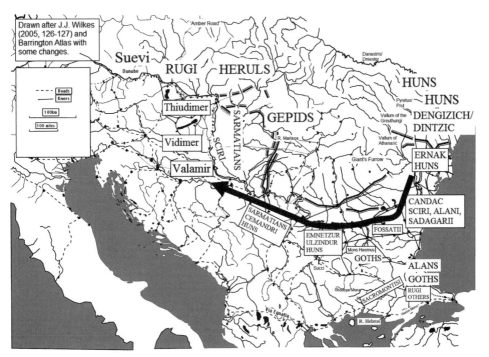

Hunnic Invasion in about 455/6.

This account and subsequent details given later prove that all of the *foederati* (or at least most of them) that had been given land east of the Ostrogoths from Castra Martia up to Scythia were still loyal to the remaining sons of Attila and/or their East Roman masters and that all of them united their forces against the Ostrogoths and marched, presumably along the southern shore of the Danube, against them. The important point here is that the attack against the Ostrogoths would have meant the breaking of the *foedus* with the East Romans if it had been done without their acceptance. It is therefore clear that this was not the case, because the East Romans did not punish the Huns or any of the tribes that had been settled along the Danube frontier.

The fact that Valamir was able to defeat the Huns and their allies speaks volumes of his skill as a commander. He needed only a third of the Ostrogoths to defeat the Huns in a situation in which they had previously felt unable to defeat the Huns with all of their forces. The defeated force appears to have become scattered so that at least some ended in Roman territory while others ended just north of it. Subsequent events prove that the Sadagarii under their leader Sadagis found a place of refuge somewhere in the interior of Pannonia (presumably somewhere between the Danube and Gepids) while Dintzig, one of the sons of Attila, took the other remnants somewhere between the Danube and

Dnieper. Even though Jordanes does not mention any Roman involvement in these events, it is clear that the Roman field army under Anthemius must have connived with the Huns for them to be able to march through Roman territory against the Ostrogoths, and it is likely that the Roman forces would have at least shadowed the Huns while they were in the area.

The usual view is that the Ostrogoths in Pannonia revolted against Leo in 459 because he had not paid the subsidies agreed with Marcian and because he had shown favour to the Ostrogoths in Thrace who were under Theoderic (or Theodericus or Theodoric) Strabo, the son of Triarius, and that this revolt ended in 461 when Leo reinstated the payments. However, I agree with Blockley (1992, 71–2, 209) that the revolt could easily have started under Marcian as stated by Jordanes (*Get.* 270–271). The fragment of Priscus (Blockley, fr.37) unfortunately fails to name the emperor who received the Ostrogothic envoys and agreed to pay them 300 lbs of gold each year so that it cannot be used to prove any dating. In fact, I would go so far as to state that the revolt of the Ostrogoths under Valamir, Thiudimer and Vidimer started precisely under Marcian as claimed by Jordanes, and that it should be connected with the events described above.

It is because of this that we need to analyse Jordanes' *Getica* in detail by taking into account the *Panegyric of Anthemius* by Sidonius, which sheds light into the techniques used by Jordanes to hide the reversals suffered by the Amali. According to Jordanes' *Getica* (270–71), after Valamir had defeated the Huns, Valamir and his brothers Thiudimer and Vidimer sent an embassy to the Emperor Marcian. The reason for the embassy was that they had not received the usual gifts which they received every New Year (likely to mean 456) as presents from the Emperor. The deal was that they would keep the peace in return for these gifts; but they had not arrived. The second reason was that they had found out that Theoderic, son of Triarius, a man of Gothic blood but not of the Royal House of the Amali, was in great favour in Constantinople. It is possible that in this case Jordanes actually referred to one of the reasons for the war that took place at some time in about 459–463. This Theoderic, the son of Triarius also known as Theoderic Strabo, was allied with the Romans and received an annual bounty, with the result that the Amali felt their conceited pride hurt. I would suggest that it is more likely that the Ostrogoths had sent their envoys to Marcian already before the Hunnic attack rather than after it as implied by the order of the text in Jordanes. Jordanes claims it was this that aroused the Amali brothers to frenzy so that they took up arms, but I would suggest that it was actually the Hunnic attack that caused the frenzy. Jordanes stated that the Amalis marched through almost the whole of Illyricum and pillaged it in their search for spoils. In this case Jordanes purposely mixes events that took place under Leo so that it was possible for him to hide the defeat of Valamir by Anthemius. In truth the areas which the Ostrogoths attacked in 456 appear to have been those with which Leo was unable to communicate in 457. Jordanes then claimed that it was this that caused the Emperor to change his mind quickly and return to his former state of friendship. This implies that this took place while Marcian was still Emperor. The Emperor sent an embassy which gave to the Goths both past gifts and those which were now due, and promised to give these gifts in the future without any dispute. This is actually the end of this war, but Jordanes has purposely left out at this point the subsequent renewal of the war against the East Romans in about 462/3, which ended disastrously for the Ostrogoths and led to the handing of Theoderic, son of Thiudimer, as a hostage in about 463 and which is described by Sidonius in his Panegyric of Anthemius 223ff. (see the reign of Leo). In return for the agreement with the Goths, the Romans received as a hostage Theoderic, the young child of Thiudimer better known with his later name of Theoderic the Great. According to Jordanes, Theoderic was then 7 years of age and was entering upon his 8th. According to Jordanes (*Get.* 268–9), Theoderic was born from a concubine Erelieva on the same day as Thiudimer received the news of Valamir's victory over the Huns, which dates the event roughly to 463. Thiudimer hesitated to give his son as a hostage, but his uncle Valamir managed to convince him to do so anyway in the hope that this would secure peace between the Romans and the Goths. In this context it is important to note that hostages were typically given to the Romans only in situations in which the enemy had been defeated. Jordanes then notes that Theoderic was given as a hostage by the Goths and then brought to Constantinople to the Emperor Leo and that Theoderic went on to gain imperial favour thanks to his goodly behaviour. This portion of Jordanes' account does indeed refer to the ending of the war that had been successfully conducted by Anthemius and which was described by Sidonius.

In short, I would connect all of the above with the occupation of the two Pannonias by Avitus in 455, which then caused the East Romans to use the Huns against the Ostrogoths in 456. When this failed, the Ostrogoths naturally laid waste to East Roman territory. I would suggest that it is in this light that we should see the above referrals to the cities that were in communication with Constantinople in 457 and 458. As noted above, the only areas where the Emperor Leo did not send letters in 457 were Dacia Ripensis, Dacia Mediterranea, Moesia Superior, and Praevalitana. I would suggest that it was these areas that the Ostrogoths ravaged in 456 and which returned to Roman control by the next year, 458, as a result of the return of the payments by Marcian which the Ostrogoths would have received on the New Year of 457. The unfortunate thing about this is that my theory is equally as unprovable as the other one which dates the end of the conflict to 459–61, but at least this version has the benefit of explaining why the areas that were troubled in 457 were back in Roman control by 458 and why the Romans failed to punish the Huns, and where Ricimer conducted his campaign in 458 (see later) and why the Ostrogoths handed Theoderic as a hostage, something that would not have happened if the Ostrogoths had been victorious, and when the victories of Anthemius took place. Furthermore, the fragment of Priscus (Blockley fr.37) does not refer to any counter-attack by the Romans, but merely to the sending of envoys to the emperor who then agreed to pay 300 lbs of gold each year so that the Goths would not ravage Roman territory. In short, there is no referral to any successful Roman counter-attack by Anthemius, which must therefore have taken place during the reign of Leo I (457–74).

The modest Eastern help for the West during 455–457

As noted above, contrary to what modern works and historic works of Eastern origin suggest, it is probable that Marcian continued, in his modest way, the previous policy of supporting the tottering western half of the Empire even after Valentinian III had been killed. However, the help against the Vandals was far more modest than before. There was no military action at the beginning of Marcian's reign, but as we have seen on the basis of Hydatius' text it is possible that Marcian did send some naval detachments to assist Ricimer to reconquer Sicily and Corsica, in addition to which Marcian put diplomatic pressure on the Vandals after 455 for them to release Eudoxia and Placidia from Vandal captivity. Malalas claims that both had been sent to Constantinople already when Marcian was still ruler, but Priscus' fragment implies that this actually took place later, under Leo in about 461. It was then that the future emperor, Olybrius, got back his wife Placidia with whom he sired a daughter called Juliana at Byzantion (i.e. at Constantinople).[7]

The Caucasus and the Persian Border in about 455–457

Marcian was fortunate that the peace with Persia was mutually beneficial and that the Persians needed peace with Rome just as much as they did. The division of Armenia at the end of the fourth century (see vol.2) had brought with it a number of policy adjustments in the East. The most important change was that the division of Armenia had increased the strategic importance of Lazica/Colchis immensely. Lazica and Pontus Polemoniacus were now the only territories that separated the Persians from the Black Sea. This meant that the Roman Emperors had to pay close attention to any disturbances there. In about 455/6 the King of Lazica Gobaz crowned his son co-ruler without Roman permission. The Romans defeated Gobaz, but were forced to withdraw due to the difficulty of supplying the forces in the absence of proper harbours. This may mean that the Roman expedition to the area had been a naval one, but it is equally possible that this refers only to the supply problems. Consequently the Romans decided to use the land route close to Persarmenia. Since the Romans knew that the Persians would note the buildup of forces near their borders, they dispatched an embassy to Persia to ask for their permission to march the Roman army close to the Persian border. At the same time, the Lazicans had dispatched their embassy with a proposal to change sides if they were assisted by the Persians against the Romans. Yazdgerd II refused to help the Lazicans and granted his permission to the Romans. The Kidarites threatened the Persian possessions in the East and Yazdgerd needed peace on his western frontier to be able to deal with them. The Lazican crisis was finally solved through agreement according to which Gobaz was to resign his throne in favour of his son after which he was to visit Constantinople where he was expected to explain his behaviour.[8]

Marcian's Troubles in Arabia, Egypt and Africa in 450–457

While fighting against the Huns Marcian was also facing troubles all along his eastern and southern frontiers in 450–53, but, as noted above, his first priority was the solving of the Hun problem. In the north there was the revolt of Persarmenia which the Persians were crushing. This did not involve the Romans directly, but it is still clear that the Romans needed to post troops to secure the frontier just in case. Just south of it the Romans faced Arab forces along their entire frontier south of Damascus up to the tip of the Sinai. This is proven by fragment 26 of Priscus and Church History (15.9.32C) of Nicephorus Callistus. Priscus notes that when the *strategos* Maximinus was on his way to crush the Blemmyes and Nobatae, who were ravaging the south of Egypt, he met en route the *MVM per Orientem* Ardaburius at Damascus in 453. The *Life of Daniel the Stylite*

(10) also proves that the Samaritans had revolted against the Christians in Palestine in about 453 which therefore appears to have taken place immediately after the Romans had used them in Palestine against the Monophysites, which is mentioned by Zachariah (3.5–6). To me this suggests a probability that all of those groups in the East that had grievances against the Romans were in revolt at about this time and that Ardaburius was in charge of fighting against all of them. When Maximinus arrived, Ardaburius negotiated with the Arab envoys who were suing for peace, which means that Ardaburius had inflicted a defeat on them. Nicephorus in his turn mentions that the *Comes et Dux Palestinae* Dorotheus had to abandon his campaign against the barbarians (i.e. the Arabs) in Moabitis and march to Jerusalem because the Monophysites had driven its patriarch, Juvenal, away from the city. As noted by Irfan Shahid, it is probable that the fighting in this area involved also the *Dux* of Arabia, who would have been left in charge of the campaign against the Arabs while Dorotheus dealt with the religious disturbances in the interior. It is not known whether the Arabs who threatened the East Roman frontiers in the north and south consisted of the same or different tribes. Likewise the identity of the enemy is not known, which makes it possible that the Persians could have incited one of their client tribes against the East Romans, to keep the Romans too busy to interfere in Armenia and Caucasus. It is possible that these Arabic incursions could also have been the result of the same adverse weather phenomenon that affected Yemen and Nubia at this time (see below). Shahid has speculated that the Arabs in question could have been the Kindites or two independent groups. What is certain is that the East Romans once again managed to defeat the Arabs and force them to sign a peace treaty and that they also defeated the other enemies in the area at the same time.[9]

Maximinus continued his march from Damascus to Thebaid in Egypt where he inflicted a heavy defeat on the Nobatae and Blemmye invaders. The probable reasons for this invasion had been the rise of Nobatae power before the year 450, which in combination with the adverse weather and the blocking of access to the Temple of Isis at Philae caused the barbarians to invade Roman territory. The reasons for these conclusions are given below. The defeated Blemmyes and Nobatae sued for peace. Maximinus negotiated a peace for 100 years. The barbarians promised to hand over the prisoners, plunder, pay war damages, and give as hostages children of the nobility. In return for this, the Romans promised free access for pilgrims to the Temple of Isis at Philae and promised that the cult statue would once again start to make annual voyages on a barge to Lower Nubia. The death of Maximinus soon after this made the treaty void in barbarian eyes. They released their hostages by force, which implies some sort of daring commando operation. After this, they resumed their raids. It was presumably then that the *Alexandrinae urbis procurator* or *Comes Aegypti et Praefectus Augustalis*, Florus, took matters into his own hands by assuming command of the troops with which he defeated the Blemmyes and Nobatae invaders and expelled them from Egypt in late 453 or in 454.[10] This was not the end of troubles, however.

As noted above, the greed and abuse of Bishop of Alexandria Proterius led to serious hostility towards him. Consequently, when the deposed previous bishop Dioscorus died in 456, there was much mourning and rioting, and the locals considered the prospect of appointing a new bishop of their own. The only thing that prevented them from doing this was the known stance of Marcian. When the news of this was brought to Marcian he sent John, chief of the *Silentarii*, with a letter to the Alexandrians in which he urged them to unite behind Proterius. When John saw the large numbers of monks united in their stance with the even larger crowd of common people and heard of what Proterius had done, he did not carry through the orders of Marcian but promised the locals to take their case before Marcian. When Marcian then learnt of the conduct of Proterius, he blamed him for the troubles, but before he could come to a decision what to do he died in 457.[11]

Himyarite 'Knight' and Axeman
Drawn after Yule and Robin Fig. 159 with the reconstructed lower half of the relief (below dotted line).

Nubian king Silko's (early 5th century) victory over the Blemmyes. Note the Roman and Egyptian influences in the Nubian Kingdom. The illustration also suggests that the Nubians may also have used cavalry to great effect against the Blemmyes.

The reasons for the above conclusions arise from analysis of the information of the events that took place in Nubia, Ethiopia and Yemen after ca. 430. At some point in time before c. 450, Silko, 'the King of the Noubades and all the Aithiopians', described in inscription his three campaigns against the Blemmyes. He defeated the Blemmyes twice and on the third occasion he conquered their cities. This marked the end of Blemmye rule in Lower Nubia, and the last of the Blemmye rulers in the area, Phonoin/Phonen, became Silko's phylarch. The fact that Silko called himself a *Basiliskos* (kinglet) in his Greek inscription proves that he still considered himself as a client king (*foederatus*) of the Eastern *Augustus/Basileus*.[12]

The letter of Phonen to Silko's successor Abourni in c. 450 (tr. in Burstein 126–8) shows that Silko's victory over the Blemmyes had essentially consisted of the forcible eviction of the Blemmyes from the cities, which he had used to extort a payment of sheep, cattle and camels from Phonen. In return Silko had promised to give the lands back, but after he had received the gifts he failed to fulfil his promise. After Silko's death Phonen conquered one city but was once again defeated, this time by Abourni. Phonen had then sent his brother as ambassador to sue for peace, but Abourni had killed him. Despite this breach of the truce, Phonen was still prepared to accept peace if Abourni retreated from the cities as promised by his father. It is unfortunate that we do not know what happened next, but it is probable that Abourni won and annexed the Blemmyes because Phonen is the last known Blemmye king. It was this united force of Nobatae and Blemmyes that the Romans faced next in 452/3.

The annexation of the Blemmyes had made the Nobatae too powerful for their own good. This was even more so because the Kingdom of Silko and Abourni did not consist solely of the northern branch of the Nobatae (Nobatia) and Blemmyes, but also of the other Nobatae (later known as the kingdoms of Makuria and Alwa). This is proven by the fact that Silko had also (tr. of the inscription in Burstein, 123–5) subdued the 'other Nobatai' in the 'upper countries' (= Upper Nubia) together with rulers of other peoples so that Silko could call himself the King of all Aithiopians. It is in fact quite probable that Silko subdued the kingdom of Aksum in the 430s because its ruler was called *Basiliskos Mikros* (minor kinglet) by a Roman traveller at this time with the implication that the King of Aksum held lesser rank and was subject to the *basiliskos* of the Nobatae. The rise of the Nobatae was short-lived because they made the mistake of invading Egypt. The Romans crushed both of their invasions in 453 and 454. It is probable that it was thanks to this that the Romans once again switched their support to the Aksumites. This is proven by the fact that the Aksumites invaded Yemen after 456 and installed a Christian ruler there. It is clear that they were no longer subjects of the Nobatae. The ability to operate in Yemen also suggests Roman naval involvement or at least Roman neutrality. See below.

The Leiden Papyrus, which is a petition from the Bishop of Syene and Contra Syene Appion to the emperors Theodosius II and Valentinian III, makes a complaint concerning the raids made by the Blemmyes and the Anoubades (i.e. the Nobatae) and asks the emperors to send military assistance against them. It is unfortunate that the Papyrus cannot be dated more accurately than to the general period of c. 425–450, but since Silko was a client king and the Roman military response came only in 452/3, one can perhaps speculate that the petition took place in about 447–50. In this context the information provided by Evagrius (chapters 1.7 and 2.5), Priscus (Blockley frgs. 4.4, 26–27.2) and Jordanes (Rom. 333) are of the greatest value for the dating of these events. These sources suggest that the Austuriani, Mazices, Blemmyes and Nobatae ravaged Libya and Egypt in the late 440s and early 450s, which does once again suggest the possibility that the Sahara and the deserts of Nubia were suffering from drought, or from devastation caused by locusts after years of good harvests, or from floods that would have resulted in the loss of harvests and spread of diseases. What is notable about these problems both with the Germanic and Hunnic peoples and with the desert dwellers is that these troubles coincide with the severe cooling of the climate which took place in the fifth century. The fact that the famous Marib dam burst open in Yemen in about 449 suggests flooding, because the likeliest reason for the destruction of a dam is that it was broken by masses of water. We do not know with certainty whether the Austuriani were still causing troubles in the early 450s after their defeat by Armatus/Armatius, but this is possible because we find their neighbours ravaging Roman territory.

The extant circumstantial evidence from the fifth century suggests that the Aksumite Empire broke into pieces at some point between 390 and 440. Firstly, the foregoing proves that the Aksumites had lost their nominal control over the Blemmyes and Nobatae together with the land route to Egypt because the wars between the Romans on the one hand and the Blemmyes and Nobatae on the other could not have taken place if the Aksumites had still retained tight control over the land trade routes. Secondly, the Sabaeo-Himyarite kingdom was ruled by Abakarib Asad during the first third of the fifth century (I would date his reign to the period after c. 432) and he is considered to have been the greatest ruler of south Arabia in Arabian tradition. He extended his kingdom into Central Arabia and according to tradition was converted to Judaism at Medina. The conversion is a clear indication that he had broken relations with the Aksumites and with the Romans who had previously sponsored the conversion of the Himyarite kings into the Christian faith. I would suggest that we should connect the rise of Abakarib Asad with the Persian invasion under Bahram V Gur in about 431–34 so that Bahram would have invaded Yemen to oust the Aksumites after which he would have installed Abakarib as his client king in the area. However, it is possible that Bahram actually acted as Roman ally while the Romans marched another army to Mecca. Thirdly, there exists a letter by Bishop of Helenopolis Palladius (who lived between 368 and 431) which describes the travel of a *scholastikos* of Thebes to India to study under the Brahmins. The *scholastikos* made a stop at Adulis where he waited until he was able to catch an 'Indian ship' for his travel to India. Even when one takes into account normal Roman racial prejudices, the title *Basiliskos Mikros* that the *scholastikos* used for the king of Aksum leaves little room but to conclude that at that time the king of Aksum was no different from the kinglets of Nubia.[13]

On the basis of the above, I would suggest that the Aksumites first lost control of the Blemmyes and Nobatae because the Romans under Theodosius I and Arcadius no longer considered it necessary to bolster the Aksumite kingdom they were allied with Persia, and that the Aksumites lost control of Yemen and the Horn of Africa as a result of Bahram's invasion. If Bahram and the Romans conducted a joint campaign in Arabia, Ethiopia and Africa, then it is clear that the Aksumites would have turned against the Romans before this date (probably because they had not received any help from the Romans against the Blemmyes and Nobatae), which would mean that the aim of the superpowers was to restore the previous status quo in the area. What appears to be certain, however, is that the kingdom of Aksum was a client kingdom of Rome in about 437. It is not known whether we should connect the Persian campaign in the area with the inscription of King Silko which states that he was ruler of all Ethiopians, because his campaigns in the area cannot be dated securely, but it is quite possible that he campaigned on behalf of Rome against Aksum at the same time as Bahram invaded Yemen and the Horn of Africa. On the other hand, it is also possible that Silko just exploited the weakened state of Aksum and invaded the area after the Persians had left, but I would still consider the former to be more likely.

In short, the Aksumite rulers had probably already lost their grip on the Blemmyes and Nobatae in the 390s. The likeliest reason for this would have been that the Romans would not have considered it necessary to prop up the position of their Aksumite ally when they themselves were allied with Persia. This would certainly have been the case after Arcadius made Yazdgerd I a guardian of his son, and the latter sent eunuch Antiochos to act as guardian for the young Theodosius II. The final nail in the coffin of the empire status of Aksum was the invasion of Yemen, the Horn of Africa and East of Africa by

Bahram in about 431–4. It is in fact probable that in the aftermath of these disasters the Aksumites were temporarily subdued to tribute-paying status by King Silko as suggested by his inscription. The maritime trade via the port of Adulis continued as before, but it is still probable that thanks to the peace, the Persian merchants were able to offer their wares and services at more affordable prices than before, which undoubtedly increased their market share at the cost of the Roman, Aksumite and Himyarite merchants.

As with everything in life, this situation did not last. The *Book of the Himyarites* states that at some point in the fifth century, the Aksumites under Hiuna conquered Himyar. Munro-Hay notes that the name Hiuna bears close resemblance to the Greek name of one Aksumite ruler who was called Eon. On top of that, the title used by this King Eon can be interpreted to mean *Basileus Habasinon* (King of Habaschat), which was one of the titles used by the rulers of South Arabia. In addition to this, his coins have been found in South Arabia and so have those of his successors until the reign of Kaleb (ruled during the first half of the sixth century). Munro-Hay notes that stylistically the coins of Eon belong probably to the early fifth century and therefore the identification is uncertain. On the other hand, since the dating of coins on the basis of their appearance is an uncertain art, we can perhaps make the assumption that the coins of Eon are later and are to be dated to the 450s. It was then that the Jewish Kingdom of Himyar began its downfall.

In about 449 or 455 a large section of the economically vital Marib dam in Yemen collapsed. These damages were repaired, but in 450 or 456 the dam suffered even greater damage and 20,000 men were detailed to repair it. This happened during the reign of Shurahbiil Yafur, son of the great Abukarib Asad. It is impossible to know whether this contributed to the events that followed, but despite the fact that the dam was apparently repaired again, it is still clear that the damage to the economy had been significant just before the Aksumites invaded. According to Arab-Islamic tradition, Shurahbiil's successor Abdkulal converted to Christianity.[14] I take this to mean that it was then (probably the late 450s) that the Aksumite King Eon/Hiuna reconquered Himyar. We do not know whether the Aksumites were allies of Rome when this happened, but my own educated guess is that the invisible hand of Roman diplomacy was behind these events – but this is obviously improvable even if the fact that the Romans were by then enemies of the Nobatae and Blemmyes would have made this quite natural. The reason for this conclusion is that the next time we have any information regarding the relationship between Rome and Ethiopia, they were clearly amicable.[15] Despite both superpowers preferring to maintain peace (there were only short outbreaks of hostilities during Leo's reign), the Romans no longer felt it necessary to respect the Persian position after c. 449. It was in the Roman interest to prop up the position of her allies and to improve the relative position of her own merchants and allies in the Arabian Sea and Indian Ocean.

The fact that Dionysius, the *Comes Aegypti*, was in Upper Egypt until the very end of Marcian's rule suggests that there was once again trouble on the southern frontier of Egypt. When the Alexandrians learnt of the death of Macrian, they exploited this by appointing Timothy Aerulus as their archbishop.[16]

Marcian (25 August 450 to January or 30 April 457), the unsung Saviour of the Western Civilization

Marcian died at the age of 65 in January or on 30 April 457, officially of gangrene of the feet. At the time of his death, the position of the Eastern Empire was secure despite the troubles with the Ostrogoths. He left his successor an empire in excellent condition, much better than when he inherited it. The Hunnic threat had been crushed permanently and there was peace with Persia.

The two pivotal decisions of Marcian's reign were the decision to abandon the appeasement of the Huns of Attila and the convening of the Council of Chalcedon. Both had far reaching results. Contrary to what is usually assumed, Marcian was not merely lucky in his dealings with the Huns. It was not just because Attila was fighting in the west that he achieved his victories. The sources make it absolutely clear that the East Roman forces trashed the Huns that they faced in Thrace and in the Balkans twice in 451 and 452. This was not a coincidence. This time the Romans were better led than they had been in 447. The real anomaly in the wars between the Romans and Huns is actually the events of that year and to a lesser extent the events of 441. Marcian, Ardaburius and other East Roman commanders deserve full credit for their successes, which they have not received so far. It is equally clear that Marcian did not only save the Eastern half, but also the Western half. It was thanks to his reinforcements that Aetius was able to weather out the invasion of Italy by Attila, and it is even possible that Marcian was behind the death of Attila (note his dream). It is quite clear that Marcian and Aetius had saved Western civilization from the barbarian nightmare represented by the Huns, and we can all be forever grateful to them for that.

The decisions taken at the Council of Chalcedon were at least equally important, even if the power behind them was actually Pulcheria. Marcian gave her his full moral and military backing and it was thanks to these decisions that the Eastern Church was divided into Monophysite and Orthodox, with far-reaching consequences – it was thanks to these divisions that the Romans could not always put their full trust in the loyalty of the populace and alliances with the Arabs and Armenians. Furthermore, it increased the rift between the Archbishop of Constantinople and the Pope of Rome.

As far as domestic policies are concerned, Marcian's reign was on the whole a great success. Under his rule the relationship between the federate block lead by Aspar and the native Romans remained trouble free, but in such a way that Aspar's relative power still increased so significantly that he was able to decide who would succeed Marcian. In other words, the relationship between the two factions remained stable because Marcian did not attempt to overthrow Aspar and his federate/barbarian military block. But it is precisely this that can be criticized. Under Theodosius II Aspar's position was not as strong, which is well demonstrated by the fact that Aspar was simply brushed aside by Theodosius when he became angry over Aspar's poor performance against the Huns. In other words, Aspar and Areobindus had no influence on Theodosius in 449. They owed their return to power entirely to the influence of Pulcheria and Marcian. The situation was entirely different when Marcian died. Aspar's position was now so strong that he decided who would succeed Marcian. This should have been Marcian's job. He should have decided in advance who would succeed him and he should have made his successor's position so strong that Aspar could not have challenged it, but so that it would not alienate the barbarian block. One possible way to achieve this would have been to replace Aspar with another barbarian.

Marcian was also able to unite the upper classes behind his rule and limit corruption. Most importantly, it was thanks to his prudent financial and anti-corruption policies and military successes against the Huns that Marcian was not only able to lower taxes for upper classes but also to leave the state coffers full. According to John of Lydus (*De Mag.* 3.43), Marcian left his successor with 'ên de hyper tas chilias hekatontadas tou xhrysiou litrôn' – in other words, with well over 100,000 pounds of gold. It was with very good reason that Marcellinus Comes (a.456–7) included Marcian among the good emperors.

Thanks to the efforts of Marcian and Aetius, the Romans were in a position to begin their road to full recovery by crushing the Vandals, which would then enable the West Romans to revive their fortunes so that they would have been able to pacify the other barbarians living within their territory. The next book in this series explains how the Romans sought to achieve this, what happened and why the militarily superior East Romans failed to defeat the Vandals in the fifth century while they managed to do that in the sixth century, and why it was that East Rome was to become the real successor of Rome.

© Dr. Ilkka Syvänne 2014

Bibliography

Primary Sources:

Most of the primary sources (e.g. Annales Ravennates, Jerome, Jordanes, Cassiodorus, Paulus Diaconus, Priscus, Malchus, Nonnosus, Zosimus, Zonaras, Socrates, Sozomen, Theodoret, Vegetius, various Armenian sources etc.) are now available on the web either as old editions (e.g. FGH, MGH AA, PL, PG etc.) and translations or as html documents. Good places to start seeking those are Robert Bedrosian's Armenian Resources, the Internet Archive, Google Books, and the Tertullian Project. Whenever possible I have used Loeb or Budé editions and translations, excepting when I have been writing where I have had not access to my books or library. The following list (Select Primary Sources) refers only to those modern editions/translations that I have cited in the text or notes.

Select Primary Sources and Translations
ACC = *The Acts of the Council of Chalcedon*, tr., intr. and notes R. Price and M. Gaddis. Liverpool 2002.
Blemyomachia, *Anonymi fortasse Olympiodori Thebani Blemyomachia (P.Berol.5003)*, ed. Henricus Livrea (Enrico Livrea) Meisenheim am Glan (1978); *Select Papyri III* (1941), ed. and tr. by D.L. Page. Loeb.
Blockley R.C. (tr. and com.), *The Fragmentary Classicising Historians of the Later Roman Empire Eunapius, Olympiodorus, Priscus and Malchus.* 2 Vols. Liverpoool 1983. A very useful collection of sources with comments.
Candidus, see Blockley.
Chalcedon 1, *The Acts of the Council of Chalcedon*, tr. R. Price and M. Gaddis. Liverpool (2005).
Chalcedon 2, see secondary sources.
Chronica Minora, see *Monumenta*.
Codex Justinianus, ed. P. Krueger, Berlin 1877.
Constantius of Lyon, The Life of St. Germanus of Auxerre (Vita S. Germani), see Hoare.
CTh = Theodosian Code, Latin text available on the web, English tr. by C. Pharr, *Theodosian Code and Novels and the Sirmondian Constitutions.* Princeton 1952.
Evagrius, *Ecclesiastical History*, ed. J. Bidez and L. Parmenties London 1898; The *Ecclesiastica History of Evagrius Scholasticus*, tr. M. Whitby, Liverpool 2000.
FRMG = *From Roman to Merovingian Gaul*, ed. and tr. by A.C. Murray. UTP 2008 (very useful collection of translated sources).
Gallic Chronicle, see Chronica Minora and FRMG.
Gordon C.D., *The Age of Attila*. New York (1960). A very useful collection of translated sources (Candidus, Olympiodorus, Priscus, Malchus, Ioannes Antiochenus/John of Antioch) with commentary.
Gregory of Tours, *The History of the Franks*, tr. by Lewis Thorpe. London 1974.
Hydatius, *The Chronicle of Hydatius and the Consularia Constantinopolitana*, ed. and tr. by R.W. Burgess. Oxford (1993).
The Irish Annals = Annals of the Kingdom by the Four Masters from the Earliest Period to the Year 1616. Vol.1, Dublin 1856.

John of Antioch, *Ioannis Antiocheni Fragmenta ex Historia chronica*, ed. U. Roberto. Berlin and New York (2005). Partial English tr. in Gordon.

John of Lydus, *see Lydus*.

Joshua the Stylite, *The Chronicle of Joshua the Stylite*, tr. by William Wright (Cambridge, 1882); *The Chronicle of Pseudo-Joshua the Stylite*, tr. F.R. Trombley and J.W. Watt (Liverpool, 2000)

Julius Africanus, Kestoi, *Les 'Cestes' de Julius Africanus*, ed. and tr. by J.-R. Vieillefond. Paris (1970).

Kedrenos/Cedrenus, *Georgii Cedreni Historiarum Compedium*, ed. I. Bekker, CSHB. Bonn (1838) and in PG (fragments also translated in Zonaras/Banich).

Lydus, John, *De magistratibus, Ioannes Lydus On Powers or The Magistracies of the Roman State*, ed. and tr. by A.C. Bandy. Philadelphia (1983).

Malchus, see Blockley.

Marcellinus Comes, *The Chronicle of Marcellinus*, ed. (Mommsen's text) and tr. by Brian Croke. Sydney (1995).

Monumenta Historia Germaniae, several volumes

Monumenta Historia Germaniae Auctores Antiquitissimonum Fontibus Tomus IX (*MGH AA IX, Chronica Minora Volumen I*), (includes: *Anonymi Valesiani pars posterior* which I have also used from the Loeb ed.; *Fasti Vindobones priores and posteriores; Paschale Campanum; Prosperi continuation Havniensis* which is also known as *Auctarium Prosperi Hauniensis* sited either as *ordo prior* or *ordo posterior*; Agnellus).

Moses Khorenatsi, *History of the Armenians*, tr. R.W. Thomson. Cambridge and London (1978).

Nonnosus, fragments in ed. C. Müller, *FGH 4*, 178–81.

Olympiodorus, see Blockley.

Paul the Deacon, see Paulus.

Paulus Diaconus, *Historia Romana* (available online e.g. from Internet Archive).

Philon, Mechanike Syntaxis 5, in Y. Garlan (1974) *Recherches de poliorcétique grecque*. Paris., pp.279–327 (with French tr. by Garlan), commentary etc. pp.328ff.

Possidius, The Life of St. Augustine of Hippo, see Hoare.

Priscus of Pannium, see Blockley.

Procopius of Caesarea, *Wars, Buildings, Anecdota/Secret History*, ed. and tr. H.B. Dewing, 7 vols. Loeb, London 1914–1940.

REF2 = *The Roman Eastern Frontier and the Persian Wars. Part II* AD 363–630. Eds. G. Greatrex and S.N.C. Lieu. London and New York (2002). A useful collection of sources.

Salvian (Salvianus), *On the Government of God*, tr. by E.M. Sanford. New York 1930.

Sidonius Apollinaris, *Poems and Letters*. 2 vols., tr. and ed. W.B. Anderson. Loeb ed. Harvard 1936/1965.

Strategikon, *Das Strategikon des Maurikios*, ed. G.T. Dennis, German tr. by E. Gamillscheg. Vienna 1981; *Maurice's Strategikon*, tr. by G.T. Dennis. Philadelphia 1984.

Theophanes, *Chronographia* ed. C. de Boor (Leipzig 1883) and PG version both available online; *The Chronicle of Theophanes Confessor*, tr. by Cyril Mango and Roger Scott with the assistance of Geoffrey Greatrex. Oxford 1997.

Vegetius, *Flavius Vegetius Renatus, Epitoma Rei Militaris*, ed. and tr. by Leo F. Stelten. New York 1990.

Vita S. Germani, Constantius Lugdunensis (The Life of St. Germanus by Constantius of Lyons), ed. in *Acta Sanctorum* July 31; tr. in *The Western Fathers* by F.R. Hoare London and New Yrok 1954, 283ff. (references are to The Western Fathers, which is based on a modern critical *MGH* edition of Constantius' text unlike the *Acta*).

Zachariah of Mitylene, *The Syriac Chronicle known as that of Zachariah of Mitylene*, tr. by F.J. Hamilton and E.W. Brooks, London 1899.

—— *The Chronicle of Pseudo-Zachariah Rhetor*, ed. Geoffrey Greatrex, tr. by R.R. Phenix and C.B. Horn with contributions by S.P. Brock and W. Witakowski. Liverpool (2011).

Zosimus, *Zosimus. New History.* (1990), tr. by R.T. Ridley. Melbourne; *Nea Historia*, tr. and ed. Paschoud. Budé Paris. 4 Vols. (older English tr. available from the web).

Secondary Sources

Anderson, see Sidonius

Aquileia. Città di frontiera. Fondazione Aquileia (a fragment available as a PDF on the web).

Ariño B.D., 'Las murallas romanas de Cartagena en la segunda mitad del siglo I a.e.', (available from academia.edu).

Ayvazyan A. (2016), Армяно-Персидсая Война 449–51 гг. Erevan.

Bachrach B. (1973), *A History of the Alans in the West.* Minneapolis.

Bajenaru C. (2010), *Minor Fortifications in the Balkan-Danubia Area from Diocletian to Justinian.* Cluj-Napoca.

Barbera G. (1999), 'La valle dei Templi: il mandorlo e il 'Museo vivente", in *ANGKN 26*, 177ff.

Barrington Atlas of the Greek and Roman World (2000). Ed. R.J.A. Talbert. Princeton.

Bernardes P. and Martins M., 'Computer Graphics and Urban Archaeology. Bracara Augusta's case study.' (available at academia.edu), highly recommended for its nice computer graphics of the city.

Blockley R.C. (tr. and com.), *The Fragmentary Classicising Historians of the Later Roman Empire Eunapius, Olympiodorus, Priscus and Malchus.* 2 Vols. Liverpool 1983.

Blockley R.C. (1992), *East Roman Foreign Policy. Formation and Conduct from Diocletian to Anastasius.* Leeds.

Burstein S. (2009), *Ancient African Civilizations Kush and Axum.* Princeton.

Bury J.B. (1905), *The Life of St. Patrick and His Place in History.* London.

—— (1923) *History of the Later Roman Empire.* 2. vols. London.

Capasso B. (1905), *Topografia della Città di Napoli.* Naples.

Chacedon 2, *Chalecedon in Context* (2009), eds. R. Price and M. Whitby. Liverpool.

Clover, F.M. (1971), *Flavius Merobaudes: A Translation and Historical Commentary.* Philadelphia.

Croke B. (1977), 'Evidence for the Hun Invasion of Thrace in A.D. 422', in *GRBS 18.4*, 347–67.

Dodgeon M.H. and Lieu S.N.C (1991), See REF1.

Downey G. (1958), 'The Size of the Population of Antioch', *Transactions and Proceedings of the American Philological Association 89*, 84–91.

—— (1941), 'The Wall of Theodosius at Antioch', in *AJP 62.2*, 207–13.

Escher K. (2006), *Les Burgondes Ier-Vie siècles apr. J.-C.* Paris.

Filippo R. de, 'Nouvelle définition de l'enceinte romaine de Toulouse', *Gallia 50*, 181–204.

Fotiou A. (2000), 'Introduction Part Two', in *Kaminiates. The Capture of Thessaloniki*, tr., Intr., Comm. by D. Frendo and A. Fotiou. Perth, xli-xlix.

Freeman E.A. (1894), *The History of Sicily. Vol. IV.* Oxford.

Giovanni G. Di (5th ed.), *Agrigento.* Agrigento.

Greatrex G. and Bardill J. (1996), 'Antiochus the Praepositus: A Persian Eunuch at the Court of Theodosius II', in *DOP 50*, 171–97.

Grenier M.A. (1955), 'Essai de topographie narbonnaise', in *Comptes rendus des séances de l'Academie des Inscriptions et Belles-Lettress 99*, 352–62

Haarer, F.K. (2006), *Anastasius I. Politics and Empire in the Late Roman World.* Cambridge.

Haase, Barbara S., see Ennodius.

Heather P. (1996), *The Goths.* Oxford.

Hendy M.F. (1985), *Studies in the Byzantine Monetary Economy c.300–1450.* Cambridge.

Hippone, see Laporte.

Hoare F.R. (1954), *The Western Fathers.* London and New York.

Hodgkin T. (1892), *Italy and Her Invaders vols 2–3.* Oxford.

Holum K.G. (1982/1989), *Theodosian Empresses. Women and Imperial Dominion in Late Antiquity.* Berkeley, Los Angeles, London.

Hughes I. (2010), *Stilicho. The Vandal Who Saved Rome*. Barnsley.
—— (2012), *Aetius Attila's Nemesis*. Barnsley.
italicapress.com (webpage).
Jones A.H.M. (1964/1986), *The Later Roman Empire 284–602*. Oxford.
Jones M.E. (1986), 'The Historicity of the Alleluja Victory', in *Albion 18.3*, 363–73.
Kelly C. (2008), *Attila the Hun*. London.
Kouznetzov V. and Lebedynsky I. (2005), *Les Alains*. Paris.
Laporte J-P. (2005), 'Hippone Vandale et Byzantine' (un état de la recherché), in *Hippone*. Sous la direction de Xavier Delestre. Aix-en-Provence. pp.37–40.
Laroche D., 'La refondation de la cité', in d'Izmir à Smyrne. Louvre, 40ff.
Lawrence, A.W., 'A Skeletal History of Byzantine Fortification,' *Annual of the British School at Athens 78 (1983)*, 171–227.
Lebedynsky I. (2011), *La campagne d'Attila en Gaule*. Clermont-Ferrand.
MacGeorge P. (2002), *Late Roman Warlords*. Oxford.
Maenchen-Helfen O.J. (1973), *The World of Huns*. Berkeley.
Mayor A. (2003), *Greek Fire, Poison Arrows & Scorpion Bombs*. Woodstock, London, New York.
Milne J.G. (1913), *A History of Egypt Under Roman Rule*. London.
Munro-Hay S. (1991), *Aksum. An African Civilization of Late Antiquity*. Edinburgh.
Murray, see FRMG.
Nathan G.S. (1999), 'Theodosius II', in DIR (luc.edu/roman-emperors/theo2.htm).
Nathan, G.S. (1998), 'Marcian', in DIR (luc.edu/roman-emperors/marcian.htm).
Oost S.I. (1964), Aëtius and Majorian, CP 59.1., 23–29.
Paulinus, see web.
Petrikovits von H. (1971), 'Fortifications in the North-Western Roman Empire from the Third to the Fifth Centuries AD', in *JRS* 61, 178–218.
Pharr, C. (1952), *The Theodosian Code and Novels and the Sirmondian Constitutions*. Princeton.
PJROPL = Palet J.M, Julia R., Riera S., Orengo H.A., Picornell L., Llergo Y, 'The role of the Montjuïc promontory (Barcelona) in landscape change: human impact during Roman times', in Variabilités environnementales. Antibes 2012, 323ff.
PLRE1, (1971/2006), *The Prosopography of the Later Roman Empire*, A.H.M. Jones, J.R. Martindale & J. Morris. Volume 1 A.D. 260–395. Cambridge.
PLRE2, (1980/2011), *The Prosopography of the Later Roman Empire*, J.R. Martindale. Cambridge.
Ribeiro J.M.P. (2010), *Arquitectura romana em Bracara Augusta*.
Richmond L. A. (1931), 'Five Town Walls in Hispania Citerior', *JRS* 21, 86–100
Schippmann K. (2001), *Ancient South Arabia*. Princeton.
Shahid I. BAFIC (1989, 2006), *Byzantium and the Arabs in the Fifth Century*. Washington.
—— BASIC (1995–2010), *Byzantium and the Arabs in the Sixth Century*. Washington.
Syvänne I. *Military History of Late Rome*. Vols. 5–7, Pen & Sword, Barnsley forthcoming in 2020–2021. *Britain in the Age of Arthur*, forthcoming in 2019.
'East Roman Naval Warfare and Military Treatises,' forthcoming in 2019.
—— *The Reign of Emperor Gallienus. The Apogee of Roman Cavalry*, Pen & Sword, Barnsley 2019.
—— *Military History of Late Rome. Vol.2 (361-395)*. Pen & Sword. Barnsley 2018.
—— *Caracalla: A Military Biography*, Pen & Sword, Barnsley 2017.
—— *A Military History of Late Rome 284–361*, Pen & Sword, Barnsley 2015.
—— 'Scutarii' in the Wiley-Blackwell's *Encyclopedia of the Roman Army*, edited by Yann Le Bohec, 2015
—— 'Excubitores' in the Wiley-Blackwell's *Encyclopedia of the Roman Army*, edited by Yann Le Bohec, 2015
—— (2004), *The Age of Hippotoxotai*. Tampere.
—— Other articles etc. available online at academia.edu.

Syvänne, Ilkka and Maksymiuk, Katarzyna, *A Military History of Fifth Century Iran*. *Forthcoming*, Siedlce 2019.

Szuppe M. (2002/2012), 'Herat iv. Topography and Urbanism', in *Encyclopaedia Iranica* available at iranicaonline.org.

Tarraco, Archaeological Visual Guide (available e.g. from academia.edu).

Torres C. (1992), 'Povoamento antigo no baixo alentejo de Mertola', in *Arquelogia Medieval 1*, 189–202.

Trombley F.R. and Watt J.W. (2000), *The Chronicle of Pseudo-Joshua the Stylite*. Liverpool.

TTFP = A. Teodor, E.S. Teodor, M.S. Florea, M.A. Popescu, Noviodunum Roman Fortress. A Survey on a City Wall Section, Available on academia.edu.

Welsby D.A. (2002). *The Medieval Kingdoms of Nubia*. British Museum, London.

—— (1998), *The Kingdom of Kush*. Princeton.

Whately C. (2013), 'Jordanes, the Battle of the Catalaunian Plains, and Constantinople. *DHA supplements 8*, 65–78.

Whitby, *see Evagrius*

ZZG = Zirone D., Zanovello P., and Giglio R. (2004–2005), *Lilibeo fortificata*. Padova (Padua).

Notes

Chapter 1

1. I have discussed these matters in greater detail in a research paper at ASMEA Conference in 2015 and in the article dealing with East Roman and Persian security apparatuses (generously supported by ASMEA Research Grant) which was published in *Historia i Swiat* in 2016.
2. This chapter gives only the bare outline of these topics. The reader is advised to consult the previous volumes (esp. vol.3) in the series if he/she seeks a more detailed discussion. I will include in the following text only the skeleton version of the administrative and military matters into which I will add new fifth century material.

Chapter 3

1. Hughes (2012) has made the educated guess that Felix would have been an Easterner, but in my opinion it is more likely that he was a Westerner because the new administration needed to reward those who had betrayed John and Felix is a likely candidate for that. It should be noted that no concrete evidence exists for either conclusion – both of us have just made an educated guess.
2. Hughes, 2012, 32.
3. See e.g. the commentary in Croke (1977) who lists some of the views.
4. In other words, I do not accept Croke's (1977) interpretation of the events. He uses Olympiodorus' fragment 27 to redate Theophanes to the year 421, but in my opinion the evidence he presents is not conclusive.
5. For an analysis of the conversion, see Maenchen-Helfen (82–85) and Escher (25–28).
6. It should not be forgotten that during this date the Catholic Church was not really an independent entity but part of the imperial administration.
7. In other words, I do not agree with those who lower the figures given by Procopius.
8. Reconstruction of the events of the siege is based on Procopius and Laporte (37–38).
9. This is the reason stated by Procopius, but it is also possible that the reinforcements sent by West and East Rome collectively had already arrived, making it necessary for the Vandals to seek a more suitable place for combat.

Chapter 4

1. I have here adopted the same approach as Ian Hughes and use an annalistic approach to stress the fact that the West Romans were facing continuous and simultaneous troubles all over their Empire. The sources for the events described can be found in the PLRE2 under each person mentioned. I include them in the discussion only if they are important for the sake of argument or I use the source or sources mentioned to argue something new.

Chapter 5

1. Once again, sources for the events can be found in the PLRE2 under the name of each person mentioned.
2. i.e. I agree with Ian Hughes (*Aetius*) that the likely reason for the reinstatement of Aetius was that the army refused to fight for Sebastianus.

3. For a different analysis of the sources, see MacGeorge (17–67). She argues that Dalmatia and possibly the entire of western Illyricum without Noricum would have been under East Roman control from 437 until about 481/2. I find her analysis utterly unconvincing. Her argument is entirely based on the unfounded dismissal of Procopius's referral to the cause of Marcellinus's revolt in 454 which was the murder of Aetius, and on the assumption that if Marcellinus was ready to obey the wishes of Constantinople that he would have been an East Roman military commander. This doesn't take into account the referrals to Marcellinus's independent position. It was and is entirely possible for a small nation or military power to take into account the wishes of the more powerful neighbour or neighbours without actually being part of that nation/empire. A good modern example of this is Finland in the post WWII period.
4. For the date of the raiding see Prosper a. 437 with Ian Hughes' analysis (2012, 98–99).
5. Note that I date the events differently from that adopted by the PLRE2, which has made a mistake in the dating of Hydatius' text.
6. Prosper dates this campaign to 436 and Hydatius to 437.
7. Prosper dates the campaign to 435 and Hydatius to 437. I, like most others, follow the latter. See also Hughes 2012, 97–98; Escher; PLRE2. I do not agree with those who suggest that the Huns under Rua crushed the Burgundians alone and that Aetius was not involved. The fact that Prosper fails to mention Aetius when he stated that the Huns destroyed Gundichar and his people is definitely not conclusive when all the other sources mention that the Burgundians were crushed by Aetius. For an analysis of the various views, see Escher. The PLRE2 dates this war to 436, but this is clearly a mistaken reading of Hydatius, who does not date it to 436 but to 437.
8. Hughes 2012, 97–98.
9. Hughes 2012, 99–100.
10. Hughes (2012, 103) after Halsall.
11. Bachrach (1973, 32–3). The reason for the quarrel between Aetius and the PPG suggested by Hughes (2012, 113).
12. Jacobsen 114ff., Hughes 2012, 111ff.
13. The illustrations are adapted from Torres. Note that the reconstructions of the walls of the inner city on top of the ridge are slightly different. I have not attempted to reconcile those as that is a question best left to archaeologists.

Chapter 6
1. The sources for each event can be found in the PLRE2. I include those only when it is important for the argument.
2. Hughes 2012, 121–2, 130–1; Jacobsen 134–5.
3. Clover 42ff.; Hughes 2012, 130ff.; PLRE2. I do not accept Hughes' view that the Franks would have besieged Majorian at Tours (too far south and, most importantly, not mentioned by Gregory of Tours), but have adopted Clover's view that the enemy would have been the Bacaudae.
4. In other words I redate the death of the famous bishop even earlier than others. The other suggested dates are 31 July 445 or 448 (see Clover).
5. The importance of this *Novella* was recognized by Maenchen-Helfen (104).
6. Oost.
7. Procop, *Wars* 3.5.8ff.
8. Kelly, 174–6.

Chapter 7
1. The sources can be found in the PLRE2 or in the secondary sources mentioned, except when I have considered the naming of the source important for the argument.

2. This chapter is based on Holum 1982, 147ff.
3. A useful summary in Nathan, Theodosius II.
4. A useful summary in Nathan, Theodosius II. See also Holum 1982.
5. Jones, 948–50.
6. Maenchen-Helfen, 86ff.; Blockley, 1992, 59–60. Note that I disagree with Manchen-Helfen and accept that Aetius handed over territory in return for soldiers.
7. Maenchen-Helfen, 90ff.; Blockley, 1992, 59–60.
8. This is a quote from my *Historia i Swiat* (2015) article dealing with the reign of Bahram. For the sources, see BAFIC.
9. Holum 1982, 183ff.
10. The usual interpretation is that no additions were made to the walls of Antioch during the reign of Theodosius I because sources do not mention any Antiochus Chouzon as *PPO* for his reign but mention Antiochus Chouzon (*PPO* in 430–431) for the reign of Theodosius II. It is actually quite problematic to connect the building of the walls in 430/1 with the statement that they were built at the request of Eudocia because Eudocia visited Antioch only in 438 en route to Jerusalem and presumably also when returning back in 439, and also possibly in about 444 if she visited Jerusalem for the second time as indicated by Evagrius – it is of course possible that Eudocia could have requested that the walls were to be extended even at a time when she was at Constantinople in 430/1 or that Antiochus was put in charge of the construction in 438/9, but it is inherently more likely that she would have made the request at the time she was visiting Antioch because she reconstructed the Wall of Jerusalem precisely at the same time as she visited the place.
11. The different pieces of evidence for the size of the population have been collected by Downey (1959). The estimates range from the low end of 150,000–200,000 all the way up to 300,000 to 500,000 or even 800,000.
12. Holum 1982, 189ff.
13. Bardill in Greatrex and Bardill.
14. Most of the sources conveniently translated and collected in REF2.
15. Most of the sources usefully collected in REF2, 44–45. Joshua the Stylite (18) claims that when Valash/Balash made a request for financial assistance from the emperor Zeno in 484, the latter answered that the taxes which Valash received from the city of Nisibis should be enough for Valash because they had by then been due to the Romans for many years. The same argument was also used by Anastasius.
16. The sources for this chapter are usefully collected and analyzed by Maenchen-Helfen (108ff.) and the narrative and analysis is mostly based on this and on the PLRE2.
17. Tr. by Blockley, 1983, p.233.
18. Fotiou and Lawrence, 184–5.
19. Fotiou.
20. Fotiou.
21. Full analysis of the *Novella* in BAFIC, 49–50.
22. The best account of the fates of those in the court of Theodosius II is still Holum (1982, 176ff., esp.191ff., the sources mentioned therein). The following is based on his analysis even if I sometimes adopt a very different view, for example by accepting the apple story as accurate – far stranger things have happened and will happen in the future.
23. The sources are once again usefully collected and analyzed by Maenchen-Helfen (108ff.) on the basis of which I have developed my own theory (which is slightly at variance with his version) regarding the course of the war. Editions and translations of the sources can be found from the web or for example from Blockley or Gordon.
24. PLRE2 Armatius/Constantius 7.

Chapter 8

1. Sources collected, translated or referred to in: Gordon 104ff.; PLRE2; Blockley 1983, esp. fragments of Priscus fr.16ff.
2. Priscus fr. 15, Blockley ed. fr. 20.1.
3. Sidonius's Bellonoti is often thought to refer to Valerius Flaccus's (6.161) Ballonoti and is therefore thought to be a literary referral and therefore imaginary. The Geloni, Neuri/ Neurians, and Bastarni are also thought to refer to peoples that had disappeared (the case for the Bastarni is not so certain) and are therefore often considered imaginary. However, I am inclined to follow those who like Lebendynsky and Anderson (Loeb; Bellonoti are Sarmatians) think that Sidonius simply used archaic terms to refer to real existing tribes in those areas. The reason why I have given the Bructeri 20,000 men is that Tacitus claims in his Germania that the Chamavi and Angrivarians defeated the Bructeri in battle at the turn of the second century AD and that more than 60,000 Bructeri fell (the tribe was supposedly destroyed), which means that they could easily have collected this number after they had revived their fortunes. I have also made the educated guess that since the war was fought right next to the Franks, Burgundi and Thuringians that they would have been required to put into the field a greater number of men than those nations (Sciri, Bastarnae) bordering the Danube. It is possible to identify the Geloni as steppe nomads on the basis that they (Claud. Against Ruf. 1.313) tattooed their limbs and milked their mares (Sid. Epist. 4.1.4). The Geloni would have represented several nomadic tribes. The Neuri lived in north-west Ukraine/south Belarussia, which may imply that they were either Balts, or Slavs, or Celts. The Bastarnae (Bastards) lived north of the province of Scythia and were originally a mixed group of Celts and Germans, but one may make the educated guess that they would have become even more mixed by the fifth century. The Sciri were pure-bred Germans who were neighbours of the Bastards. Sidonius fails to mention the Ostrogoths. The probable reason for Sidonius's unwillingness to use the Getae for the Ostrogoths would been Avitus's close relationship with the Visigoths. It was not prudent to include the Goths among the enemy forces. I have based my estimate of Aetius's own retinue on Belisarius's sixth century retinue (7,000 horsemen), but since it is actually probable that Aetius possessed more men than Belisarius on the basis of the position he held in the Empire, I have added an extra 8,000 to the figure. In light of the fact that Fredegar 2.62 considered it plausible for Belisarius to have 12,000 retainers, this figure seems quite conservative for the de facto ruler of West Rome. On the basis that the expeditionary citizen levy of Bourges (Avaricum, Bituriges) was 15,000 men in 583 (Greg. 6.31), one can suggest that the Armoricans could have easily collected a levy of 30,000 men for war which was fought right next to them. I have calculated the regulars in the ND as follows: cavalry units ca. 500 horsemen, legions 2,000 men, and *auxilia palatina* 1,000. These are only rough estimates, because the legions could consist of more men if the units in question were created during the Tetrarchy and because the *auxilia* could in practice possess considerably less men if the government had been unable to obtain sufficient numbers of tribesmen as recruits. For the sizes of tribal armies, see vols.1–3 with my *The Age of Hipptoxotai* and *Gallienus*.
4. This is unlikely to be Narbonne/Narbo.
5. Hodgkin 2.116–18; Hughes 2012, 156–59; Kelly, 190–92; Lebedynsky 2011, 35–40; the interpretation of Nymaie as Nijmegen is my own.
6. Replacement of Goar with Sangiban: Bachrach 1973, 65.
7. Description of the walls: Lebedynsky 2011, 47–48;
8. Jord. *Get.* 186ff.; Sid. *Pan. Avit.* 315ff.
9. This analysis is fully based on the analysis and reconstruction that I already made for the *Age of Hippotoxotai* (the latest partially corrected version 2005), but with the difference that I am now inclined to accept the larger figures for the armies. However, since I have noted that most readers do not necessarily understand my line of reasoning if I merely present the results, I have here included a long quote with an analysis of the contents because in my opinion it is

important that the public finally get the right idea of what happened in the course of this very important battle. For an excellent analysis of Jordanes's literary and 'propagandistic' purposes in describing the battle of the Catalaunian Plains in detail and its intended Constantinopolitan audience, see Whately.

10. Lebedynsky (2011, 57ff) collects the various theories.

11. See vols. 1–2 with intro to the 3rd vol and Syvänne (2004).

12. Fredegar includes a complex plot according to which Aetius first visited Attila and then Thorismund and managed to convince both to abandon the battlefield, but this is likely to be a later legend woven around the real event. It should still be remembered that one cannot entirely rule out that such events and plotting took place as Aetius was definitely an expert at plots and schemes.

13. In Fredegar's confused account the Visigoths suffered 200,000 dead and the Huns 150,000. The figures are probably invented, but in my opinion still reflect the fact that both nations suffered terribly.

14. For an analysis of the Council in its context, see Chalcedon 2.

15. Mainly based on Procopius and John of Antioch.

16. For a fuller discussion, see MacGeorge 52ff. Note however that I disagree with her in regard of Marcellinus's standing vis-à-vis the East and in her analysis of the naval potential of Marcellinus's forces. She, like many other modern commentators, is guilty of underestimating the military value of civilian levies of ships. She thinks that the naval levies would not have constituted a navy; in her opinion only a standing professional fleet would have. This is a projection of modern realities into the past. The difference in military worth of a professional fleet and levy of civilians was not as pronounced in the past as it is today. The cases in point are the successes of the levied fleets of Republican Rome. They faced professional fleets all over the Mediterranean and bested all of them. The decisive thing was the type of ship used, as is well demonstrated by the East Roman Edict (CTh 9.40.24 on 24 Sept. 419) which legislated against the teaching of naval building techniques to the barbarians. This is confirmed by the ancient sources. The key to Roman victory over the Carthaginians was the copying of their naval building techniques which were then improved upon by additional features like better grappling techniques (i.e. the famed *corvus*). Civilian captains, sailors and rowers learned all the necessary sailing and rowing skills as civilians and could then employ these when using war galleys. The land forces in their turn could be used as marines. It should also be stressed that the larger civilian transport galleys were quite usable as large warships either without the ram or with some kind of attached ram. It is also probable that the Dalmatians would have kept some true war galleys in existence for anti-pirate use, in addition to which they would have kept warships in their docks in readiness just as the Republican Romans did.

Chapter 9

1. Most of the sources mentioned in this chapter can be found in chronological order in Gordon or Blockley (fragmentary). I add an exact location only when one cannot be found from these sources in chronological order. The PLRE2 also lists the sources for each of the persons.

Chapter 10

1. Most of the sources mentioned in this chapter can be found under the names of the persons mentioned in the PLRE2 and/or in the *MGH AA Chron. Min. 1–2* (these include several chronicles which are organized annalistically and are therefore quite easy to check up). I include referral to the original source only when I think that this adds something new to the discussion or is otherwise interesting for the reader, but I have always included references to the secondary literature if I have used it.

2. Priscus fr.24/31.

3. Prisc. fr. 24/31.1–2; Sid. Carm. 2.367; Giovanni, 5.

4. This is how Burgess translates the text, but Murray's translation (FRMG) is actually more accurate. Hydatius doesn't state specifically that the victory over the Vandals was achieved by the Easterners off Corsica, but he includes the referral to the victory of Marcian's army immediately after his referral to Ricimer's victory off Corsica, which makes it probable that the victory was actually achieved by an East Roman fleet operating under Ricimer.

5. Hughes 2015, 60, 63, 65, 68–9.

Chapter 11

1. For the Persarmenian revolt and war against the Persians in 449–51, see now Ayvazyan's groundbreaking study.

2. Zachariah 3; Malalas 14.27ff.; Nathan, Marcian; Haarer, 120.

3. Zachariah 3; Priscus fr. 28.1–2; Evagrius 2.1–8 (esp. 2.5).

4. See MLHR Vol.1 p.282; Jones (1.110); Hendy (339–341); Evagrius 3.40–41. Evagrius, however, claims that Zosimus lied when he stated that Constantine instituted the *chrysargyron* tax and many other measures against every class of people. In fact it is possible that Evagrius is partially correct, because there are indeed indications that at least some of the taxes had been in use before, but at the same time it is still quite probable that Constantine did make the tax laws harsher than before to obtain money for his many projects.

5. Sid. 2.199–209; PLRE2; Jord. Get. 264ff.; Maecnhen-Helfen, 143ff.

6. Jordanes (Get. 268ff.); For the locations, dates etc. see the discussion in Maenchen-Helfen, 152ff.

7. Malalas 14.31; Priscus (Blockley fr.38); with the account provided previously.

8. Blockley (1992, 70) on the basis of Priscus (Blockley fr. 33.1–2).

9. Shahid, BAFIC, 55–58.

10. Jordanes Rom. 333/Priscus fr. 27.2 with comments of Blockley p.392; Milne, 100–101.

11. Zachariah 3.11.

12. Welsby 2002, 17.

13. Based on information provided by Munro-Hay (Chapter 4.6) and Schipmann (64), but conclusions drawn from their information are mine. It should also be noted that Schipmann considers the evidence for the conversion of Abakarib in Judaism to be uncertain. For further discussion, see my article on Bahram V Gur in *Historia i Swiat*.

14. Munro-Hay Chapter 4.6; Schippmann 64–65.

15. For example, Welsby (2002, 19) notes that the Romans once again subdued the Ethiopians and Nubians at some unknown point in time because they were in a position to give orders to both in about 523–5.

16. Evagrius 2.8 with comments of Whitby pp.84–5. Whitby lists all the authors (Socrates 7.13.2, SHA Firmus 8.1; Dio 51.17.1–2) which included Evagrius that noted the propensity of the Alexandrians for violence and unrest.

Index